Dance's Duet with the Camera

Telory D. Arendell • Ruth Barnes
Editors

Dance's Duet with the Camera

Motion Pictures

palgrave
macmillan

Editors
Telory D. Arendell
Missouri State University
USA

Ruth Barnes
Missouri State University
USA

ISBN 978-1-137-59609-3   ISBN 978-1-137-59610-9   (eBook)
DOI 10.1057/978-1-137-59610-9

Library of Congress Control Number: 2016939228

Cover illustration: © Trigger Image/Alamy Stock Photo

Printed on acid-free paper

This Palgrave Macmillan imprint is published by Springer Nature
The registered company is Macmillan Publishers Ltd. London

PREFACE

We spoke first about the possibility of this manuscript in a backyard full of grass, bugs, and a fervent desire to let film and dance speak in a stage conversation that gives equal weight to each of these media. Our collaboration follows on the heels of Douglas Rosenberg and his 2012 Oxford University Press publication, *Screendance: Inscribing the Ephemeral Image*. And yet, whereas Rosenberg approaches this duet from a more filmic perspective, we ourselves are more firmly located in the dance space. As should be clear in our own text, a choreographer who employs video for production makes physical movement primary to the creation of all products. Film is therefore an equal partner in this dance, but it is most definitely a dance we present rather than a screened image. We say this with all due respect to Rosenberg, whose efforts are duly noted and appreciated as seminal contributions to the field. We want merely to offer another set of perspectives as practitioners and scholars committed to dance's contribution to the duet that is relatively recent in dance and film, both on stage and on the printed page.

ACKNOWLEDGEMENTS

The Missouri State University Graduate College, Provost, and Department of Theatre and Dance have provided financial and moral support.

Faculty and peers at the University of California, Riverside, Dance Department stimulated and challenged my understanding of screen dance, thereby encouraging me to explore a new path of research.

Dance Base (Edinburgh), 87 Dance Productions (North Carolina), the dancers, and composer Dmytro Morikyt devoted time, space, and creative energy that helped me make new objects for study.

– R.B.

To my extended family.

– T.D.A.

CONTENTS

Notes on Contributors

Telory D. Arendell (co-editor) is Associate Professor of Performance Studies in the Missouri State University Department of Theatre and Dance. Her publications include *Performing Disability: Staging the Actual* (2009) and *The Autistic Stage: How Cognitive Disability Changed Twentieth-Century Performance* (2015).

Ruth Barnes (co-editor) is Professor of Dance in the Missouri State University Department of Theatre and Dance. Her recent mixed media choreographic work includes *A Proper Container* (2011—in collaboration with Vonda Yarberry and Sheryl Brahnam), *Homing/In* (2008) and *On Reflection* (2004).

Heather Coker is a choreographer and filmmaker who makes personal work combining the media of dance and film into a collage of memory, imagination and subjective reality. She choreographs and directs for the stage and screen. Her piece *Pretty Good for a Girl* combines video projection and live performance, bringing past and present, approximate and specific into visual conversation while following an experimental narrative structure. She earned an M.F.A. in Dance from UCLA's Department of World Arts and Cultures.

Cara Hagan is Assistant Professor of Dance Studies at Appalachian State University. She is a professional artist of many genres, including dance, film, storytelling and community engaged art. Hagan has presented her work across the United States and abroad on stage, on screen and in educational settings. The recipient of several awards, her most recent award is the 2014/2015 North Carolina Arts Council Choreographic Fellowship. In addition, she is founder and curator of Movies By Movers, a film festival dedicated to the celebration of the conversation between the camera and the moving body.

Frances Hubbard completed her (AHRC-funded) PhD in Film Studies in 2014, and worked as a full-time teaching fellow at the University of Sussex, UK. She teaches across a wide range of Film Studies modules, at both undergraduate and postgraduate levels, and is currently teaching at Brighton University. Hubbard holds a BA (Hons) in Drama and Film Studies and an (AHRC-funded) MA in Film Studies. Her research interests are interdisciplinary in nature, mainly focusing on the sensuous, kinesthetic experience and analysis of film, particularly screendance. She is interested in how dance (and/or choreographed movement) can enhance a film's agency and its ability to cross time and space, "touching" the viewer and thereby working to transform historical objectification and liminality into embodied interaction. Her doctoral thesis, "Screendance: Corporeal Ties Between Dance, Film and Audience," examines a range of screendance genres, from avant-garde feminist film, to a Spanish flamenco trilogy, experimental short films, and popular Hollywood cinema.

Angela Kassel is a teacher of Dance and certified Pilates trainer in Germany. She studied at the Dance Academy in Rotterdam before earning a Master's degree in Theatre, Film, and Television studies at the Academy for Music and Dance at the University of Cologne.

Melanie Kloetzel is Associate Professor at the University of Calgary, and holds an MFA in Dance from the University of California at Riverside in addition to a BA and an MA in History from Swarthmore College and the University of Montana, respectively. Kloetzel is the artistic director of kloetzel&co., which she founded in New York in 1997 and which has traveled with her across the US and now into Canada. Since its inception, kloetzel&co. has moved between theatres and more unconventional sites, seeking out distinctive spaces and artistic collaborations along the way. Her research has been presented at/published in numerous journals and conferences and her anthology, *Site Dance: Choreographers and the Lure of Alternative Spaces* (2009), is edited with Carolyn Pavlik.

Carol-Lynne Moore is Director of MoveScape Center in Denver, and has been involved in the field of dance and movement analysis as a writer, lecturer, and consultant for over 30 years. She is the author of *Movement and Making Decisions* (2005), *The Harmonic Structure of Movement, Music, and Dance According to Rudolf Laban* (2009), and co-author with Kaoru Yamamoto of *Beyond Words: Movement Observation and Analysis*, 2nd edition (2012).

Izabella Pruska-Oldenhof is Assistant Professor at the School of Image Arts and a member of the graduate programs in Communication and Culture, and Documentary Media at Ryerson University. Her doctoral work at York concentrated on identifying the feminine aesthetics in the avant-garde cinema and body art by drawing on Julia Kristeva's and Luce Irigaray's theories on vanguard poetry and language. Izabella's films and videos have screened internationally and have received several awards.

Peter Sparling is Thurnau Professor of Dance at the University of Michigan and an active independent dance artist. As former principal dancer with the Martha Graham Dance Company (1973–1987), chair of the University of Michigan Department of Dance from 1988 to 1993, and Artistic Director of Peter Sparling Dance Company since 1993, he has had extensive experience as a director, choreographer, performer, teacher, lecturer, video artist, writer, collaborator, administrator and dance/arts consultant.

Philip Szporer and Marlene Millar have been immersed in the Canadian dance world for many years. Currently, Szporer teaches in the Contemporary Dance department at Concordia University and is a Scholar-in-Residence at the Jacob's Pillow Dance Festival in Massachusetts. In 1999, he was awarded a Pew Fellowship (National Dance/Media Project), at the University of California, Los Angeles. In 2010, he was the recipient of the Jacqueline Lemieux Prize awarded by the Canada Council of the Arts. Montreal filmmaker **Marlene Millar** created her first award-winning film *The Woman and the Sink* in 1989. Millar received her BFA in Film Production from Concordia University, studied at the School of the Art Institute of Chicago and in 1999 received a Pew Dance Media Fellowship at the University of California, Los Angeles. In 2001 Philip Szporer and Marlene Millar co-founded the production company Mouvement Perpétuel, directing and producing acclaimed arts documentaries and dance films.

CHAPTER 1

Introduction: Dance and Film as Siblings

Telory D. Arendell

Dance and film share an uneasy relationship with each other when it comes to primacy in the performance space. There is a long history of American Musical Theatre's use of dance on film for industry greats such as Fred Astaire and Busby Berkeley. Technology that is currently available for intermedia performance has moved beyond these early examples, and yet there is great benefit to a project that traces these steps to arrive at historical awareness of this relationship. We see in this anthology the ways in which early practitioners such as Loïe Fuller and Maya Deren began a conversation between these media that has continued to evolve and yet still retains certain valuable unanswered questions about the potential interactions of film and dance: Who is more real—the film image or the live? Can the camera dance with the dancer? Can we capture motion with words? What happens to the gaze when both live and recorded bodies fill the space? Do motion and filmed recording leave the same image traces in our memory? Is there image residue from the dancing body that can be re-enacted in our minds like a film sequence? Can you 'zoom' in a dance piece? How?

The authors in this collection contemplate these various questions from multiple directions. Some take a more dance historical approach. Others fix on more mechanical considerations when tackling screens and dancing

T.D. Arendell (✉)
Missouri State University, Springfield, MO, USA

© The Editor(s) (if applicable) and The Author(s) 2016
T.D. Arendell, R. Barnes (eds.), *Dance's Duet with the Camera*,
DOI 10.1057/978-1-137-59610-9_1

1

bodies that share performance space. All on some level take on the difficult task of verbalizing how the live aspects of present, sweaty, energy-driven dancers might collaborate with the more staid, focused, and digitally manipulated forms of either 2D or 3D film. The camera in these interactions becomes more a partner, a disembodied portion of a multiplied self that looks back in order to reflect on motion that has come before, to mirror or double the movement in real time, or to presage movement that follows. The images we create with dancing bodies on stages or in environmental locations function differently than those brought to bear in both edited film and the more recent category of video dance. We have not dismissed the legacy left by Fred Astaire with regard to maintaining the integrity of the full dancing body, and yet, what postmillennial technology can do with these full bodies operates in a mode and at a pace somewhat unimaginable to Fred Astaire, or only in the dreams of Loïe Fuller and Maya Deren.

SCREENDANCE: A SHORT HISTORY

While cinema studies and dance studies have each enjoyed their own histories as separate entities, screendance or dancefilm has a far shorter historical record. This is due in part to these more historical fields and practices needing to establish clear boundaries, differentiating their theories and practices to build stability for their own independent fields. Their combination can be traced back to early experiments by, for instance, the Lumière Brothers, or Loïe Fuller, or Maya Deren. However, these examples in their own time frame were pioneers, and any theory they may have written about such a combination was sure to sound like a foreign language to either side of the divide. For the purposes of our collection, I would like to establish our dance/film perspective with discussions from Sherril Dodds, Erin Brannigan, and Douglas Rosenberg. Their publications are, in order, texts from 2001/2004, 2011, and 2012, just to give you a sense of currency. When Sherril Dodds published *Dance on Screen: Genres and Media from Hollywood to Experimental Art* first in 2001 and then a later version in 2004, she was in effect plotting the ground for a brand new field. The texts by other authors on similar subjects owe her a debt of gratitude for opening the door. Therefore I will begin my map of screendance theory with Sherril Dodds.

DANCE ON SCREEN: GENRES AND MEDIA

Dodds warns us fairly early in her text that in theorizing dance on screen we need to keep an equal eye on both sides of this juncture. 'There are some critics who use stage criteria to evaluate screen dance and overlook the role of the film or televisual apparatus. This is clearly a problematic mode of analysis in its partial point of view.'[1] Let me be equally clear up front that we certainly do not mean to overlook the role of film or video in our anthology. Rather, we offer dance scholar/artists' understanding of how film and video can supplement, optimize, and extend the boundaries of what it means to be a moving body on either stage or screen. Dodds cleverly gives dance credit where it is due to Busby Berkeley and Fred Astaire: 'In Berkeley's work the camera is very much a participant in the dance.' And of course, 'The dance was of paramount importance to Astaire and for this reason he insisted on full body shots, the dancers being captured in a 'tight frame,' and a limited number of cuts. ... The result is that the dance is seen as clearly as possible without being distorted through the filmic apparatus' (6). In our anthology, Carol-Lynne Moore's chapter is the one that devotes itself to Astaire's legacy for these very reasons.

Dodds works effortlessly throughout her text to pinpoint what is meant by a 'video dance body.' By this phrase, I am not referring to MTV's short history of music videos that included dancers as a way to elucidate the content of popular music. As Dodds explains,

> The video dance body is a body that is technologically mediated. It is situated at an intersecting point between the medium of dance and the technology of television, and this convergence suggests that the video dance body constitutes a hybrid form. It is a technological construction that can only exist within the temporal and spatial frameworks of television (or film) and cannot exist outside this site. ... In video dance, the televisual technology is inextricably linked to the dancing body in order to create dance that plays on, utilizes and is determined by the televisual apparatus. (146)

In fact, says Dodds, 'In video dance, the camera work and the style of the edit are essential components of the dance itself' (89). Dodds here establishes the same sort of connection between dance and film that we ourselves use in our title; dance and film are partners with an equal investment in a final product that does justice to a camera that dances and dancers who inhabit televisual space.

One of the modern age's best film theorists is a scholar who viewed all arts as elements in an age of mechanical reproduction. Dodds calls on this scholar, Walter Benjamin, to tackle issues very much at the heart of our own discussion: what counts as real in dance and film? She writes,

> Although authenticity is a particularly slippery concept in relation to dance, nostalgia for the live performance and the authenticity of a unique dancing body form the basis of some arguments that seek to criticize dance on film and television. ... It is interesting that [Walter] Benjamin conceptualizes the 'original' in terms of uniqueness and permanence, and the 'copy' in terms of transience and reproducibility. In the case of dance, the live performance may be unique, but it is far from permanent, while video dance aligns itself more with permanence. ... Benjamin goes on to assert that as an aura implicitly assumes an original, it is therefore always characterized by 'distance.' Although it may be a short time-scale, the auratic work develops a heritage from its original state through to its current existence. Benjamin suggests that, in contrast, the reproduction eliminates distance. The reproduction can be defined by its immediacy. (154)

From here, Dodds goes on to argue that, 'although it is problematic to define live dance performance in terms of authenticity, it is nevertheless possible to acknowledge an original movement on a live body, because it undergoes a loss of aura in its reproduction' (155). This whole dialectic sounds at times a bit like a "Who came first, the original or its reproduction?" debate, which of course exists at the same level as its chicken/egg model, and yet, such a question seems best solved by deconstructive philosophies involving the body as a cultural construct rather than a material reality. But this thinking negates the primacy of somatic experience and leaves us with a ghosted aura that infinite reproduction of the original will always strive to make concrete again. Apparently, Benjamin would like to claim the film audience as more 'critical and receptive' than viewers of original, auratic art, where 'the viewer is "lured" into the auratic art work' without much critical distance. Film, 'he suggests, produces an autonomous spectator' as well as 'an ideologically motivated artificiality' (158). So, to tally this vote, Benjamin believes that Dance = Original = Authentic = Auratically Impermanent = Distant, whereas Videodance/Dancefilm = Copy = Reproduced   Permanence = Immediacy.   Granted,   even Dodds admits that Benjamin might be a bit outdated in his theory here, but she also warns us that video dance may be 'closer to Benjamin's theory on the production of a distracted, critical viewer' and that on this point his theory continues to be on point.

In any event, 'The centrality of the body within these discourses is extremely pertinent to video dance's construction of a technologically mediated body,' which perhaps suggests a continuing importance of material considerations. However, 'A central polemic to emerge is whether the video dance body, as a technologically mediated form, may constitute a threat to the material body or signify a potential extension of its capabilities' (161). Here, the chicken/egg, live/recorded, authentic/cyborg standoff is poised at a point of tipping scales either in the direction of cursing the techno-dance-body as cheap imposter or welcoming it as an evolutionary improvement on what humanity has thus far been physically capable of achieving. Dodds reassures us that, 'the video dance body is not simply an electronic representation that can mutate in endless configurations. It is a material body that has flaws, quirks, strengths and limitations, but which is open to reproduction, multiplication, distortion and augmentation by the televisual technology in order to become a video dance body' (162–3). In her version of these events, 'If a body is technologically mediated this poses the question of whether it is the same body as the one prior to its reconstruction and where the so-called "natural body" begins and ends' (164). And at the end of the day, 'The "enhancing" cyborg technology is the category in which the video dance body most appropriately belongs' (165). So, for dancers who have opted for hip and/or knee replacements, is video dance the final frontier? It can certainly become what Dodds refers to as a 'prosthetic techno-body' where technology acts as prosthesis to support rather than replace the dancing body. It is in this vein that *Dance's Duet with the Camera: Motion Pictures* wishes to begin its dialectic. See Ruth Barnes's chapter in our collection for a discussion on Benjamin's notion of aura in terms of live motion capture.

DANCEFILM: CHOREOGRAPHY AND THE MOVING IMAGE

Erin Brannigan states from the very beginning of her text that 'The dance that is realized in dancefilm did not exist prior to the invention of film and needs to be considered entirely in terms of its cinematic manifestation.'[2] This statement does not automatically rule out conversations about auratic performance. However, it does place Brannigan clearly in a regulatory position: "...we leave the 'actual' body and the terms relevant to such bodies behind when we consider the screened body and our experience of its 'presence.' ...It is a body created through the cinematic machinations of light, dust, and duration" that leaves a sort of "luminous dust" (11).

I wonder if this sort of dust has any relation to what Dodds refers to as the complication of videated representation that 'gives the video dance body an additional texture, a layer of "technological signification"' (149). In simple terms, this conflation might suggest that dance film bodies carry a light dusting of technological significance that we are still trying to decipher. After all, Brannigan argues that 'Film theory offers approaches to the moving body and the moving image that are particularly valuable for developing discussions of dancefilm in relation to screen performance, cinematic presence and gestural articulation, categories of cinematic movement, framing and editing, spectatorship, and the historical film avant garde' (6). Here we have the markers of presence, gesture, spectatorship, and movement that are both physically actual and cinematically framed.

Brannigan calls on pioneer Maya Deren to explain the notion of 'screen choreographies.' Deren's location in the historical film avant-garde is part of what makes her ability to let film frames dance such a vital link to the dance community. In fact, 'One of the most significant film makers, located within the avant-garde, in relation to dance on film is Maya Deren. … Deren is cited as being an innovator of "chore-cinema," an art form in which the dance and the camera are inextricably linked' and 'her work is often described in terms of a dance sensibility' (Dodds, 7). This sensibility entirely determined what Deren had her film cameras do. As Brannigan suggests:

> *Vertical film form* is a concept developed by Deren to account for the different film structure in non-narrative films—what she calls 'poetic film.' Rather than progressing 'horizontally' with the logic of the narrative, vertical films or sequences explore the quality of moments, images, ideas, and movements outside of such imperatives. *Depersonalization* refers to a type of screen performance that subsumes the individual into the choreography of the film as a whole. Actors become figures across whom movement transfers as an 'event.' The manipulation of gestural action through *stylization* occurs through individual performances as well as cinematic effects—the two levels of filmic performance combining to create screen choreographies. (101)

Furthermore, 'Deren's repeated use of the term *dancefilm*' has directly informed Brannigan's own 'use of the term in referring to a cinema of movement where the dance and film elements become indistinguishable' (104). For both Deren and Brannigan, dance must meet film in the middle, using images in ways that speak both languages.

Brannigan credits anthropologist Jane Goodall for considering 'how bodies think and how movement might be a form of thinking' that provides us with a somatic intelligence, or a 'term that overcomes the mind/body binary' (188). This produces, in William McClure's way of imagining it, a 'body which feels where thought fails' (cited on 189). This somatic model 'provides a site for the playing out of… gestural exchange, from the component gestures to the affect of the gestural thrust, to our gestures of response' (189). Brannigan summons this image as a 'site of the affective encounter where bodies collide with bodies rather than thought, where the transcription of signifiers into the component gestures of the work of art are met by the gestures of the "living bodies" who are capable of feeling' and forming what Jean-Francois Lyotard refers to as a "polyesthetic" site…' (cited on 191). Brannigan goes on to explain that none other than Loïe 'Fuller's dancing prefigured the role of the moving body in dance-film as that which can exceed language-based representation and deny the reduction of the body to a definable totality' (192). In our anthology, Isabella Pruska-Oldenhof's chapter best captures Fuller's hide-and-seek mechanisms for the escape of the moving body's subjectivity on film.

ROSENBERG'S SCREENDANCE: INSCRIBING THE EPHEMERAL IMAGE

Douglas Rosenberg's 2012 monograph on screen dance is to date the most concentrated and accurate assemblage of historical and theoretical explorations of dance made for film. Coming from a perspective that leans more heavily toward screen than dance, Rosenberg's book weaves together film, dance, photography, visual arts, and performance studies to arrive at a guide that defines dance's relationship to the camera. Although this author traces a number of pathways along various multimedia methodologies, his introduction to the inscription of hybridity between screen and dance is of most use for our anthology.

Rosenberg begins his book by detailing the relationship of camera to dancing bodies. He likens the movement of dance to camera as a process quite similar to contact improvisation—a multi-person dance practice in which partners constantly rely on each other for physical support to create and achieve their movement. At the center of this motion is of course the body:

…there the camera fixes its gaze. And there the camera allows for a kind of engaged looking at the body that is unique to that device. [In fact,]…

screendance speaks of the *end point* or the *point of reception* by the viewer and not of the material form of the production in the way that 'videodance' refers to the actual production media or method of inscription.[3]

This discussion goes on to make clear that all the names for screendance such as filmdance, cine-dance, dance for the camera, video-dance and others should be considered subcategories of this larger genre. Rosenberg is quick to point out that rather than duplicating vision per se, cameras '*replace* how we see the world with a mediated version of what we desire the world to look like' (9).

Rosenberg describes the body caught in motion by film as an 'impossible' body, one unencumbered by gravity or time. In relation to this body, the camera is 'a carnivorous image-prosthetic device' that merges the languages of dance and film as a 'mediated duet with the body.' As our own title for this anthology suggests, the camera itself dances with the dancer it records. Editing techniques allow the dancing image to multiply, shrink or expand, speed or slow motion, and transform backdrops. We applaud Rosenberg's self-conscious 'attempt to initiate a theory that defines screendance, to open screendance up to further theorization, and to filter it through a set of lenses that can provide new and renewed perspectives on the form' and hope to add our own voices to this nascent conversation.

TAKES AS MULTIMODAL DANCE

We now have the capability on film to let a dancer start in one movement or location and pass through several others sequentially. The dancing self in projected form can be multiplied, divided, enhanced, sped up or slowed down, and positioned in ways that explode the notion of traceable self. It is not unusual to see live dancers interacting with each other in the middle of a series of screens on which fragments or relics of their live performance get replayed in new relation to each other. One such performance took place from 5 to 8 January 2012 at 3LD Art & Technology Center, 80 Greenwich Street in NYC:

> Conceived by choreographer Nichole Canuso and Multimedia director Lars Jan, TAKES immerses you in a shimmering world where live action and lost moments intersect. Barely separated from the audience by the thin membrane of a room-size projection box, the audience is free to wander and shift perspective around the installation. Canuso performs alongside Dito

Van Reigersberg (Pig Iron Theatre Company) in this panoramic marriage of choreography and live film.[4]

In this production, dancers Canuso and Van Reigersberg are separated from their audience only by projection scrims that trace walls of a box around their figures. A live video-feed projects images of the dancers as they move, and also loops their previous movements with new images of themselves. This means that at moments, the live projection of a dancer repeats a gesture that we have seen previously as a movement contained within the self but which then extends to interact with another filmed version of her reaching toward the gesturing version of herself. This creates at least three layers of perception: the original image of live dancer performing movement that is mediated live and appears as slight afterimage on the scrims; the after-image as it is projected; and another hybrid of that image plus the next live mediation of the dancer, whom we still see dancing in the middle of the space. It is thus (at least) a triplicate version of the self on stage. There is also the blending/synthesis of the images and the live dancer, which the spectator sees as a composite kaleidoscopic whole.

Nichole Canuso sets *TAKES* as a performance in the round, which allows this triplication to replicate and splinter itself even further by adding circumambulatory angles of spectatorship that alter each viewer's perception of the piece, depending on the position from which they choose to look. *New York Times* reviewer, Brian Seibert, found this aspect of their staging somewhat vexed by a choreographic content that troubled the technology:

> 'Takes' may be theater in the round, but the going in circles reads as artistic limitation rather than artistic choice. Similarly the halting rhythm of the show, skipping like a scratchy record tended by someone preoccupied with other matters, comes across as more an artistic defect than a representation of the couple's stuttering, stuck relationship. (Seibert, p. C7)

While appreciating Seibert's attention to choreographic detail in this review, it is possible that he may have lost sight (literally and figuratively) of what concessions movement makes in order to accommodate surround video with live feed. His opinion is that 'The technology of "Takes" effectively delivers Ms. Canuso's message, but the content doesn't communicate enough to make us care' (C7). Of course, had the choreography existed free of combination with this technology, Canuso might have tailored it with more phenomenal styles of motion, recognizing that the live dancer was her only medium. However, in efforts to avoid thoroughly disorienting her audience in the round, Canuso made the necessary adjustments to her movement and that of her partner in order to let the body dance with its filmed image(s).

Every multimedia performance is a set of dialogues: at times one medium takes the foreground as in the solo riffs of a jazz ensemble; at other times the various elements perform in complete conversation with each other, letting the viewer construct whatever meanings for the piece he or she manages to glean. What this multi-element conversation demands on the part of its viewers is patience and an ability to actively read layers of information and image as a conglomerate text. Apparently reviewer Brian Seibert expected to follow this conversation in *TAKES* from a single perspective that was upset by rather than open to multiple voices in combination. Granted, multimedia demands a different sort of audience, hopefully one that is willing to put forth increased effort to process and arrange the multifaceted performance they witness.

DANCE AND FILM IN CONVERSATION

The scholars in our anthology discuss and interpret the art of other multimedia practitioners. Our practitioners offer details of their artistic process in trying to place dance and film in complex conversation with each other. The scholar/practitioners talk across boundaries about both what they witness in others' work and how they approach these challenges in their own productions. With both a nod of appreciation to what has come before this moment in the history of film and dance, and an equal recognition of the new versions of film's relationship with dance in live and recorded performance, we offer a range of articles that address the ever-shifting relationship between live bodies in dance and recorded images of these bodies on film.

SITE/SIGHT AND THE BODY

Our first part, 'Site/Sight and the Body,' explores connections between the site of looking and what is seen. From prison yards to travelling performances, these authors investigate the ways in which the camera captures movement as a record of identity and a means of (re)defining the category of dance film. Melanie Kloetzel draws clear connections between site-specific dance and dance film and even cites 1930s–1950s filmed musical theatre's influence on our contemporary narrative link to location. In effect, dance for the camera 'can transform a place from... backdrop into... collaborator,' sharing the following mechanisms with site-specific work: alternative contexts, alternative perspectives, and a democratization of dance that diversifies both dancer and audience demographics. In discussing her own site-specific dance films and the work of others who have inspired her, Kloetzel traces powerful pairings between body, site, film, and dance.

Cara Hagan explores a feminist and womanist approach to the presentation of bodies of color in her own dance films and those of fellow diverse female artists. Hagan details the foundation of her own film festival, Movies by Movers, which uses dance film as a 'sophisticated platform for social commentary.' Her goal in personal work and in studying that of other women of color is to rectify the presentation of all female bodies within both dance and film. She bemoans the lack of racial diversity in dance film, and acknowledges her own process of learning to 'speak dance film theory' from an alternative perspective. Both authors challenge subjectivity as the camera throws the location of embodied self into question within the filmic frame.

Frances Hubbard adds to our discussion of diversity in dance film with an essay on the Hollywood film *Black Swan* (2010), starring Natalie Portman as a ballerina with a psychiatric disability. Portman's character Nina has a psychosis of paranoia that leads finally to her suicide while playing the black swan. In the midst of hallucinations and other obsessive-compulsive behavior, 'the arguably cynical and gratuitous inclusion of the two-minute soft-core lesbian sex scene' with Nina's alternate dancer Lily relies on a 'psychoanalytic theory of lesbian psychosis' promoting 'the patriarchal, heterosexist, and homophobic assumption that lesbianism is a "phase" that should be outgrown, and a desire based only on gender dysfunction rather than autonomous desire.' Through film theory and a psychoanalytic reading of dance shots, Hubbard consciously 'increases the visibility of and discussion about queer/lesbian desire in a space in which lesbianism still remains relatively invisible.' She thus successfully queers both film and dance in this timely discussion.

Movement Beyond the I/Eye

Our second part, 'Movement Beyond the I/Eye,' presents two artist/scholars whose work lets the relationship between theory and practice change according to approach and perspective. Izabella Pruska-Oldenhof puts theory into practice with her piece *fugitive l(i)ght* while Peter Sparling introduces practice *as* theory in a conversation about his choreography.

Pruska-Oldenhof explores the notion of shifting viewership in a return to Loïe Fuller's *Serpentine Dance*. Her own piece, *fugitive l(i)ght*, is a filmic response to Fuller's desire to make her dances somewhat impossible to locate or fix on film. Pruska-Oldenhof reclaims Fuller's work as a performance that presents itself through absence in evocative ways. She compares Fuller to the work of her contemporary, poet Stéphane Mallarmé. She cites these two artists as exemplary in their destabilization of subject/author positioning to set this standpoint in a state of continual flux. Employing an 'unmoored, mobile, and multiple I,' Fuller offers an historical basis from which contemporary female artists have unfixed the gaze through their play on visible/invisible and present/absent subject positions. Feminist theorist Julia Kristeva's expansion of subjectivity in excess that subsequently leads to full dispersion allows for what Mallarmé considered a movement beyond the self.

This notion of movement beyond individual self-conception finds an echo in Peter Sparling's 'Naked Came I/Eye.' Sparling borrows art theorist T.J. Clark's words on Cézanne's nudes that evoke a plurality in visual response in which our experience of our own bodies gets beyond us as viewers. Sparling wonders if the naked dancing body demonstrates a Modernist poetics of dance rather than being trapped in an aesthetically proscribed rubric of interpretation. He prompts us to reclaim the gaze (whether by proliferation or other means) inside the space of the camera. In some ways, Sparling calls forth the I/eye of the camera as a spectator in its own right. This spectator, he reminds us, is a privileged way of looking that holds its own control over perspectives. When moving from the live stage or studio to the flat screen, Sparling identifies an essential shift from human form to a 'purely sculptural morphology and the negative space it inhabits.' He encourages us to move toward a screen version of 'the body electric' that engages the dancing form as a kinetically charged element of film, no matter what its costume.

QUERYING PRAXIS

Our third part, 'Querying Praxis,' begins with a dialogue between the editors of this collection, Ruth Barnes and myself. In 'Theoretical Duet' we struggle to pin down a more exact theoretical relation between dance film and live dance. This conversation then ventures into uncharted territory with the work of two artist/scholars struggling with equal representation for dance and video in live and recorded performance. Heather Coker recounts her methods for tackling and gaining mastery of the camera's wandering eye while Ruth Barnes revises theory and practice through the lens of promenade performance.

Heather Coker takes on wrestling with the beast of integrating live dance and projected video footage on a stage floor in her own work. She likens this process to a translation of meaning that crosses media. Claiming that dance and film do indeed belong in the same space together, she continues to strive for equanimity while the two share stage space. Essentially, she juggles what she considers to be three distinct elements: live dance composition, video composition, and stage composition. A mixture and juxtaposition of these three charges in itself offers a third meaning altogether, one the multimedia artist presents in complex combinations that direct audience perception of all elements as a whole. Coker details the differences demanded of an audience for each element in its own environment: while video has a 'hot' quality that focuses visual imagery in ways that leave audiences in a somewhat passive state of receivership, live dance's 'cooler' medium encourages audiences to make their own assumptions about the connections they witness. Her argument suggests that the hybrid of these forms should try to combine each of their strengths to elevate each other.

In Ruth Barnes's look at ways to turn around or multiply vantage points for an audience through a combination of live-feed video and dance on stage, she layers images in ways that complicate spectatorship and the location of the gaze. Her premise is an investigation of how performance environments may be changed in ways that alter both spectators' and performers' viewpoints in the perception of meaning. She encourages a sort of 'heightened engagement' in her use of a 'promenade performance-in-the-round.' She likens the observer/participant as one form of *flâneur*, a figure who, while detached and contemplative, shifts vantage points in ways that change the meaning of a dance piece by re-framing the movement in radically alterable perspectives.

BODIES, SPACES, CAMERA

Our fourth part, 'Bodies, Spaces, Camera,' looks more closely at the ways in which dance and film trade secrets and work to fortify each other's media. Angela Kassell uses discussions of space, time, and body to describe how film helps dance in practice. My own piece goes back to Maya Deren's historical precedent to better understand how dance helps film in fundamental ways. And Carol-Lynne Moore details the importance of Fred Astaire's demand that the musical camera follow dancers using full-body shots.

Angela Kassel pinpoints the ways in which film has amplified dance, covering the categories of space, time, body, perspective and montage. A spatial setting, for example, might alter audience perception of the movement shown on screen. The surrounding can even proffer meaning for the dance. Perspective in film, or an intersection of framing choices and point of view, has the potential to alienate movement such that the laws of gravity are contested and the manipulation of time either gives the audience an opportunity to watch movement in slow motion or give the image sequence a more narrative feeling. Kassel explains various techniques used in dance film to give moving bodies a different look: duplications, change of size, mirroring or reproduction, fragmentation, and visualization of energy patterns all make these film versions of the dancing body ones that cannot exist without editing the motion. If one were to reverse this process in live performance, the result might be one in which the perspective itself is duplicated, changed, mirrored, or fragmented.

Whereas Loïe Fuller has been touted as what Pruska-Oldenhof considers a dance equivalent representative of the Symbolist Movement, Maya Deren worked consciously to counter symbolist tendencies and named herself instead an 'Imagist.' I argue in my own piece that Deren's use of movement in films during the 1940s drew parallels between the language of film and that of the unconscious. Resisting both symbolist and psychoanalytic interpretations of her work, she let images speak their own language, as one would in a dream. Deren's resistance to interpretive models meant that her films displayed dream imagery that purposefully lacked signification beyond the bodies it presented. Much like Loïe Fuller's evasion of the gaze, Deren presented what Pruska-Oldenhof refers to as a 'fugitive self.'

This self for Deren was always split, at times in two and at others three parts, enacting a literal replication of her form that divided subjectivity and displayed her as both the subject and object of her own gaze. She literally embodies the multiple vantage points that Barnes attributes to the *flâneur*, giving audiences a self that both invites and defies the camera's gaze. She makes use of the space and time distortion that both Coker and Kassel mention, operating with a less than logical kinesthetic sensibility. As she herself tells us, 'motion in a slower speed has no room to hide,' a statement that recalls Martha Graham's phrase, 'movement never lies,' one that Peter Sparling assures me this modern dance maven never let her dancers forget.

Carol-Lynne Moore takes a more dance historical approach in her chapter on Fred Astaire's contribution to the film industry. Moore argues that whereas on the one hand film has radically changed dance's nature as an 'artifact-poor' art, dancers and choreographers such as Astaire laid a strong groundwork for the protocols involved in filming dancing figures. This luminary performer essentially compensated for what might be considered the missing third dimension in 2D film with a demand that cuts in camera angles be minimized and that when the camera tracked the dancers, it showed full body shots only. In some respects, Astaire's absolutes for the film industry paved the way for all Musical Theatre films beyond his own oeuvre. Moore reasons that the 'Astaire style' offered a bit of a paradox for the ballet world that loved him: while carriage in ballet has total vertical balance in most movements, Astaire's axis leaned a bit forward on the dance floor, making him resemble a spinning top. She argues that counter to balletic legs that are usually straight, Astaire worked with his legs always bent and fluid. His ludic essence was essentially what played so well to the camera, which followed his every move, giving audiences what Moore calls a 'privileged view of the dance as it unfolds.'

NEW TECHNOLOGIES: DANCE AS 3D'S ULTIMATE AGENT

Our fifth and final part, 'New Technologies: Dance as 3D's Ultimate Agent,' plays with the use of dance in a three-dimensional film format in order to recognize the acute relevance of moving bodies to the capture of motion on screen. We pair Philip Szporer and Marlene Millar's discussion of their professional work as choreographers for 3D film with Ruth Barnes's further rumination on dance's position in a multimedia world that includes the embodiment of three dimensions.

Philip Szporer and Marlene Millar offer a practical discussion of how film can determine the body's landscape by creating images in 3D that give the body a stronger stereoscopic presence and the editing a slower pace in order to fully experience the dancing form. These authors share not just a dance film project but also a poetic sensibility of dance in three dimensions. They remind us that cinema grounds itself in a movement of light and sound waves wherein what translates to its audiences is a kind of pure but manipulated motion. Dance in many ways is thus the ideal medium to represent in 3D film.

Ruth Barnes tracks us back through a history of multimedia performance and makes clear connections with past experiments and the work of current artists in our collection and beyond. She selects Wim Wenders's 2012 film on choreographer/dancer Pina Bausch entitled *Pina* as a perfect example of how dance and film go hand in hand. Essentially, Bausch's choreography pops off Wenders's 3D screen in ways that breathe new life into old work that illustrate both dance and 3D film's dependence on alive presence, a live presence of bodies in motion that astounds its viewers and brings breathtaking presence to any audience no matter their own physical location.

In this anthology, we invite dancers, filmmakers, and readers of all kinds to experience the thrill, frustration, and complexity of merging camera and motion. We have tried not to privilege either side of this dance/film duality, but rather to explore the many ways in which these two artistic languages might argue with each other, concur, borrow techniques, and act as each other's doppelgangers when thrown into close contact. In some respects, their relationship appears oddly familial; perhaps they share a sisterhood that reflects both a deep and constant contention as well as an enduring love that weathers any and all infractions. As Douglas Rosenberg attests, we need to see dance and film not 'as incompatible forms but rather as siblings with a great deal in common.' He credits Amy Greenfield's notion that 'Film and dance are the only two art forms that move in both time and space. That is a strong basis on which to form a common language' (Rosenberg, 7). We hope that our readers will recognize both ends of this extreme, and forgive us our sibling rivalries. As my students say, without the dancers there would be no video dance. We hold that a history of mixed media beginning with practitioners such as Maya Deren and Loïe Fuller demonstrates that dance and film are powerful partners, but we need to retain and maintain a primacy of the dancing body in even the most cutting edge new technologies.

NOTES

1. Sherril Dodds, *Dance on Screen: Genres and Media from Hollywood to Experimental Art* (New York: Palgrave Macmillan, 2004), 35.
2. Erin Brannigan, *Dancefilm: Choreography and the Moving Image* (New York: Oxford University Press, 2011), viii.
3. Douglas Rosenberg, *Screendance: Inscribing the Ephemeral Image* (New York: Oxford University Press, 2012), 2–3.
4. Brian Seibert, *The New York Times* 9 January 2012, C7.

PART I

Site/Sight and the Body

Where do dance and the moving image meet, and why? How do such encounters alter the viewer's perspective on the dancing body, and on place? Whose bodies dominate the screen dance landscape? This section contains two chapters that look at site, the body, and what we see. Melanie Kloetzel addresses the notion of dance films as site-specific works, and presents an overview of the history of dance and the moving image, as well as an explanation of how language and labels of the dance and screen genre have changed over time. Cara Hagan sizes up the exclusion of women of color in first-, second- and third-wave feminism and carves out a screen space for these excluded bodies to form their own identities in response.

CHAPTER 2

Location, Location, Location: Dance Film and Site-Specific Dance

Melanie Kloetzel

A scarred torso of a man, cracked and peeling paint on an old wall. Verbal descriptions of the smell, look, and feel of a place. Adult men create a long line of monochrome, prostrate bodies leading up a set of stairs and into darkness. Seemingly hundreds of white square cloths display the pocket contents of male trousers, contents that have been forcibly removed as the men move into another realm of existence—imprisonment. In grey tones and slow-moving footage that fades in and out of focus, marching bodies and unison gestures weave with physical markings of time and desperate efforts to communicate through impenetrable walls. This is the world of Alcatraz, a memory of a past place and the reminder of a present reality.

In *Well Contested Sites* (2013), a film by choreographer Amie Dowling, filmmaker Austin Forbord, and performers from the San Francisco Bay area, some of whom had suffered incarceration, we experience the emotional, sensory, and physical conditions of prison through a combination of tight rhythms, palpable stillnesses, athletic partnerings, and, most of all perhaps, searing images of place. In fact, without the location of Alcatraz as the setting for the film, the impact of this filmic and physical rendering of the experience of imprisonment would be decidedly less. Yet, due to the presence of the solid metal bars, dark confining cells, monotone palette, and that overwhelming sense of rigidity from a concrete and steel

M. Kloetzel (✉)
Department of Dance, University of Calgary, Calgary, Alberta, Canada

© The Editor(s) (if applicable) and The Author(s) 2016
T.D. Arendell, R. Barnes (eds.), *Dance's Duet with the Camera*,
DOI 10.1057/978-1-137-59610-9_2

structure, we cannot help but feel how time served might register on the human body.

Dowling and Forbord's contribution is a dance film, a dance made specifically for a two-dimensional screen (whether for television, computer, movie theatre screen, or other virtual display). In this relatively new genre, the dances themselves are typically filmed outside the usual context for dance performance, meaning the stage or the studio. Rather, the majority of dance films are set in (and created for) "real world" locations—in a living room, down an alley, by a lake, in a café, etc. As Katrina McPherson, a dance filmmaker muses, '[v]ery often, people will remember video dance by the location in which it was filmed. Test this out on yourself: how often do you refer to a work as "the one set in a…".'[1]

In this sense, the dance film genre has much in common with another dance genre—site-specific dance. In the 1960s, the era in which both genres found their footing, site-specific dance and dance film tried to find a new direction for dance, away from the studio and the proscenium arch. Instead, both genres turned to alternative contexts as an avenue for realizing their aims. A comparison of the genres offers much to our understanding of both forms in terms of their respective histories, techniques, and impacts. And a fuller investigation of the forms reveals just how important location has become as these genres attempt to recontextualize the dancing body. In this chapter, I will examine dance film and site-specific dance as genres that have embraced both alternative contexts and altered perspectives on the body, and, by doing so, have worked towards a democratizing of Western dance practice on a societal level. Building on a previous argument that I have made regarding the significance of place in the dance film genre,[2] I will demonstrate how dance films, similar to site-specific dances, have dehierarchized the relationship between trained and untrained movers, as well as between performers and place, effectively transforming our notions of how movement can connect populations to one another and to the environments in which they reside.

ORIGIN STORIES AND PARALLEL AIMS

The dance film genre has had its origin story repeated multiple times; for example, in 2002, Virginia Brooks put together a timeline of the genre for the compilation, *Envisioning Dance* and, in 2012, Douglas Rosenberg offered a more in-depth understanding of this history in *Screendance: Inscribing the Ephemeral Image*.[3] Yet, certain key developments bear repeating for the sake of understanding the links between dances made for the camera and site-specific dance. Certainly, dance was coupled with film almost from the first moment film technology took off. Some of the earliest experiments with film made by Thomas Edison and the Lumière Brothers had an inherent interest in how the dancing body figured inside the camera frame. For example, Edison captured Spanish dancer Carmencita's popular act in 1894 and Annabelle Moore's Loïe Fuller-inspired performance in 1895, while the Lumière Brothers turned to Loïe Fuller herself for an impressive rendition of her "Serpentine Dance" in 1896. By the time film began to reach the masses, people found enjoyment in Irene and Vernon Castle's elegant waltzes (made popular in the silent film *The Whirl of Life* in 1915), in Busby Berkeley's swarms of bodies making intricate patterns in the early 1930s, and in Fred Astaire and Ginger Rogers's romantic dancing escapades of the late 1930s. The same can be said for independent cinema, where Maya Deren's experiments in avant-garde films, such as *A Study in Choreography for the Camera* (1945) and *Ritual in Transfigured Time* (1946), joined dance and the camera in new and inspiring ways. Deren's focus on the dancing body venturing through domestic and outdoor spaces helped set the stage for dance films in the generations to come, and Deren's efforts continue to be lauded decades later.[4] Building on Deren's work, as well as the work of such filmmakers as Norman McLaren, Hilary Harris, and Shirley Clarke, choreographers were set to take filming into their own hands when Sony released the first home video cameras in the 1960s. Since this revolutionary development, independent choreographers have been making dances specifically for two-dimensional viewing, spurring the creation of a new genre variously called dance for the camera, videodance, dance film, cinedance, or screendance.[5]

Of course, the dance film genre was not the only new genre to take shape in the 1960s. Many other artistic efforts flourished in this era of experimentation. One of these new genres was site-specific dance. With the influence of Merce Cunningham, Anna Halprin, and others, choreographers associated with the Judson Church movement began taking their dances outside of the theatre space, attempting to uncover connections between the body, movement, and alternative venues. Choreographers including Lucinda Childs, Deborah Hay, Steve Paxton, and Simone Forti took some of the first steps into this genre in the early 1960s, siting their work along busy city streets, on golf courses, in the forest, and in art galleries, to name a few. Two women, often considered the founders of the genre, Trisha Brown and Meredith Monk, took these efforts further. For Brown's pieces, *Man Walking Down the Side of a Building* (1970) and *Walking on the Wall* (1971), dancers in harnesses traversed the walls of buildings, walking as though they were merely meandering down the street; in Monk's works, *Juice* (1969), *Needlebrain Lloyd and the Systems Kid* (1970), and *Vessel* (1971), audiences embarked on tours of a site (or sites) sometimes over the space of week or a month. Through Monk's and Brown's efforts, as well as through other choreographers who entered the genre, site-specific dance developed particular characteristics that have remained cornerstones of the field for the last five decades. As outlined in *Site Dance: Choreographers and the Lure of Alternative Spaces*, these include: an attending to site that encourages audience awareness of and engagement with non-theatre sites, an investment in experimenting with the audience-performer relationship, an interest in pedestrian movement (walking, standing, sitting, and so on), and a focus on the relationship between humans and their surroundings.[6]

On the surface, these two genres—site-specific dance and dance film—would seem to have little in common. One genre expects audiences to venture physically to various sites and to experience a hands-on connection to these places; the other involves sitting and watching a two-dimensional screen. One offers audiences a multisensory experience of place, encouraging audiences to smell, touch, see, hear, and sometimes taste the dimensions of place; the other relies heavily on the visual and aural to convey an idea, unable to access the other senses through its virtual medium. One expects audiences to travel to a specific performance place (and sometimes even during the performance) to personally experience the details and totality of a place; the other brings audiences up close to the miniscule textures and shapes of both dancing bodies and places without the audience having to move a muscle. Yet, upon closer examination, the similarities between the two genres, as well as the motivations behind their creations, are striking, and, I would argue, these similarities bear inspection for the sake of advancing and theorizing both forms.

A New Context for the Dancing Body

At the root of both site-specific dance and dance film lies an interest in recontextualizing the dancing body; in very basic terms, this involved a turning away from the stage space and an embracing of alternative venues for dance. In 1945, when Maya Deren propelled Talley Beatty through multiple indoor and outdoor spaces in *A Study in Choreography for the Camera*, she was foreshadowing the efforts within both genres to find this new context for dance. Dissatisfied by the limitations of the proscenium arch, artists in both genres sought a reframing, a new perspective on dance that could develop via the camera or via unusual sites or both.

For site-specific choreographers, the turn towards new contexts initially stemmed from the 1960s artistic efforts to disrupt the boundaries between art and everyday life. However, site-specific choreographers such as Trisha Brown, Meredith Monk, and others wanted to take this interest further, to find contexts that could not only offer a new frame for the dancing body, but could also provide rich fodder for the work itself in terms of theme, aesthetics, significance, and so on.[7] For Trisha Brown, this meant using the structure of a site to guide the structure of a performance. As she created *Man Walking Down the Side of a Building* (1970), for example, she made sure that artistic agenda was secondary to the strictures of a site— the performance length was determined by how long it took a dancer at a typical walking pace to traverse the outer surface of a building from the roof to the street, not by how long Brown wanted the performance to last.[8] Meredith Monk's ideas on what alternative venues brought to her work are captured particularly well in her article, "Meredith Monk as Site Pioneer." Monk notes that she enjoyed bringing audiences to new sites in order to break up the expectations around performance and the everyday. As she expresses, 'I wanted to make art that was useful, experiential, rather than presentational. At that time, theatrical conventions such as the frontal orientation of the proscenium, the one- to three-hour duration… seemed limiting to me.'[9] But Monk links this idea of disrupting conventions more particularly to her dialogue with space and the specifics of various spaces. As she says, '[w]hat satisfied me most about working in a nontheatrical space was that the process became a dialogue between an environment that already existed and me. My task was to listen to what a particular space was saying to me. I liked that I was not constructing a reality that would be the same no matter where I went.'[10]

Interestingly, within her site-specific explorations, Monk also began to make direct connections to the film medium, a step that she saw as two sides of the same coin. By the 1970s, Monk was frequently referring to film and filmic techniques as inspiration for her live work. In her discussion of *Needlebrain Lloyd and the Systems Kid* (which she subtitled *A Live Movie*), the concept of filmic framing comes to the fore: 'I wanted to play with the filmic notion of time and space in a live performance. I thought that using the techniques of film—close-ups/long-shots, wipes, dissolves, cuts, simultaneity, and framing—would be an intriguing way to explore the time and space of outdoor environments.'[11] By the time Monk started making dance films such as *16 Millimeter Earrings* (1979), *Ellis Island* (1980), and *Book of Days* (1988), it seemed a natural extension of her continued experimentation with film techniques and framing in live site performances.

Framing is, naturally, the very essence of film creation and one of the most fundamental considerations when making dance films.[12] When choreographers began to use the camera as a device to recontextualize the dancing body, they, like site-specific artists, zeroed in on the importance of framing to help define the new genre. But, dance filmmakers were forced to consider not a singular framing of the body within the space of the camera; rather, they had to address the dual framing that was implied in the dance film genre. Rosenberg discusses this dual reframing as a doubling: 'In the last decade at least, the screen has clearly become a well-understood site for dance. However, it is always a site that is doubled: the initial layer is the built environment or landscape in which the body (dance) is located; the secondary layer is the media by which the performance is inscribed, bonded into one screenic image.'[13] Sherril Dodds, author of the well-known *Dance on Screen*, specifies that for dance filmmakers this doubling typically meant a rejection of the stage or studio in order to designate a clear separation between dance film and live performance. As she puts it, 'part of the agenda of dance designed for the camera is to avoid the transposition of a stage context to screen. One way in which this can be achieved is to locate the performance in a site that would not bring to mind, or normally be associated with, a stage setting.'[14] This embrace of "real world" settings for the dancing body lies at the root of the dance film genre, as Deren's *A Study in Choreography for the Camera* so clearly indicates. As Talley Beatty performs a singular phrase for Deren to capture, rather than a consistent background to frame his dancing body, Deren chose a multiplicity of non-studio settings. Seeing his body traverse a forest, a living room, and a courtyard helped the nascent dance film genre carve out a new space for the dancing body, an alternative context that demonstrated that dance film was not akin to live performance documentation.

In truth, for either genre, the choice of context figures as one of (if not, *the*) critical decisions for a project's development. Clearly, for site-specific dance, the initial choice of context ends up determining the majority of all subsequent decisions for a project. Due to the fact that the work derives its themes from a singular site (meaning, from a site's history, design, aesthetics, and surrounding community) and that it is performed at that location (a fact that often determines what performers may be able to do choreographically, as well as decisions about audience size, configuration, sight lines, and the potential need for technical equipment), the audience experience revolves around that initial decision of place. And, even though these experiences of the site may involve the use of the site as a vector to explore larger issues of the day or even the possibility that the site itself is mobile (for example, when the site is a bus, train, or some other transportable one),[15] it is that first consideration of place that guides all future development of the work. For example, for Martha Bowers's *On the Waterfront* (1993), the decision to make the work on the Red Hook piers in Brooklyn, New York ended up influencing the realization of each part of her work: the theme of the work stemmed from the history of the Red Hook waterfront itself, the fact that the site consisted of a succession of piers meant she could treat her mobile audiences to an episodic version of Red Hook history (each pier representing an era of that history), and her decision to work at the piers encouraged her to involve Red Hook community members, whose memories and understanding of the site influenced the work itself.[16]

The decision around which location is chosen for a dance film seems less essential at first glance. I could argue that it would be possible for Beatty to appear against a backdrop of, say, a quarry or bedroom or perhaps a suburban street and still have a similar effect. Yet, the choice of location is not so simple and its effects can be far-reaching for a given film. McPherson, in her how-to manual *Making Video Dance*, warns that the choice of filming location brings with it certain associations and great care must be taken when choosing the context of a film; in truth, a poor choice could ultimately undermine the work. She goes so far as to say, 'In many respects, you can't really properly begin to imagine what your video dance is going to look like before you decide in what sort of environment it will be filmed.... This is because location not only affects what your work communicates, but it also impacts greatly on the way that you can shoot and, most crucially, the dancers' ability to perform.'[17]

The validity of this statement becomes clear as soon as you witness films such as Peter Anderson and Rosemary Lee's *boy* or Chelsea McMullan and Yvonne Ng's *Slip*. In *boy* (1995), a coastal setting of sand dunes and lapping waves fundamentally defines the movement of the lone boy who leaps with abandon off the dunes, digs determinedly in the sand, and gallops through the shallow water like a wild colt. For *Slip* (2008), a single tracking shot of a woman's pool changing room allows audiences to jump to the theme of private female spaces, and the crowded and steamy interior of the changing room brings out both the freedoms and the restrictions that are enacted upon the female form. For both of these films, considerations of choreography, theme, and audience comprehension would have been impossible to determine without having made that initial decision to film on the coast or in a woman's changing room, respectively.[18]

In my own dance film, *The Sanitastics*, which has since its inception been called a "site-specific" film, the initial inspiration for the film stemmed from my experience with a particular place, the Calgary Skywalk system, a series of pedestrian bridges that hang 15 feet above street level in Calgary's downtown core. Intrigued by this unusual spatial phenomenon, I began a research and development process that resulted in a film where the themes, movement phrasing, characterization, camera work, and postproduction choices all sprang from my dialogue with the site. In many ways, the site itself became the main protagonist of the film as the surveillance superheroes (inspired by the security personnel and oodles of surveillance cameras on site) employ powerful traveling movements and performative cleaning tactics that expose the dictates of the place.[19]

As Monk has pointed out, and as can be seen in other site works, site-specific artists have often borrowed from cinematic strategies and terminology to help further their work. Yet, in a curious reversal, dance film scholars have turned to the lexicon of site-specific art and performance to discuss the intricacies of the dance film genre. Rosenberg, in his oft-cited article from *Leonardo* that has functioned as a guide for the theorizing of dance film, turned purposefully to site-specific art to describe the genre: 'Video dance is a site-specific practice, its site being video itself.'[20] When discussing the ground-breaking work of Deren and Merce Cunningham, Rosenberg goes further to state that '[t]he importance of these works can be found in their use of the camera in creating an architecturally and/ or geographically specific site that contextualizes the choreographer's vision in a way not possible in the theater,'[21] yet another nod towards the importance of recontextualization and alternative location. Even in recent writings, Rosenberg continues to be quite frank about borrowing terminology; in 2012, he stated that 'screendance culture is an expanded culture, a site-specific practice that, if true to form, moves beyond the simple migration of dance from the stage... and re-sites bodies in motion in a filmic or screenic space.'[22] As both dance film and site-specific dance continue to reframe the dancing body in terms of alternative contexts (as well as to theorize this reframing), I expect to see further cross-fertilization of the lexicon, a development that could, I would venture, advance the ability to analyze both forms.

ALTERING PERSPECTIVES ON THE BODY (IN PLACE)

Another point of similarity between these two genres resides in their common interest in shifting perspectives and perceptions of the dancing body. In a large part, due to *where* dance films and site-specific dance take place, these forms can offer perspectives on the body that are at odds with what is typically on display in a theatre setting. In a theatre, we rarely have a choice about what we can see from our assigned theatre seat. We cannot (or at least do not) change our distance from the performer. We almost always view the body as an entire entity. And, due to the fixed nature of the proscenium arch and the seats in the theatre, the frame, background, and setting for the dancing body remain static.[23] While stage performances may awe audiences with the virtuosity of the total performing body, the separation between audience and viewer as well as the laws of space and time impose boundaries on the dancing body that can have little variation between one live performance and the next. But in both site-specific dance and in dance films, bodies and their capabilities often appear fundamentally altered, particularly in relation to their surroundings. As bodies interact with diverse sites in both real and actual time, a viewer's awareness of what a body can do shifts: vulnerabilities of the body may be revealed, impossible feats may seem commonplace, and/or unusual dialogues between bodies and place can change our assumptions about what bodies could or should do.

On a basic level, dancers in site-specific works can surprise audiences by blending into an environment in pedestrian ways much as in Lucinda Childs's *Street Dance* (1964); in this work, the trench-coated dancers often seemed indistinct from the trench-coated passersby, undermining our assumptions about which bodies are (or could be) performing. As Steve Paxton said when he reflected on seeing this work in 1964, 'People on the street continued to walk. But now I doubted them. Were they "real"?... The whole city joined the duet Childs made.'[24] Some performances push this merging much further, employing integrative techniques that turn inanimate objects into performing bodies or performing bodies into non-human beings or even inanimate objects that reside at a site. Marylee Hardenbergh, a site choreographer based in Minneapolis, for example, has worked with large machinery in a number of works, with the machines themselves acting as the performers for the audience to witness. On the other side of the coin, in *River* (1995), the choreographers Eiko and Koma Otake float downstream into the audience view at the beginning of their work and continue the journey downstream out of sight of audiences at the end. This entrance and exit are done in the "real time" of the river with the performers allowing the river to carry their still bodies; as such, the performers seem like logs or leaves merely continuing their river journey. For *Junebug* (1998), Leah Stein discovered a divot in the earth where an animal had burrowed and where a child rolling down a hillside during the performance could fit perfectly; this small moment put the divisions between who inhabits a place, animal or human, into question. Site-specific choreographers' awareness of the falseness of such divisions helps guide their work, and their use of such tactics, which I call "techniques of integration,"[25] are evident in a range of site works. As Leah Stein puts it, '[m]y body instinctually reacts and tells me that I am more "a part of," rather than "apart from," the landscape.... That inseparability is at the core of my passion for making dances on site.'[26]

In site work, perceptions of bodies may also alter due to site choreographers' interest in playing with scale, distance, and time in extreme ways. Dancers may move both very far away and/or very close to audience members during the course of the work, or even seemingly break the dictates of time. This playing with scale was particularly evident in Meredith Monk's *Vessel* (1971) where dancers began almost on top of the audience in the intimate space of Monk's loft, making them appear larger than life. But, in the third installment of the work, these dancers ended up in a Soho parking lot far from the viewing audience, and looking more like miniature figures than the performers encountered in the initial segment. Sometimes scale is played with in terms of numbers of dancers, with performing bodies overwhelming audiences with the possibilities of what an active body can do in "daily life." In Stephan Koplowitz's *The Grand Step Project*, for example, which occurs on large sets of steps of museums, libraries, or other grand institutions, 50 or more dancers roll down the steps, sit, fall, and get lifted back up towards the imposing entrances, shifting our impressions of typical pedestrian routes into and away from such buildings.

Site choreographers also toy with experiences of linear time. In Ann Carlson's *Night Light* (2000) project, she restaged eight historical photos in the exact likeness and place of the original photos around the Chelsea neighborhood of New York; audiences took guided tours to see the restaged photos and the performers held completely still positions for upwards of an hour, often in pouring rain, to create the desired effect. As Carlson tells us,

> it created a space-time collision. What's there now, what was there—that kind of history/present juxtaposition... The *Night Light* strategy asks, what was here before it was a Starbucks? The photo being staged on and as close as possible to the site where it was originally taken is vital. It's that collision between a historical moment and what's there in contemporary life, and it points to the fact that we're making history right now. The *Night Light* strategy emphasizes the circular continuum of historical events.[27]

In similar fashion, Rogoff's *The Ivye Project* brought people back to the 1940s, and in particular, to the experience of the Jewish residents of the town. Taking place in a forest in Belarus where 2500 Jews from the town had been murdered and buried in a mass grave in 1942, audiences wandered through the forest witnessing reenacted scenes of private family occasions, meals, love scenes, card games, and so on. As they encountered these quotidian scenes, audiences came to identify with the characters, sensing that these same lively characters walked the very same path to their deaths in 1942.[28] This palpable sense of the past can change our comprehension of time and what performing bodies can access on the temporal continuum.

In dance films, the options for altering perspectives of the body are even more extreme. Spectators can watch the body from a 360° view; they can see the smallest parts of the body in minute detail, such as Bettie de Jong's hip or thigh in Hilary Harris' *Nine Variations on a Dance Theme* (1966); or they can watch dancing bodies perform impossible feats in space and time, such as Liz Aggiss's unbelievably fast movements in a white box or her giant and instantaneous leap into a completely new setting and costume in *Motion Control* (2002). As Rosenberg notes, 'the camera has no permanently fixed point of view, rather the camera in motion has the ability to create a type of intimacy with the dance that can only be imagined by the viewer in the theater.'[29] These shifts of perspective forbid carrying over assumptions about the body from live performance—what it can do, where it can be, and what it can interact with.

Certainly, in dance films, the most obvious methods filmmakers use to shift perspectives of the body are suspending the laws of gravity and altering the flow of time. The dancing body can appear impervious to the downward pull of gravity and dancers can be made to fly, boogie on the ceiling, rest in mid-air, or perform movements forward or backward in extreme fast- or slow-motion. Such efforts were being made with the dancing body in Hollywood already in 1951 with Fred Astaire's famous "Dance on the Ceiling" in MGM's *Royal Wedding* (1951) and they continue today in such experimental films as Liz Aggiss and Billy Cowie's *Anarchic Variations* (2002), and, on at least a minimal level, in the vast majority of dance films where a body's speed and placement almost always undergo some kind of alteration in the editing booth. These seemingly superhuman possibilities for the body emerge due to the very different nature of screenic space and time, which are, by definition, illusionary— products of the live moment as much as products of post-production manipulations. As Rosenberg puts it, 'While viewing a screendance it is clear that bodies *were* in motion in some prior temporal moment, and that those same bodies *did* perform in real space in real time. But those phenomena are in the past in a dimensional, temporal space…'. Rather than witnessing the live moment, the audience sees a recasting into a screenic time and space, where all manners of physical laws are disrupted and audience members function as "secondary witnesses" to a former event.[30]

Many dance filmmakers are enamored with upending physical laws in their work; yet, they just as often make choices that demonstrate an altered perspective on the body in relation to its environment. Specifically, these shifts of perspective rely on framing techniques that—as I mentioned before in relation to site-specific dance—I refer to as "techniques of integration." In a recent article in the *International Journal of Performance Arts and Digital Media*, I discuss how filmmakers, in addition to employing techniques that defy physical laws, are drawn to techniques that provide a new perspective on the dancing body as intimately connected to place. In particular, filmmakers have turned to the use of close-up and long shots, as well as to rapidly changing or unusual angles in order to highlight the relationship of human bodies and place. With a nod to Gabri Christa's film *Quarantine* and Ana Cembrero Coca's *Cinética*, I argue that 'close-ups that show a body's influence on place or *vice versa* often stand out in terms of kinesthetic impact.'[31] For example, when the soft flesh of a hand unfolds against the rough surface of peeling paint in the Dowling and Forbord's *Well Contested Sites*, our own physicality cringes at the sense of what such a dangerous surface could enact on our own flesh; or when the young boy's feet land heavily on the sandy dunes in *boy*, we can sense that satisfying give of the sand softening our impact. Rosenberg describes it well: 'A gesture that on stage may seem small and insignificant may become, when viewed through the lens, grand and poetic, while the dancer's breath and footfalls may become a focal point of the work.'[32]

Erin Brannigan, borrowing from Giles Deleuze, has discussed such close-ups as a method for dehierarchizing the relationship between body parts, so that fingers or elbows or toes can have an equal dramatic import as the face.[33] For dance films such as *boy* and *Well Contested Sites* described above, the close-up certainly enacts this physical dehierarchizing. However, I argue that the dehierarchizing extends much further in the dance film genre, in particular, through the use of the long shot. In examining the films *Horizons of Exile* (2007) by Isabel Rocamora and *Away From Here* (2011) by Katrina McPherson, I assert that the long shot 'has become more common as filmmakers try to highlight the environment as a key contributor to the work, not only in how it relates to the body, but also in how it exudes its own changing and moving characteristics. Instead of merely underlining the diminutiveness of the body, the long shot often acts to boost the import of the site.'[34] After ample close-ups of an intimate couple on an outdoor bench in Shantala Pèpe's *Embrace* (2014), for example, the film rests at the end with a long shot that captures the fact that the couple's embrace was facilitated by the loneliness of the bench in a beautiful and isolated coastal environment. The beauty of the environment, which was shown as background during the majority of the film, grows in stature as the ripples of the water and the playful wind become the main actors for a full 35 seconds at the film's close. In this way, body and site become joint players or protagonists in a dehierarchized relationship between humans and place.

These tactics of dehierarchization are also evident in the use of rapidly changing or unusual angles, so that the body seems to wholly blend into a site or *vice versa*. In Eiko & Koma's *Wallow* (1984) and Carolyn Pavlik's *Lady-boy* (2004), shots from a low or high angle, canted angle shots, and/or revolving shots end up disorienting viewers, making them question the distinctions (and possible hierarchies) between site and body. This becomes eminently clear in Joris Hoebe's *Val* (2010), where bodies, viewed from above as well as from very tight low angles, surface as if growing directly out of the earth's soil, or in Kim David Arrow's *Wave Action* (2014) where a lone and passive body gets tossed about in the waves that lap a shore, appearing more as a discarded mollusk left on the beach than a living human figure. When bodies and environment blend in such films, Leah Stein's comment on the body as more '"a part of," rather than "apart from," the landscape' seems ever more pertinent.

As site-specific dances and dance films employ techniques of integration, as they question the dictates of space and time, as they toy with expectations about who is performing and the possibilities of the performing body, they are also interrogating how our bodies function in everyday life. They are making the case for the endless possibilities of a responsive body, a body that does not have to bow to the pressures and preconceptions that limit what our bodies (can) do in the places we inhabit. Elsewhere, I have noted, borrowing from Susan Foster's work on choreographic empathy, that when we view dance films (and, I would here argue, site-specific dances) with the strategies outlined above, our bodies sense what it means to interact with a site; we can feel the prickliness of the peeling paint or the buoyancy of water supporting our physicality. Foster has discussed this kind of physical empathy at length in her work, *Choreographing Empathy*. Investigating the research being conducted on mirror neurons, corporeality, and choreographic strategies, Foster demonstrates how kinesthetic empathy arises by seeing how a dancing body interacts with other bodies, objects, and its surroundings.[35]

In the dance films and site works discussed above, filmmakers and choreographers capitalize on the reality of kinesthetic empathy by placing the body in sensual and often unusual relationships with specific sites. Observing such relationships triggers a kinesthetic response that allows viewers to imagine themselves responding to and integrating with place; or, to put it another way, dance films provide the spark for viewers to go off and engage in their own new and unexpected dialogues with a variety of spaces. It is through this dialogue, a dialogue that models the potential avenues for our own phenomenal bodies, that dance filmmakers and site-specific choreographers attempt to enact a fundamental shift in how we perceive our bodies and their capacities as integrated with place.

DEMOCRATIZING GENRES

As dance film and site-specific dance make strides to take dance out of the cloistered environments of the studio and stage, to shift perspectives on the body, and to dehierarchize the relationship between body and place, they also make strides in "democratizing" the dance experience. Helena Wulff, a social anthropology professor in Stockholm, has discussed the "democratizing" effect of dance on screen in the volume, *New Technologies at Work*. Examining dancers' views of dance on screen, she notes their disappointment with the lack of sensation when live performance gets reduced to the two-dimensional screen. But Wulff argues that such a response by dancers overlooks the very important fact that dance on screen makes dance as a form much more accessible, democratizing dance for the masses. Wulff asserts that this expansion of audience is a revolutionary step for dance, and one that also demonstrates that bodies and machines are tightly joined in a 'social relationship.'[36]

Without a doubt, due to the fact that dance film and site-specific dance have both expanded beyond the bounds of the theatre space, the level of accessibility for the forms tends to increase. Theatrical productions of dance often attract limited audience attendance due to ticket prices, a lack of familiarity with dance as a discipline, and/or societal assumptions about a theater-going public. But site-specific dance and dances made for the camera typically exist in spaces that anyone can and will frequent. For site works, they may materialize beside you on the sidewalk, in a neighborhood parking lot, or as dancers suspended off the local library; for dance films, they can pop up with ease on your computer or television screen, or sometimes at the local cinema during a dance film festival. As such, the number of spectators who access these forms may far surpass the typical dance performance, and the audience itself is often more diverse.

But this "democratizing" of dance in both forms extends much further. For one, the performers involved in the work often changes; no longer limited to the trained performer, dance filmmakers and site-specific choreographers have expanded their idea of cast to include audiences and/or untrained performers in the work. In theatrical settings, audiences tend to expect professional dancers to perform virtuosic feats that they themselves would never attempt; they also assume that they will have no physical involvement in the work. However, in both dance films and site dances, non-dancers often get involved in the work. This is partly due to alterations in framing (site choreographers often see the frame of their work including the audience and audience movement, while dance filmmakers employ close-ups or long shots that can mean less of a need for virtuosic movement), but it is also due to both genres' interest in seeing broader populations represented in the work.

In site works, audience members are frequently enticed into direct participation in the work and/or people with no dance training may become the performers. At times, this inclusion may be very simple, not pushing audience participation, but rather inviting them to join if interested. In my own site-specific dance works with live musicians *Rock* (1998), set in Brooklyn on the Carroll Street Bridge over the Gowanus Canal and in *The Gate City: Rail Town Reflections* (2007), set in a vacant hotel in downtown Pocatello, Idaho, I asked the performers to continue the live music after the performance was over so that the dancers could bring the audience into the experience of dancing on site. This is a tactic widely used in the site world, as remarked on by Sara Pearson and Patrik Widrig in *Site Dance*[37] as well as viewed in the recent work, *The River* (2014), performed by the Barrowland Ballet along the Clyde River in Glasgow. Audience involvement is a tactic Marylee Hardenbergh has used at great length in her work; for example, in multiple works, she has asked audiences to manipulate props or fabrics to create large-scale patterns in space. In Hardenbergh's *One River Mississippi* (2006), audience members in seven sites along the Mississippi River (spanning thousands of miles) found themselves performing a gestural, learned unison phrase up and down the river at the exact same moment.[38] This involvement breaks down the fourth wall and upends common ideas about who can don the title of performer.

This audience involvement may also surface unexpectedly, in the form of verbal feedback or surprising audience antics. A number of site choreographers remark on these surprising moments, noting how upending theatrical conventions makes audiences feel empowered to become directly involved in the work. Heidi Duckler, in her creation process at a Los Angeles Laundromat, remembers how involved the people who used the Laundromat got during rehearsals for the piece. They would comment on the process and took a certain pride in seeing the work develop. Even during the performance itself, a local man, who refused to wait the 20 minutes for the length of the piece to be performed, did his laundry in the middle of the performance, thereby becoming an unintentional performer in the work and delighting the audience with his involvement. As Duckler comments, 'It is hard not to have interactions develop on site because the audience isn't passive… Site work plays with boundaries. We have had audiences travel down hallways, and suddenly some started opening doors. They couldn't control themselves; they were giddy. They felt free to express themselves, to make choices. And they had to rethink, "What exactly are the boundaries here?"'[39]

At times, such involvement may be less comfortable for audience members, but perhaps more impactful. For example, in Heidi Duckler's *Most Wanted* (1997), when audiences entered the abandoned jail in Los Angeles where the piece was going to take place, they discovered that they would be fingerprinted and their mug shots taken as part of the piece. Through this mechanism, audiences directly experienced the physical techniques that prisoners undergo and Duckler treated these audience members as characters involved in the performance throughout the subsequent viewing of the work. Tamar Rogoff's methods for audience involvement in *The Ivye Project* were perhaps a bit subtler, but no less direct, as she exposed everyone's culpability in the actions that had taken place in 1942 in that Belarus forest. At the very end of the work, the audience members—all of whom had slipped on green capes at the beginning of the piece effectively uniting them in that common role of audience—had to remove these capes in order to enter the memorial (gravesite) itself. Rogoff recalls this experience,

> It was in this moment that their status as audience dramatically changed. In rehearsing this piece, I spoke with elderly survivors who knew my family and who also had family buried in Ivye's mass graves. Often they recounted with great difficulty how their loved ones were forced to take off their clothing and whole families, mothers, and teenage sons saw each other naked in their last seconds together in that very same forest. Having worn their capes throughout the piece, taking them off for the last scene became a significant act. The audience now represented themselves; they became visible as individuals. Did that play any part in why a layer of self-consciousness and responsibility descended on my audience as they stepped in this sacred space?[40]

Such moments may function as uncomfortable democratizing moments, moments that force audiences to question how we collectively attend to both site and community.

Site-specific choreographers may also move beyond audience involvement and attempt to recruit non-trained dancers as the main performers in the work, either to match the grand scale of a site, or to demonstrate the potential of involving wider populations in dance, or both. For example, for Monk's *Juice*, she wanted to match the impressive scale of the Guggenheim Museum, so she incorporated 85 performers in the piece, including whole families and friends of friends who wanted to try something new.[41] In *The River*, choreographed by Natasha Gilmore, she aimed to explore multiple sites along an impressive river, so she incorporated large numbers of community members into the cast itself (150 total), with children and senior citizens ushering audiences along the river and performing in substantial sections of the work as both movers and musicians.

Often this style of performance may grow out of workshop-based involvement with local communities. In such instances, choreographers contact local groups at schools or community centers or the like in order to develop the work; then, after participating in the workshops, members of the groups take on major roles in the performance itself. Martha Bowers, for example, has created a number of pieces solely for non-trained dancers based on this workshop model. For her work *On the Waterfront* in Red Hook, local schoolchildren and seniors from the nearby housing projects acted as highlighted performers portraying the various episodes of Red Hook history. Bowers feels strongly about the implications of involving local community in her projects, and she bemoans how such work has too often been dismissed in the United States, 'where the lines between what was considered high art and community art were clearly drawn. Artists whose work involved community members were often devalued as amateur.'[42] But this does not dissuade Bowers from continuing to be inclusive in her work. As she states, site work and its ability to incorporate community members into the performance process has allowed her to address the key concepts of 'public space and participatory democracy,'[43] themes that she sees as the essential ingredients for building better communities.

Ann Carlson attempts such inclusion in a different way. For her *Real People* project, she has made a series of pieces for people grouped in certain non-dance professions or activities, for example, for lawyers, fly-fishermen, nuns, security officers, or poker players. Typically these pieces are performed where the work or activities take place—such as a pond or office—in order to, as Carlson says, 'invite people… to participate in these performances by siting the work where they were comfortable.'[44] To make the work, Carlson would draw on the participants' familiarity with the movement associated with their communal activities. As Carlson describes, 'These works are based around people's passions, why they do what they do, and what gestures and movements define and express those passions and activities. The series examines stereotypes and looks for the vulnerability and the humanity embedded in people's work and identity.'[45]

By democratizing the dance performance experience in this way, site choreographers are often quite aware that their work has wider political implications. Bieringa, of the BodyCartography Project, voices it like this: 'I think an activist message is inherent in the process of getting people excited about their bodies. They realize that dancing is not only a physical activity for trained movers.'[46] Through Bowers's long-term experiences in working with community members in the United States and Ireland, she has begun to discuss site-specific dance in much broader terms, terms that speak directly to the democratizing experience,

> My notion of what the choreography of a project entails has expanded exponentially. It is not only what the performers are doing during the final public performances; it also includes the many interactions between artists and community members that have been part of the process of making the work. It includes people from different cultures, races, or socioeconomic backgrounds crossing cultural comfort zones to interact because they are involved in the project. It includes the journey the audience takes to reach the site and to follow the performance through a location… This is the kind of site-specific choreography that interests me—social choreography, spiritual choreography—choreography that navigates the intersections of place, heart, and public interest.[47]

Although I would argue that the democratizing of the dance experience is less evident in dance film, without a doubt, the dance film genre can be characterized as making dance more visible and accessible on a popular level. As Wulff observed, the marriage of dance and technology has opened dance viewing to the masses; and this expanded population is even measurable, with the number of "hits" on various dance films uploaded to sites such as YouTube or Vimeo able to be counted. On your average Vimeo or YouTube account, the author of a film can see how many hits they are receiving a week, with the average overall number of views on a YouTube video running around 8000.[48] Although for most dance films posted, the number of views tends to be on the lower side of this average, in a quick perusal of the dance films that have been uploaded to YouTube through TenduTV's *Essential Dance Film* series, the majority of films had between 1000 and 3000 views and some had well over 10,000.[49] And, of course, this is only one venue where these films have appeared—most having made a significant circuit to dance film festivals around the world prior to their being included in the *Essential Dance Film* series. Considering the much smaller audiences that see live contemporary dance performances—

typically ranging in the hundreds rather than the thousands—the democratizing turn for dance film is certainly quite apparent in these simple online audience tallies.

Dance filmmakers, similar to site-specific choreographers, have also become attracted to the idea of including non-trained movers in their films. While many dance filmmakers are still dedicated to displaying the virtuosic body, other dance filmmakers have veered in the direction of highlighting "everyday" people. In *Dance on Screen*, Dodds links dance film's new interest in expanded casts directly to place. As she modestly claims, 'The use of alternative locations for the presentation of dance and the exploration of pedestrian and gestural movement vocabulary, technologically mediated movement, and popular or social dance styles, undoubtedly have some impact on the type of performers employed within video dance.'[50] Sometimes this means an inadvertent role for such performers, an extreme example being Bobbie Roelofs and Tim Terhorst's 1-minute *In A Rush* (2013), where pedestrians rush by a male protagonist who walks in slow motion from a subway train to the ascending escalator; but at other times, it might mean that community members exhibit more of a supporting actor role. In Pascal Magnin's *Reines d'un jour* (1996), for example, the townspeople of the village in the Alps where the film takes place are very active participants in the film. At times, these townspeople function as observers of the main performers, looking on their antics with interest, concern, or disdain; at other times, they interact more directly with the dancers, slow-dancing with them in the village square or offering advice to them.

This interest in an expanded cast has grown in recent decades, with filmmakers recruiting people outside of the trained movement community for leading roles in their films. For example, in Chelsea McMullan and Yvonne Ng's *Slip*, which was filmed in a Toronto bathhouse, all types of female movers, young, old, trained, and untrained, were highlighted in the project; this generated the sense that these were the women who would be in the changing room on any given day, irrespective of the camera's presence. An endearing example of an expanded cast can be seen in Victoria Marks's and Margaret Williams's *Mothers and Daughters* (1994) where eight pairs of mothers and daughters participated in the film. Only 3 of the 16 performers had any dance training and, as Marks explains, '[t]he film medium supported an interest I had in working with movers who were not professionally trained.'[51] Rosemary Lee, a site-specific choreographer who also makes dance films, has taken her interest in working with non-dancers from one genre into the other. For her film *boy*, she worked solely with one eight-year-old boy with no prior dance training. She notes that for such filmmaking ventures she is inclined to curb any overly technical impulses she may have due to their appropriateness (or lack thereof) in a given setting. 'When I work in an environment,' she observes, 'I will discard anything that looks like "Oh a bit of dance!" because what I am trying to make is movement that seems right and totally apt for the environment.'[52]

Often, the democratizing turn towards an expanded cast has intertwined with the genre's investment in narrative to appeal to a wider public. As I have discussed elsewhere, dance filmmakers have embraced narrative as an important tool in the genre, one that allows them to steer away from the more abstract characteristics of contemporary dance, aiming instead for dances that are more accessible and relevant in daily life. In part, this interest in narrative has been supported through the turn to alternative contexts. Kelly Hargraves, a dance filmmaker and cofounder of the Dance Camera West festival, states that 'placing dances in dynamic locations and honing them with a narrative structure... bring[s] a heightened context and sense of reality to choreography.'[53] Dance filmmakers, keen on connecting to audiences and enjoying film's ability to access people's instinctual drive towards narrativity, have embraced story structures to link to wider swathes of audience than would typically frequent a dance theatre production. But, as I have noted, this narrativity relies quite directly on filming in alternative contexts. As I argue, 'Filming in a kitchen or on a street corner or even in a train compartment has allowed filmmakers the opportunity to make direct associations for audiences, as dances filmed in such locations instantly lose a level of abstraction and gain personal, referential meaning... Our experiences in similar sites layer our viewing and cause a sympathetic response that adds to our personal connection to the work.'[54]

In sum, the more accessible contexts for dance film and site-specific dance, as well as the efforts to diversify the bodies dancing, allow for a democratizing of the dance experience not typically evident in live stage performances. As site-specific dances appear on street corners, in parking lots, or along the river in your own neighborhood—perhaps including children, seniors, or friends that you may know and/or addressing issues that are directly relevant to your community—it may be difficult to dismiss such work as extraneous or too abstract. For dance film, the embrace of narrativity and the inclusion of all types of performers, trained and untrained, serves to broaden the playing field, making contemporary dance—a form whose abstraction seems to make it a difficult sell for the population at large—more readily comprehensible as well as enticing. In other words, as dance film and site-specific dance continue to expand the viewing (and participating) population for dance, dance as an art form becomes a democratized practice, one that grows in relevance and availability through the creation and presentation of these forms.

CONCLUSION

To be clear, while dance films *may* include an expanded cast or site-specific works *may* offer expanded understandings of what a body can perform in place, not all dance films or site-specific dances undertake these aims; they may have decidedly different goals with highly virtuosic bodies maintaining the fourth wall on site or even with photo-shopped bodies appearing on screen that fit with societal norms for particular (thin) body types. However, when viewing the works discussed above as well as a much wider swathe than I have the space to discuss here, the ability of site-specific dance and dance film to draw in wider populations and push the boundaries of what a performing body could (or should) do is quite evident. By taking audiences beyond the theater walls and encouraging them to empathize with the dancing body in alternative venues, both site-specific dance and dance film have expanded our ideas of how a body may relate to place. And this expanded notion of bodies in place helps us probe our ideas about the human-place relationship.

When Eiko and Koma Otake float downstream like two pieces of driftwood in *River* or when the dancers in *Away from Here* open their arms inviting the screen viewer into the landscape of the Scottish Highlands, we, as audience, are forced to ponder the human-place relationship in new ways. We are urged to question *what* is possible for the moving body as well as *who* has such possibility—trained bodies or the public at large. And this democratized probing figures as an invitation in both forms. 'Will you enter this dialogue?' Katrina McPherson seems to say as the dancer on screen opens her arm to the Highlands. 'Will you explore how *your* body can contribute to the discussion?' chimes in Olive Bieringa as she invites you to dance with her down the street in *GO*. As dance films and site-specific dances offer a dehierarchized understanding of the dancing body in place, we, as audience for or as performer in the work, can jump on the chance to redefine human interactions with one another and with our environments. Hopefully, we will choose to enter this dialogue, learning from both forms that it is our moving bodies—with all of the expanded possibilities modeled by these forms—that have the most to offer as we determine a future for humans in place.

Notes

1. Katrina McPherson, *Making Video Dance* (New York: Routledge, 2006), 64.
2. This chapter builds on a recent article in the *International Journal of Performance Arts and Digital Media* where I asserted that 'Owing to the absence of spoken text in most dance films, the filming strategies used in the genre (including frequent use of close-up and long shots), a keen interest in narrative and the presence of a responsive and phenomenal body, location has taken on added import in dance films.' Melanie Kloetzel, 'Bodies in place: location as collaborator in dance film,' *International Journal of Performance Arts and Digital Media* (2014), 2.
3. Virginia Brooks, 'Timeline: A Century of Dance and Media,' Judy Mitoma et al, eds. *Envisioning Dance on Film and Video* (New York: Routledge, 2002), xix–xxx; and Douglas Rosenberg, *Screendance: Inscribing the Ephemeral Image* (New York: Oxford University Press, 2012), 33–49.
4. For more on Deren, see Telory D. Arendell's chapter in this volume, or see Amy Greenfield, 'The Kinesthetics of Avant-Garde Dance Film: Deren and Harris,' in Judy Mitoma et al., eds. *Envisioning Dance on Film and Video* (New York: Routledge, 2002), 21–6 or Erin Brannigan, *Dancefilm: Choreography and the Moving Image* (New York: Oxford University Press, 2011).
5. What to title this genre has been under discussion for a number of years. I have chosen to use 'dance film' as my main term for three main reasons. First, the term 'film' has populist appeal, a characteristic much in line with my argument in this article; second, 'film' also has certain artistic connotations, an attribute that denotes an appropriate categorization for the dance works made for the screen. Finally, I have argued in previous articles for the narrative characteristics of film, something that has carried over into the dance film genre. While I secondarily use 'screendance' because it is the term of choice in theorizing dance film creations, I personally hope that 'dance film' will become the default term in years to come.

6. Melanie Kloetzel and Carolyn Pavlik, eds., *Site Dance: Choreographers and the Lure of Alternative Spaces* (Gainesville, FL: University Press of Florida, 2009). For an introduction to site-specific dance as well as an outlining of its main characteristics, see the Introduction, 1–24.

7. Kloetzel and Pavlik, *Site Dance*, 7–15.

8. Kloetzel and Pavlik, *Site Dance*, 13–4.

9. Meredith Monk, 'Meredith Monk as Site Pioneer, 1969–1971' in Kloetzel and Pavlik, *Site Dance*, 40.

10. Kloetzel and Pavlik, *Site Dance*, 45.

11. Kloetzel and Pavlik, *Site Dance*, 44.

12. Framing is a subject so vast that I do not have the space to address it here, although I will make references to some of the choices around dance film framing in the next section. For more information on framing, see Francesco Casetti, *Eye of the Century: Cinema, Experience Modernity* (New York: Columbia University Press, 2008) or, for the basics of dance film framing, Katrina McPherson, *Making Video Dance* (New York: Routledge, 2006).

13. Douglas Rosenberg, 'Excavating Genres,' *International Journal of Screendance* 1:1 (2010), 64.

14. Sherril Dodds, *Dance on Screen: Genres and Media from Hollywood to Experimental Art* (New York: Palgrave, 2001), 23.

15. Much has been written in the site-specific performance world about the definition/categorization of site-specific work, and this continues to morph as artists experiment on site. Miwon Kwon originally discussed the notion of site as a vector in her theorizing site-specific art, and this idea can be witnessed in many site-specific performances (for example, Joanna Haigood's *Invisible Wings* or Heidi Duckler's *Mother Ditch*). There has also been significant discussion around site-specific art and mobility, especially as performances such as Ann Carlson's *Geyser Land,* which took place on a moving train, force us to expand our understanding of site-specificity. For more on these concepts, see Miwon Kwon, *One Place After Another* (Cambridge, MA: MIT Press, 2002); Melanie Kloetzel, 'Have Site, Will Travel—Container Architecture and Site-Specific Performance,' *Conversations Across the Field of Dance Studies* 33 (2013), 23–9; and Fiona Wilkie, 'Site-Specific Performance and the Mobility Turn,' *Contemporary Theatre Review* 22:2 (May: 2012), 203–12.

16. Martha Bowers, 'Choreography for Uncontrollable Contexts' in Kloetzel and Pavlik, *Site Dance*, 280–2.
17. McPherson, *Making Video Dance*, 64–5.
18. These two films are exemplary of dance filmmakers' choice to film in alternative contexts. However, not all filmmakers make the choice to use settings that register as everyday locations. Some use studios, stages, green screens, or very bare white rooms that are difficult to place. However, in conducting surveys of dances made for the camera, an everyday context outnumbers the studio or theatre context by a large percentage. For example, on the two well-known *Dance for Camera* DVDs, all of the films are sited in non-theatre contexts; and, a survey of Vimeo's Dance on Camera "channel" (which features work from the amateur to the professional), 80 percent of the dance films are clearly not in a theatre or studio and at least 70 percent are located in places where an everyday realism outside of a theatre context is integral to the film's theme. See https://vimeo.com/groups/danceoncamera. Accessed 18 March 2015.
19. *The Sanitastics* has been selected for presentation at the 2011 Third Coast Dance Film Festival (Houston, TX), the 2011 Sans Souci Festival of Dance Cinema (Boulder, CO), the 2011 Oklahoma Dance Film Festival (Tulsa, OK), the 2011 Festival Internacional de Videodanza de Uruguay, the 2013 Sans Souci Festival of Dance Cinema on Tour in San Marco, TX, for a three-month run at the EPCOR Centre in Calgary, AB through the Gallery of Alberta Media Artists, and was selected for TenduTV's *Essential Dance Film* series. For more about the creation process for *The Sanitastics*, see Kloetzel, 'Bodies in place,' 13–5. Curiously, another dance film of mine, *Icarus Fried*, developed in quite a contrasting way, with many of the film's themes deriving from a stage version of the piece, which came before the film, rather than from the film site. However, the film setting, an abandoned egg farm, ended up deepening the theme material and then drastically influencing subsequent live presentations of the piece. See Kloetzel, 'Bodies in Place,' 7–8.
20. Douglas Rosenberg, 'Video Space: A Site for Choreography,' *Leonardo* 33:4 (August 2000), 275.
21. Rosenberg, 'Video Space,' 275.

22. Douglas Rosenberg, *Screendance: Inscribing the Ephemeral Image* (New York: Oxford University Press, 2012), 155.
23. Rosenberg, 'Video Space,' 279.
24. Steve Paxton, 'PAST*Forward* Choreographers' Statements,' in Sally Banes, ed., *Reinventing Dance in the 1960s: Everything Was Possible* (Madison, WI: University of Wisconsin Press, 2003), 207.
25. I have employed the moniker 'techniques of integration' in relation to dance film in a recent article, but I would argue that such techniques have existed for decades in site-specific performance, perhaps before they became a strategy in dance film. See Melanie Kloetzel, 'Bodies in place: location as collaborator in dance film,' *International Journal of Performance Arts and Digital Media* (2014), 2–8.
26. Leah Stein, 'Of Grass and Gravel,' in Kloetzel and Pavlik, *Site Dance*, 150–1.
27. Ann Carlson, 'An Interview,' in Kloetzel and Pavlik, *Site Dance*, 108.
28. Tamar Rogoff, 'Carriers of Consciousness,' in Kloetzel and Pavlik, *Site Dance*, 260–7.
29. Rosenberg, 'Video Space,' 262.
30. Rosenberg, *Screendance*, 155.
31. Kloetzel, 'Bodies in place,' 4.
32. Rosenberg, 'Video Space,' 277.
33. Erin Brannigan, *Dancefilm: Choreography and the Moving Image* (New York: Oxford University Press, 2011), 44.
34. Kloetzel, 'Bodies in place,' 5.
35. Susan Foster, *Choreographing Empathy: Kinesthesia in Performance* (New York: Routledge, 2010), 1–2. Foster's work includes a deep genealogy of the terms choreography, empathy, and kinesthesia in order to demonstrate that choreography has a way of 'summon[ing] other bodies into a specific way of feeling about it.'
36. Helena Wulff, 'Steps on screen: technoscapes, visualization and globalization in dance,' in Christina Garsten and Helena Wulff, eds. *New Technologies at Work: People, Screens and Social Virtuality* (New York: Berg, 2003), 199–200.
37. Sara Pearson and Patrik Widrig, 'An Interview,' in Kloetzel and Pavlik, *Site Dance*, 225.
38. Marylee Hardenbergh, 'An Interview,' in Kloetzel and Pavlik, *Site Dance*, 161.

39. Heidi Duckler, 'An Interview,' in Kloetzel and Pavlik, *Site Dance*, 86–9. Duckler describes another moment when a group of audience members unintentionally got stuck in a freight elevator during a performance and their struggle to deal with their panic, including spontaneous singing, ended up making them seem a part of the performance itself. 'They had gotten inside and become part of the show' (92).
40. Tamar Rogoff, 'Carriers of Consciousness,' in Kloetzel and Pavlik, *Site Dance*, 266.
41. Meredith Monk explains that, '[e]verybody that was in *Juice* would get 10 more people involved; whole families and kids got involved.' Meredith Monk, 'An Interview with Meredith Monk,' in Kloetzel and Pavlik, *Site Dance*, 39.
42. Martha Bowers, 'An Interview with Martha Bowers,' in Kloetzel and Pavlik, *Site Dance*, 271.
43. Kloetzel and Pavlik, *Site Dance*, 275.
44. Ann Carlson, 'An Interview,' in Kloetzel and Pavlik, *Site Dance*, 107.
45. Kloetzel and Pavlik, *Site Dance*, 105.
46. Olive Bieringa and Otto Ramstad, 'An Interview,' in Kloetzel and Pavlik, *Site Dance*, 135.
47. Martha Bowers, 'Choreography for Uncontrollable Contexts' in Kloetzel and Pavlik, *Site Dance*, 287–9.
48. In one statistical accounting, the average number of YouTube views was 8332 per video. http://www.reelseo.com/average-youtube-views/. Accessed 14 July 2015.
49. See Essential Dance Film https://www.youtube.com/show/essentialdancefilm/featured
50. Dodds, *Dance on Screen*, 86.
51. Victoria Marks, 'Portraits in Celluloid,' in Judy Mitoma et al, eds., *Envisioning Dance on Film and Video* (New York: Routledge, 2002), 209.
52. McPherson, *Making Video Dance*, 67.
53. Hargraves, 'Europeans Filming New Narrative Dance,' 167.
54. Kloetzel, 'Bodies in place,' 9.

References

Aggiss, L., & Cowie, B. (2002). *Anarchic variations*. London: Arts Council Capture 2.

Anderson, D. (2002). *Motion control*. London: ACE/BBC Dance for Camera.

Anderson, P., & Lee, R. (1995). *Boy*. London: MJW Productions. As seen on *Dance for Camera 2* (2008). New York: First Run Features.

Arrow, K. D. (2014). *Wave action*. Philadelphia: Kim David Arrow.

Brannigan, E. (2011). *Dancefilm: Choreography and the moving image*. New York: Oxford University Press.

Brooks, V. (2012). Timeline: A century of dance and media. In J. Mitoma et al. (Eds.), *Envisioning dance on film and video* (pp. xix–xxx). New York: Routledge.

Christa, G. (2007). *Quarantine: Another building #1*. New York: Danzaisa.

Coca, A. C. (2009). *Cinética*. Spain: La ignorancia.

Deren, M. (1945). *A study in choreography for the camera*. New York: Mystic Fire Video. As seen on Stieber, D. A. (Ed.). *Envisioning dance on film and video* DVD. New York: Routledge.

Dodds, S. (2001). *Dance on screen: Genres and media from hollywood to experimental art*. New York: Palgrave.

Forbord, A. (2013). *Well contested sites*. San Francisco: Rapt Productions.

Foster, S. (2010). *Choreographing empathy: Kinesthesia in performance*. New York: Routledge.

Hargraves, K. (2002). Europeans filming new narrative dance. In J. Mitoma et al. (Eds.), *Envisioning dance on film and video* (pp. 163–167). New York: Routledge.

Harris, H. (1966). *Nine variations on a dance theme*. New York: Mystic Fire Video. As seen on Stieber, D. A. (Ed.). *Envisioning dance on film and video* DVD. New York: Routledge.

Hoebe, J. (2010). *Val*. Amsterdam: NTR and KeyFilm.

Kloetzel, M. (2010). Site-specific dance in a corporate landscape. *New Theatre Quarterly, 26*(102, part 2), 133–144.

Kloetzel, M. (2011). *The Sanitastics*. Calgary: kloetzel&co.

Kloetzel, M. (2013). Have site, will travel—Container architecture and site-specific performance. *Conversations Across the Field of Dance Studies, 33*, 23–29.

Kloetzel, M. (2015). Bodies in place: Location as collaborator in dance film. *International Journal of Performance Arts and Digital Media, 11*(1), 18–41.

Kloetzel, M., & Jeff, C. (2007). *Icarus fried*. Pocatello: kloetzel&co.

Kloetzel, M., & Pavlik, C. (Eds.). (2009). *Site dance: Choreographers and the lure of alternative spaces*. Gainesville: University Press of Florida.

Kwon, M. (2002). *One place after another*. Cambridge, MA: MIT Press.

Magnin, P. (1996). *Reines d'un jour*. Geneva: Swiss TV. As seen on *Dance for Camera 1* (2003). New York: First Run Features.

Marks, V. (2002). Portraits in celluloid. In J. Mitoma et al. (Eds.), *Envisioning dance on film and video* (pp. 207–209). New York: Routledge.

McMullan, C. (2008). *Slip.* Toronto: Vision Entertainment.

McPherson, K. (2006). *Making video dance.* New York: Routledge.

McPherson, K. (2011). *Away from here.* Nairn, Scotland: Goat Media.

Otake, E., & Otake, K. (1984). *Wallow.* New York: Eiko & Koma.

Pavlik, C. (2004). *Lady-boy.* Kalamazoo: Carolyn Pavlik.

Paxton, S. (2003). PAST *Forward* Choreographers' statements. In S. Banes (Ed.), *Reinventing dance in the 1960s: Everything was possible* (pp. 206–208). Madison: University of Wisconsin Press.

Pèpe, S. (2014). *Embrace.* Brussels: Shantala Pèpe.

Rocamora, I. (2007). *Horizons of exile.* London: Infinito Productions.

Roelofs, B. (2013). *In a rush.* Amsterdam: Cinedans.

Rosenberg, D. (2000). Video space: A site for choreography. *Leonardo, 33*(4), 275–280.

Rosenberg, D. (2010). Excavating genres. *International Journal of Screendance, 1*(1), 63–73.

Rosenberg, D. (2012). *Screendance: Inscribing the ephemeral image.* New York: Oxford University Press.

Wilkie, F. (2012). Site-specific performance and the mobility turn. *Contemporary Theatre Review, 22*(2), 203–212.

Williams, M. (1994). *Mothers and daughters.* London: MJW Productions.

Wulff, H. (2003). Steps on screen: Technoscapes, visualization and globalization in dance. In C. Garsten & H. Wulff (Eds.), *New technologies at work: People, screens and social virtuality* (pp. 187–204). New York: Berg.

CHAPTER 3

The Feminist Body Reimagined in Two Dimensions: An Exploration of the Intersections Between Dance Film and Contemporary Feminism

Cara Hagan

WHERE DO WE STAND?

When one steps into the world of dance film, she stands between two distinct artistic traditions, with two distinct histories. Where one is as old as humanity, the other is brand new in comparison. Where one is concerned with the impermanence of each moment, the other is concerned with capturing moments to be kept forever. The differences between the traditions of dance and film make for a precarious but dynamic partnership that over the past century has given way to a genre of art making that challenges the definition of each and pushes the artists who make these works to become more creative, more resourceful, and more equipped to learn and apply new skills to make what they envision. For many women and feminist allies, dance film has created a space apart from mainstream media and the traditions of professional dance to practice principles of feminism, including rectifying the presentation of the female body, confronting issues of race, class, and cultural identity, while making room for the kind of cre-

C. Hagan (✉)
Appalachian State University, Department of Theatre and Dance,
Boone, North Carolina, USA

© The Editor(s) (if applicable) and The Author(s) 2016   49
T.D. Arendell, R. Barnes (eds.), *Dance's Duet with the Camera*,
DOI 10.1057/978-1-137-59610-9_3

ative, intentional activism that has continued to characterize third-wave feminism. What is it about dance film that makes it a space that welcomes female and feminist participants to challenge gender roles, gendered and racialized stereotypes and take control of the presentation of the body that dance or film alone cannot? Where do dance and film alone fall short? Where does dance film—an admirable, but imperfect platform—fall short? Based on my experiences as a student, an artist, an educator and a curator, I will explore what it means to be a feminist in the twenty-first century and what it means to make feminist art in the context of dance film.

PUTTING CULTURE INTO CONTEXT

To explore contemporary feminism in the context of any art from, I have to first pose the question: 'What does contemporary feminism in action look like?'

As a woman born in the mid-1980s, I enjoyed many of the benefits of the triumphs of second-wave feminism. I ran cross-country and was on the softball team in both middle school and high school. Instead of home economics classes for young women, there were shop classes, photography classes and career development classes offered to everyone. I was an anchor on my middle school's cable access news show, where my college mentor, a Communications student from Syracuse University, encouraged me to explore a field that was traditionally dominated by men. I watched my mother walk to work in her sneakers; she would put on her high heels when she got to the office. My mom was making half of our family income at the time. I knew that one day, I could do that, too. Of course as a pre-teen and young teenager in the 1990s, I was not completely aware of how the innovations—and pitfalls—of second-wave feminism would continue to affect me and my peers as we journeyed toward adulthood, and what that movement had given way to for the feminism of my generation.

More than any earlier wave of feminism, contemporary feminism has harnessed the power of popular culture in unprecedented ways. The 'women can have it all' mentality of second-wave feminism has in many aspects given way to an amplified version of this ideal through the presentation and perpetuation of the glamorized super-woman in popular culture. My introduction to popular feminism as it arose in the 1990s was through the Spice Girls (1994–2008), a British pop group whose catchphrase was 'Girl Power!' Scary Spice, Sporty Spice, Baby Spice, Ginger Spice and Posh Spice were presented as individual incarnations of what we girls were encouraged to aspire to in the collective; abstrusely powerful, independent, rich—and in a departure from second-wave feminism—very sexy. There were myriad other examples that spoke to girls and young women of all ages. The *Power Puff Girls* (1992–2005)—a cartoon featuring three pint-sized cuties named Blossom, Bubbles and Buttercup created by a Professor Utonium as perfect little girls—full of sugar, spice and everything nice. Following a chemical spill in the lab, they gained extraordinary physical and mental powers to crush evil with pizzazz in every episode. *Xena, Warrior Princess* (1995–2001) touted a radiant Lucy Lawless in the title role who aptly defeated her (mostly male) enemies using wit, physical strength and sometimes her statuesque beauty. Xena's famous war cry was the icing on the cake, the proverbial 'Girl Power' shout to top them all. Clearly, the aims of second-wave feminism had stuck. This feeling of power was both inspired within and being given voice to in mass consciousness. 'Affirming female friendship, agency and physical prowess' had become hallmarks of 1990s pop feminist icons.[1]

In 2001 at the age of 17, I decided to go to art school. I had been quietly learning to dance at my local studio, where I fell in love with the raw experiences of the body. In art school, I began to learn that the world of dance was full of paradox and so much more complicated than the simple, uninhibited joy I felt when first learning to dance. I was introduced to feminist authors like bell hooks and Alice Walker. While these writers and others put feminist theory and practice into simple terms, I couldn't reconcile the information with what I was experiencing. While the adverse effects of sexism and related societal ills were at the heart of what these thinkers were commenting on, I was a dancer. In my world, my body was not only on display, but it was being scrutinized against a set of standards that were entirely out of my control. The shape of my muscles, my height, the color of my skin, my whole being in regard to a constantly shifting ideal of aesthetic beauty, depending on the whims of the auditioner, the choreographer or the instructor, were being pitched against me and every other aspiring dancer in the western art world. And this was acceptable. Acceptable, too, was the idea that staunch competition was normal, and that as a female dancer, you were easily replaceable. We were warned about eating disorders as a part of the dance landscape we would all become familiar with either directly or indirectly. Ultimately, they were acceptable. This was sexism at work and in every way, and I was on board, unquestioning.

Historically, dance has been filled with contradiction, which has served to disenfranchise many of the artists that participate in it. Take, for example, the dichotomy presented by the romantic era ballerina: A young woman chosen to represent the epitome of chaste femininity on stage was also often making a living off-stage by entertaining the sexual desires of wealthy patrons. This practice was condoned by theaters and often the only way a young woman from a poor family could have a chance at making a comfortable, upwardly mobile living.[2] One can also cite issues in professional dance regarding the perpetuation of dysmorphic practices beginning in the mid-twentieth century due to aesthetic shifts in fashion and ideas around the ideal female dancer's body (though one may argue which influenced the other). While many companies enabled this cultural phenomenon, perhaps the most notable institution to condone these ideals is the New York City Ballet under the direction of George Balanchine from 1948 until 1983, the year of his death. Not only did Balanchine emphasize an almost unattainable body ideal, but he also wielded unruly power over his female dancers, having say in what they ate, their sexual practices, and whether they could return to the ballet after having children.[3] While one may argue that the world of professional dance is full of feminists and feminist actions—it is—the fact of the matter is that those things that are *not* feminist in nature stand out as tarnishes on the art form: the exclusion of people of color from the stage, appropriation and exploitation of dance forms derived from various ethnic groups, exclusion of differently-abled movers from dance education and performance and the very current and ongoing reality of inequality in arts education.

During the years I spent in college, I did not identify as a feminist. Of course, I was in agreement with many of the ideals of feminism: equality in the workplace, eradication of sexual harassment and the perpetuation of rape culture. But like many young women of my generation, I was hesitant to be associated with the stereotype second-wave feminism had been bound by: women who hate men. In fact, until I was in my mid-twenties, I did not identify as a feminist. I felt that perhaps feminism had run its course. Of course, I had a lot of growing up to do.

KITCHEN TABLE: ENGAGING IN CONTRADICTIONS MAKES STATEMENTS

In 2010, I had just finished production on my third dance film, *Kitchen Table*.[4] In the film, catty homemakers Penny and Jo—played by myself and my sister, Mackenzie—bake, bicker, gossip, shop and dance around an idyllic 1950s world. Frivolity abounds, and a realm unfolds where spoons become dance partners and women's voices are replaced with the chatter of birds. The stage dance this film is derived from and the creation of this film was in response to both my upbringing with movies of the golden age of Hollywood and the growing resurgence of interest in domestic activities of many young women of my generation. Fashion blogs, DIY craft blogs and makeup tutorials were popping up all over the Internet. Pinterest would soon follow. Disney had regained popularity among my contemporaries and ironically enough, the college students I was teaching at the time were *obsessed* with princess characters penned long before they were born. A whole new set of princess characters would emerge from the creators at Disney during the 2010s, igniting even more interest by young girls and women in all things 'girly.' During this time, I had become curious about feminism again and my place within its aims, citing my own aesthetic interests in the 1950s—namely the womanly fashion and squeaky-clean lifestyle aesthetic in the form of colorful bakeware and household kitsch—and noticing the contrasts between the dream and the truth. The dream of the 1950s still stands as an unspoiled time in America's history, where men and women knew their places and the country was more or less at peace. Politicians and pundits like to wax nostalgic about the era when talking about the deterioration of the family in the United States in efforts to quash progress in the form of causes like women's reproductive health and same-sex marriage. The truth is, there *never was* a traditional family unit in the United States. Family has always been a varied, messy endeavor that evades definition. Additionally, much of the country was excluded from this lifestyle, idealized and touted by women's magazines and sitcoms, as women of color, single mothers and women of low socio-economic class could not afford to partake in the activities of housewifery.[5] Even women who *could* afford and participate in it felt trapped upon returning to the kitchen after having a taste of financial and social independence during World War II.[6]

Citing these realities, our tongue-in-cheek participation in this ideal presents several contrasts. First of all, my sister and I are African American. It is rare to see women of color donning circle dresses, crinolines and bright red lipstick in television and the movies these days, as the film industry is still overwhelmingly white, presenting material from an almost entirely eurocentric, heteronormative viewpoint. There certainly were no people of color represented in early TV, as the studios wanted to depict for the American public the 'least objectionable' family unit, which could only include a two-parent, heterosexual, white, suburban household.[7]

Until fairly recently, with the creation of such sitcoms like *Family Matters*, a show about the experiences of an all-black family, *Will and Grace*, about the experiences of two roommates, a gay lawyer and a straight interior designer, and *Weeds*, about a single mother who sells pot to maintain her middle-class lifestyle, the trope of the 'least objectionable' family has been held up in mass consciousness by the entertainment industry. Second, there is an absence of men from our story (save one cameo). Women in film have historically been depicted and are still often depicted as needing men to validate or save them, even in shows and movies where the female character is the heroine. Finally, there is no housework or children to speak of in *Kitchen Table*. During the 1950s the amount of housework a woman did went up immensely as compared to the previous two decades. The idea that housewives had much time for frivolity at all was not the case. With the cultural notion that homemakers were to be in charge of all aspects regarding the home coupled with the boom of the convenience appliance business, housewives found themselves making fulltime jobs out of maintaining aesthetically beautiful homes and raising children in a child-centric cultural ideological shift. While making the most obvious commentary on how times have changed, given the efforts of second-wave feminism, *Kitchen Table* also alludes to several present-day contrasts that are still within our cultural purview. The most glaring is the exclusion of women of color from second-wave (and third-wave) feminism, which I will touch on later.

During the production of *Kitchen Table* my own ideology regarding my alignment with feminism changed. I realized that using this platform of dance film, I could present myself and others through a lens that spoke to my concerns as an American woman. Outside of live, professional dance, where tradition has continued to create obstacles to success for female artists, artists of color and those without the financial capital to study or create freely, and outside of mainstream media, where women and other marginalized populations do not often get the chance to fairly represent themselves, I had found a wonderful niche in this in-between, in-the-margin art form. I had become a feminist. The years following the making of *Kitchen Table* would bear many new feminist projects, some of which have been ongoing. One of the projects is the creation of a film festival, Movies By Movers, where I have had the opportunity as artistic director and curator to see hundreds of films, many of which echo my experience of practicing feminism on screen.[8]

Movies by Movers

My path to becoming a festival director and curator was a winding one, which included growing up loving classic movies and the movie musicals of the golden age of Hollywood (1930s–1960s), being introduced to the world of independent film in college, attending my first handful of film festivals as a filmmaker and finally, desiring to create a platform to support artists who are as interested in aesthetic exploration on camera as I am.

As a child, I spent countless Sunday afternoons sitting on the couch with my mother and sister watching Turner Classic Movies and American Movie Classics. I've seen them all: *All About Eve, On the Waterfront, Some Like it Hot, It's a Wonderful Life, To Kill a Mockingbird, A Raisin in the Sun*. From these films, I gleaned bits of important film history and theory that I would learn about in greater depth later. My favorites were the movie musicals. I could watch the likes of Fred Astaire, Gene Kelly, The Nicholas Brothers, Vera Ellen, Ann Miller, Chita Rivera and Bill "Bojangles" Robinson dance for hours without losing interest. To live in a world where song and dance could communicate emotions inexpressible through simple dialogue, where a big dance number could solve the principal conflict in a story just in time for a happy ending, was the kind of world this whimsical child dreamed of living in. Little did I know, these movie musicals were to become part of the dance for camera canon that has helped to shape—and continues to help shape—the discipline of dance film.

Entering art school, I met a cohort of aspiring filmmakers who desired to participate in various aspects of filmmaking I had never considered: directors, producers, editors, cinematographers and art directors. I saw my first screening of short films made by my peers. I was blown away. I mused: 'You mean films aren't all made in Hollywood? And it's acceptable for a film to be five, ten, fifteen minutes long? Where do these films go once they're made? Who watches them? Can *anyone* make a film? Can *I* make a film?' From that first experience of a student film screening, I began watching independent movies. I found I had an affinity for documentaries and a fascination for foreign films, and I began to learn the differences between how independent films and blockbusters are made. I began to learn about the film industry as a whole, a difficult-to-navigate hierarchy that has the power to leave artists floundering and greatly influence mass perception through its constant outpouring of media. I was also to learn about the historical and ongoing struggle for parity within the film industry.

Most fascinating to me was learning about the oppressive practices of big Hollywood studios, like MGM and Paramount, beginning in the early days of movie-making, up through the mid-twentieth century. Where the stars of classic movies were concerned, their public image and in fact much of their personal lives were the subject of strict oversight. While both men and women were signed to these oppressive contracts, women saw the greater share of constraint.[9] Given the double standard in Hollywood between perceptions of women and men (which arguably still exist), events like divorce, illicit affairs played out in the public eye, and even things like public drunkenness were seen as foibles that might be punishable by being dropped by a studio. Clauses pertaining to physical appearance, behavior while in public, on the red carpet and in TV appearances were common. Furthermore, these "morality clauses" in contracts could prevent women from engaging in specific romantic relationships—like relationships with other stars that might hurt the public reputation of a starlet, or engaging in interracial relationships before the court decision to allow interracial marriage in the United States in 1967.[10] The latter, of course, would have affected both women and men. Further, the struggle for equality in the film industry is apparent in the conversation around the representation and compensation of women and other marginalized populations in today's film. While many Hollywood stars are using their public image and financial flexibility to confront institutional bias in the film industry—take the Geena Davis Institute on Gender Media, for example—women, people of color and people with disabilities find themselves severely underrepresented both in front of and behind the camera.[11] Further, when people from these minority groups *do* find themselves in front of the camera, often the images we see are ones of stereotype and objectification.

With these notions in mind, I decided to learn to make films of my own. In 2007, I enlisted the help of Brett Hunter, a cinematographer/editor I met while in college. We made several choreographic tests and in 2008, my first dance film, *Folding Over Twice*, was completed.[12] I now had the opportunity to travel to my first film festival, the Indie Grits Film Festival in Columbia, South Carolina, known for screening imaginative, experimental films of all genres made in the American South.[13] During the screening of my film, my heart was racing. How would this audience respond to a film featuring modern dance as the main form of expression? At the end of the showing, there was a Q&A with several of the filmmakers. The first question from the audience went to me. 'Tell me how you go about crafting narrative without the use of words,' one man mused.

Good question! I began talking about how movement is a language all its own, that, with the help of the camera and editing, can be crafted to create a dynamic, intimate conversation without conventional speech. Without even knowing it, I was talking dance film theory. Over the next several years, I would travel to many film festivals with *Folding Over Twice* and other dance films I'd made. Along the way, I would begin to educate myself about dance film, beginning with the movie musicals I loved so much, then moving on to independent dance filmmakers like Maya Deren. I began to seek out other dance filmmakers in my state, then around the country. It was not until 2010 that I would get the idea to start my own film festival, Movies By Movers. I was in graduate school, studying inter-disciplinary art. As a practicum project, I wanted to experiment with the process of curating. I had questions surrounding the role of the curator as a supporter of artists who desire to share their work. In addition, I had questions about how the act of curating a film screening could provide a platform for dialogue around an art form that was not widely recognized. That first year, 12 films came from the call for submissions. We presented 11 of them. Working with the panelists I had chosen to assist me, how could I frame the conversation I imagined having around this art form? Luckily, persistence won out. Over the next five years, through increased exposure via social media, independent film networks and the vast dance and film communities across the globe, Movies By Movers grew, each year seeing a significant jump in the number of submissions. In 2014, Movies By Movers featured a robust roster of films from around the globe, vary-ing considerably in cinematic and choreographic approach, subject matter, scope and production value. The conversation I imagined having with the first installment of Movies By Movers is steadily unfolding. One of the things I love most about being a curator is actively seeking work that excites me, that demonstrates thoughtfulness or inventiveness in the genre of dance filmmaking. I have the opportunity to observe artistic trends, the growth of individual filmmakers as they continue to create new work, and the experience of audience members, as they engage with this art form, many for the first time. In addition I get to see social commentary and activism in action. When I alluded to the 'kind of creative, intentional activism that has continued to characterize third-wave feminism,' I believe I have the pleasure of including dance film among those endeavors. With consistently over half of the submissions to Movies By Movers being directed by women and about two-thirds of projects being choreographed by women, Movies By Movers has emerged as a platform to spur conversation around issues of representation, individual expression, and the many ways artists define contemporary feminism. The films I will discuss in the following sections, while not all having appeared at Movies By Movers, have been found through networking in the dance film community and through my work helping to curate the University of North Carolina at Greensboro Dance Film festival, of which Movies By Movers is a collaborative, programmatic partner.

CONFESSIONS OF A LACKING PURSUIT: VULNERABILITY AND DEFIANCE

Contemporary feminism, as it applies to very young women, is a constantly evolving concept with many different facets and several definitions. These definitions play out in social media platforms, in mass media and popular music, sometimes in contention with feminist theory as presented in the university classroom. What is certain is that there are more young voices participating in this conversation than ever before, thanks to the very platforms where these conversations play out. For Generation Y, or the Millennials, harnessing the influence of digital spaces to make and disseminate statements has proved a powerful tool to keep the discussion around feminism flowing.

Maggie Bailey, a 2014 graduate of the College of Charleston, sees dance film as a place to explore feminism in ways that contradict formerly accepted patriarchal norms and highlight the ways in which a woman of the twenty-first century navigates the structures of inequity. In *Confessions of a Lacking Pursuit* (2014), Bailey choreographs and directs a powerful performance by fellow classmate, Heather Bybee, set to the recitation of Sylvia Plath's 1962 poem, 'The Applicant.'[14] The entire dance takes place in the Charleston Library Society building, a historical institution founded in 1748, with its current location in the heart of downtown Charleston, built in 1914. The environment among the confined stacks of historical, cultural gems and in the wide-open, black and white tiled foyer of the building provides an arresting setting for the piece, which explores the presentation of the female form in personhood against the satirical, objectified portrayal presented by Plath. Bailey describes the strength of the work in the vulnerability she creates in part by placing Bybee in a set of undergarments—a plain, black slip and black underwear—in a public place. For Bailey, vulnerability plays an important role in contemporary feminism. 'I think it is in a place of vulnerability that strength is gained—feminists are vulnerable in recognizing that there is gender inequality. We've expressed our expectations for the changes we want to see, and I believe we will see them, but there is always that chance it won't happen, or that it won't happen in our time frame.' Further exploring the concept of vulnerability—a concept arguably absent from many conversations around feminism—Bailey questions the process of prurient objectification of the female body, especially that of the female body in motion. 'I'm interested in how women can be portrayed as strong characters in circumstances that are not about sex, while still recognizing that movement is sensual—the idea that there can be sensuality without objectifying it. I think all movement can be provocative without being sexy or making you feel uncomfortable, without stripping away any of the humanity, self-worth or significance.'

Heather Bybee's performance is deliciously sensual, three-dimensional and full-bodied against the sharp angles of library book cases and grid-like pattern of the tiled floor. As the words of Plath's poem emanate into the space, Bybee contradicts them at every turn.

Come here, sweetie, out of the closet.

Well, what do you think of that?

Naked as paper to start

She turns swiftly, then pauses in periods of controlled suspension, only to explode outward, taking up the space around her. The camera dances with Bybee, moving around her to catch every angle of her body as it changes form at a furious pace.

But in twenty-five years she'll be silver,

In fifty, gold.

A living doll, everywhere you look.

It can sew, it can cook,

It can talk, talk, talk.

…

It works, there is nothing wrong with it.

Shapes emerge from a series of sharp poses, followed by more dizzying turning, a trip to the floor, where Bybee stays for only a moment before exploding upward, again. At several times during the piece she looks directly into the camera. Bailey claims that coupled with an exploration of vulnerability in *Confessions* is defiance. To place the dancer, powerful, inquiring, taking charge of spaces, both large and confining in the midst of this collection of words that paint a picture of subservience—albeit sardonic—is a way to demonstrate all the spaces women confidently occupy in the twenty-first century. Further, Bailey claims that using Bybee as the featured character in the film was quite intentional, not only because of her abilities as a mover, but also because she is in Bailey's view, a woman of the twenty-first century who wears many professional hats and defies societal expectations still reserved for women.

The good thing, Bailey concludes, is that young people are talking about inequality. While Bailey says she's never experienced in her lifetime a woman who was not a working woman, or inferior to men in any way, she notes that her mother's generation had to endure much to pave the way for her own. In some ways, Bailey finds it incredible that feminist concerns still need to be addressed in this day and age. However, she states that she and young women like her are ready to keep the conversation going, creatively.

YELLOW RIVER: CHALLENGING THE CONSTRUCTS OF IMPOSED IDENTITY

It is arguable that despite the difficulty of being able to define contemporary feminism in a singular way, individualism, among all else, is one of the most defining factors of third-wave feminism and has made space for people of all kinds to break out of the boxes they've been assigned and float among many nuanced definitions of self.[15] Since the 1990s, the attempt to eradicate strictly binary notions of the human experience has served to combat some of the criticisms of all waves of feminism not being inclusive enough.

Li Chiao-Ping is a dancer and dance filmmaker based in Wisconsin.[16] Her early film *Yellow River* (1992) explores concepts of discovering and defining the self while challenging notions of womanhood from a Chinese perspective and questioning stereotypes associated with being a Chinese-American woman growing up in the United States. The film begins centered around a pile of rice, a pair of hands slowly releasing grains into the top of the pile. It is revealed that these are Li's hands. She sits in a space surrounded by cultural symbols—bags of rice, red cards with Chinese calligraphy, water. We hear the sounds of traditional Chinese gypsy music, as Li begins to trace large, circular shapes in the rice on the floor. As the film progresses, Li's voice begins to ring out. In between recitations of superstitious beliefs, both Chinese and Western, which emerge from all sides of the screen in front of her face in a flurry of white letters: 'Never burn your rice, or walk under a ladder or open an umbrella indoors. If you eat every single grain of rice in your bowl, you'll bear many children,' Li interjects:

> I'm running. I'm running as fast… I'm running as fast as I can, but I can't get away…

This powerful cascade of words and the following interjection echo the experience of being bombarded with thoughts, viewpoints and imposed identities that are not your own. In many ways, this presentation echoes the struggles faced by present-day feminists, where the question of identity is concerned. Quite often in contemporary feminism, the discussion around stereotypical impressions of women of color and their derisory inclusion in feminism arises as an issue still not reconciled within feminist communities and the Western world at large.[17] This is in light of the third-wave movement being fueled largely in part by women of color who felt disenfranchised by second-wave feminism.[18]

As the film continues to progress, Li begins a sweeping, swirling, sliding dance in the pile of rice on the floor. She creates shapes in the grains, walks on the tops of her feet and picks up the rice in her hands. Li explains that the walking on the grains on the tops of her feet alludes to the centuries-old practice of binding the feet of girls in China, citing also the preference of parents to bring a son into the world, instead of a girl. I ask Li how this film connects to her definition of feminism and her definition of self. She notes that the act of presenting herself as a strong, self-aware woman moving in and out of these realities against stereotypes born of both contemporary American and historical Chinese notions of femininity is in many ways a commentary on the politics of otherness and identity imposed on individuals and groups by others. In the film, Li interjects again:

> My mother told me I was Chinese. She made it sound like a dirty word. 'Remember,' she'd say, 'you're…………in America, that's………….' At School they called me,

'Ch-ch-ch-ch..........'

My mother told me I was Chinese. 'Does that mean I have yellow skin? Are my eyes slanty? Do I have a flat nose? Do I smell of China?'

You told me I was good. You told me I was pretty. You told me I was smart.

You told me I was Chinese.

In speaking to Li about the film's message, I ask her what about it still rings true for her, more than twenty years after making it. She says, '…it's a constant process where we discover ourselves—this person coming from whatever the expectations are, fitting into one particular kind of box—you used to have to check a box, some boxes did not exist. Some identities were to remain hidden. Saying who you are still resonates.'

I ask Li if her work is a work of activism. 'Activism? In short, yes. I'm doing it the way I feel comfortable doing it, though. Some people are good at lobbying, going to protests, some people work at non-profits, run for office—for me it's smaller—it's about affecting students and the people around me who see my work.'

MORE: Contesting a Culture of Hyper-Productivity

A contemporary feminist issue that has gained traction in national conversation over the past two decades is the plight of the professional mother. While second-wave feminism argued that a woman could and should have it all—career, family, and a robust social life—the result of that notion is that women have entered the area of career building without systemic consideration for motherhood and family life. Pursuing professional success and raising children in a society that praises over-work and hyper-productivity is a precarious dance that often requires women to 'do it all,' but hide their family-centered activities from the eyes of those that might perceive them as unfocused or uncommitted to the work at hand. I believe especially where academics are concerned, the road to tenure is a difficult one, almost unattainable if one is a woman of childbearing age who wishes to fulfill desires for building a family.[19]

Filmmaker Erika Randall Beahm and her husband Daniel Beahm working as Teahm Beahm explore these concepts in *MORE* (2013).[20] While working toward tenure at the University of Colorado, Randall cites her frustration at being told she must 'do more' to be favorably considered for tenure while raising a new baby boy. She speaks of the precariousness of pumping breast milk in between meetings and in airport bathrooms while maintaining professional composure in the face of fatigue.[21] These occurrences of paradox quickly became a metaphor for her experience in 'the crazy space of hyper-production' during the years and months leading up to tenure. In the film, Randall plays essentially two characters. The first, a sci-fi-inspired creature of production, her breasts secured to a super-pump powered by a 1950s vacuum cleaner. Around her waist, a skirt of 200 plastic milk jugs which sways ominously as she moves awkwardly in a confined white, liminal space.[22] The other character is that of herself, unadorned and raw, dressed only in a white slip. She mirrors many of the movements of the sci-fi character, highlighting qualities of harshness. Many of the movements have a sensual dynamic to them, making one wonder if the intent is to contest or glamorize the idea of hyper-production. In conversation, Randall notes that several of the movements that ended up in the choreography would have made her uncomfortable in live performance and that the feeling of hyper-privacy in the film—the enclosed space, the single body in each shot, the details illuminated through the camera—gave the film high emotional stakes. As she notes in her lived experience, dualities keep presenting themselves: Provider versus collaborator, artist versus educator, and so on.

Watching the film, the viewer is struck by the stark imagery. The raw, monochrome presentation of the female body and the space around her. The candid kinetic discussion around the breasts and their function. And the notion that her meaning with this imagery does not go misunderstood. Randall notes that many women actually clutch their breasts when watching the film. Asked about her ideas surrounding feminism and how she sees her film addressing some of the principles of feminism, as she understands them, Randall comments on our society's preoccupation with presenting the female body as a romanticized object. Her aim, in this film and much of her other work, is to reveal the grotesque aspects of human beauty.

WELL CONTESTED SITES: RADICAL CREATIVITY AND ACTIVISM

One aspect that sets contemporary feminism apart from previous waves of feminism is the recognition that societal ills like racism and class inequality are feminist issues. Further, the concept of male oppression has entered the conversation, a construct that includes stereotypes of manhood upheld in mass media and mass consciousness and the silencing of male voices that have been victims of physical abuse and rape. A concern particular to the womanist movement—a movement centered around the feminist struggles of African American women—is male oppression through the mass incarceration of African American men.[23] The prison industrial complex stands as a testament to America's commitment to violence and organized oppression of a large part of the male population, which has lasting implications for families torn apart by the absence of these men and for society at large: oppression of any group of people has adverse effects for us all, economically, socially, and societally.

Choreographer Amie Dowling explores the effects of mass incarceration in her film with director Austin Forbord, *Well Contested Sites,* shot on location at Alcatraz.[24] In the film, men who have been previously incarcerated serve as the message makers and movers, most notably challenging widely-accepted notions of who might be considered to be performers in an artistic presentation.

In speaking with Dowling, I learn that she sees dance film as a way of inviting people into spaces they may not otherwise be inclined or able to explore—metaphorically or physically. For Dowling, *Well Contested Sites* is a way to start a conversation around what is, for many, an uncomfortable topic. Certainly, for those of us in the population who have never been to prison, who have no close friends or family members who have served time, prison is a mysterious place, its perception colored vividly by media and hearsay. The picture rendered by mass media is a scary one. According to Dowling, 'There's this idea that when someone is labeled, "incarcerated person," they become defined by the ways the culture defines those labels, fueled by an onslaught of imagery from TV, movies and media.'

When exploring notions of feminism as they pertain to men incarcerated in the United States, one concept that bubbles to the surface is that of gaze. As it pertains to women, the conversation about gaze most often centers on the *male* gaze, a construct that objectifies the female body and discounts the intellect within that body. In one of the first shots of *Well Contested Sites*, a pair of hands empties a wallet and a set of keys onto a white handkerchief. The shot expands to display many, many handkerchiefs, all with piles of small, personal belongings on them. Another shot shows a long row of men laying face-down on the pavement in a long line, each man holding the feet of the man in front of him. Dowling explains how the process of entering prison is one of dehumanizing objectification. One trades personal belongings for empty hands, street clothes for uniforms, names for numbers. Further, the conversation of gaze turns to the type of gaze that is ever-present within the prison, that of the guards. Many of the participants in the film commented on the experience of being the subject of such a gaze, and how the experience of participating in the making of *Well Contested Sites* as performers was an opportunity to rectify their images. Dowling states, 'When people who have been incarcerated are brought into meaning making, the process of self representation, and self expression, is realized.'

There are many luscious parts to this film, which contrast sharply the stark, raw environment of the prison. One part in particular is where a young man, shirtless, brown, begins a serpent-like journey across a set of bars. He isolates various parts of his body, highlighting a foot, a portion of the spine, a hand. The men in the film are truly dancers, not trained in studios, but utilizing the raw physicality of personal experience as drivers to their remarkable kinetic maturity. Dowling states it is because of luscious scenes like this that 'people who watch the film and connect to it, do, because of its beauty and horror, there's a kind of a voyeuristic fascination—seeing black bodies this way, and it's a tool.' Dowling alludes to the notion that showing these men in this way is a tool to open audience members up to speaking about the issue of mass incarceration through showing the viewers beauty.

For me, the most powerful images are reserved for the end. A young African American boy in black slacks and black button-up shirt holds a white basin in an open interior space, where there are no bars or cells. One of the formerly incarcerated men emerges into the space. He's in street clothes—a dark pair of jeans and a striped button-up shirt—and he washes his hands in the basin. There is a cut to an exterior space, a set of stairs, where the many formerly incarcerated men featured in the film sit, in street clothes, each one in front of his own white basin, ceremoniously washing his hands. Dowling explains how several of the men featured in the film have accomplished much following their incarceration experience, citing one man in particular, who is currently pursuing his Ph.D. and speaks publicly on behalf of the film.

In Conclusion: An Invitation for Further Dialogue

While I have only given a few examples of how feminist principle is practiced and demonstrated within the art form of dance film, I hope I have established a stage upon which further dialogue can emerge. I am excited to find so easily such rich examples that clearly demonstrate why dance film is such a sophisticated platform for social commentary in today's digitized world.

In the midst of my excitement, I also recognize those places where dance film can improve. As mentioned earlier, one of the most criticized aspects of feminism is the lack of inclusion of women and allies of color. Where I earlier cited that more than half of the films submitted to Movies By Movers in the past three seasons are directed by women, and around two thirds of those are choreographed by women, one cannot overlook the apparent lack of diversity within the art form. Of the two-thirds of women who are choreographers on projects submitted to Movies By Movers, not 10 percent are women of color; the same goes for directors. Female performers of color, again, only constitute about 10 percent of the total performers tallied, and male performers of color come in at less than 10 percent. The reasons for this, I believe, stem from how the arts are disseminated in our society. The steady decrease of public arts education in low socio-economic and minority communities is reflected in the disproportionate numbers of white students who make it to collegiate arts study versus the number of low socio-economic and minority students who study arts in a collegiate setting. Too, there are societal perceptions to combat. Certainly the world of art in the Western hemisphere is still wrapped up in what is seen as 'white' art and what is seen as 'ethnic,' 'urban,' or 'minority' art. While in truth, no one gets to decide which forms of art are for whom, the lack of historical examples of dance films made by minorities does have a hand in dictating who is compelled to participate.

In conclusion, it is my hope that feminists continue to see dance film as a place where social commentary, self-exploration and self-expression can take place. It is also my hope that artists, being able to observe the pitfalls of both feminism and the arts in our culture, will continue to work toward a collective arts community that celebrates all voices and consciously works toward being the kind of space art has always been in theory: a place where anything is possible.

NOTES

1. Kathleen Rowe Karlyn, *Unruly Girls, Unrepentant Mothers: Redefining Feminism on Screen* (Austin: University of Texas Press, 2011), 7.
2. Deirdre Kelly and Nancy Flight, *Ballerina: Sex, Scandal, and Suffering behind the Symbol of Perfection* (Vancouver: Greystone, 2012), 14–26.

3. Kelly and Flight, 29–30.
4. Brief excerpt of works (including *Kitchen Table*) from *Cara Hagan: Interdisciplinary Artist* on Vimeo at https://vimeo.com/55560509
5. Stephanie Coontz, *The Way We Never Were: American Families and the Nostalgia Trap* (New York: Basic, 1992), 25–30.
6. Coontz, 31.
7. Coontz, 30.
8. http://moviesbymovers.org. Homepage shows energetic selections from the festival.
9. Hilary A. Hallett, *Go West, Young Women! The Rise of Early Hollywood* (Berkeley: University of California Press, 2013), 205.
10. Marissa Marr, 'When a Star Implodes, Studio Execs May Recall Good Old "Morals Clause,"' *Wall Street Journal* [New York] 5 August 2006: n.p.
11. Martha M. Lauzen, 'It's a Man's (Celluloid) World: On-Screen Representations of Female Characters in the Top 100 Films of 2011,' *Center for the Study of Women in Film and Television* (2011). http://womenintvfilm.sdsu.edu/files/2014_Its_a_Mans_World_Report.pdf
12. Excerpt available at http://dancemedia.com/v/1319
13. http://www.indiegrits.com
14. https://vimeo.com/92699049. Directed, choreographed & edited by Maggie Bailey. Filmed by Paul Nguyen. Performed by Heather Bybee. Sylvia Plath's recitation of her poem 'The Applicant.' Music by Shane Carruth. Screened at Movies by Movers Film Festival (2014) and the Greensboro Dance Film Festival (2015). For Sylvia Plath's poem see http://www.poetryfoundation.org/poem/248652
15. Lilly J. Goren, *You've Come a Long Way, Baby: Women, Politics, and Popular Culture* (Lexington, Ky: University of Kentucky Press, 2009), 8.
16. http://www.lichiaopingdance.org
17. Patricia Williams Lessane, 'Women of Color Facing Feminism—Creating Our Space at Liberation's Table: A Report on the Chicago Foundation for Women's "F" Series,' *Journal of Pan African Studies* 1.7 (2007): http://www.jpanafrican.com/docs/vol1no7/WomenOfColorFacingRacism_JPASvol1no7.pdf
18. Janni Aragon, 'Teaching the Third Wave,' *Transformations* 11:1 (2005): n.p.

19. Mary Ann Mason, "The Baby Penalty," *The Chronicle of Higher Ed* (2013): n.p. http://chronicle.com/article/The-Baby-Penalty/140813/
20. Photos at http://www.teahmbeahm.com/more/publicity.html
21. http://www.teahmbeahm.com/more/publicity.html
22. http://www.teahmbeahm.com/more/publicity.html
23. Aretha Faye Marbley, 'African-American Women's Feelings on Alienation from Third-Wave Feminism: A Conversation with My Sisters,' *The Western Journal of Black Studies* 29:3 (2005): n.p. Web.
24. https://vimeo.com/52877758

Hollywood Cinematic Excess: *Black Swan*'s Direct and Contradictory Address to the Body/Mind

Frances Hubbard

Sensitive to the often-contradictory politics of representation, and how cultural texts are open to multiple interpretations, this chapter shall use a multidisciplinary approach to explore the representation of psychiatric disability and feminism in a contemporary and globally popular (albeit independent) Hollywood film, *Black Swan* (2010). This will include a phenomenological exploration and analysis of how cinematography and sound combine to literally 'touch' the viewer with the central character's psychosis. As the film attempts to break down the mirror-boundary between viewer and screen, as Nina (Natalie Portman) smashes the mirror and stabs herself with a shard of it, I will also consider the ethical implications of this embodied assault/experience. I will then utilise feminist psychoanalytic tools of analysis in order to explore the film's construction of femininity, and its complex negotiation between misogyny and feminism. Whilst none of these approaches or insights can offer any 'truths' or definitive meanings, they do work together in productively investigating the complexities of representation and (embodied) identification within a popular independent Hollywood dance film.

   Black Swan tells the transformational story of a disturbed young dancer's journey in becoming the Swan Queen in a new production of Swan

F. Hubbard (✉)
Brighton University, Brighton, UK, United Kingdom

© The Editor(s) (if applicable) and The Author(s) 2016
T.D. Arendell, R. Barnes (eds.), *Dance's Duet with the Camera*,
DOI 10.1057/978-1-137-59610-9_4

Lake, as artistic breakthrough merges with psychotic breakdown. Perfect as she is for the innocence and graceful fragility of the White Swan, she lacks the sensuality and darkness necessary for the Black Swan, recognising these qualities in her own "dark double"/understudy, Lily (Mila Kunis). Therefore, under increasing pressure to find and release these qualities within herself, and combined with the conflicted relationships she has with her mother, fellow dancers, understudy, and artistic director, Nina's paranoid delusions and hallucinations intensify, building to the film's horror climax and her hallucinatory transformation.

A PHENOMENOLOGICAL CINEMATIC PSYCHOSIS

Nina's frightening and climactic descent into a psychosis of paranoia is first implied in the film's use of mirrors and phantasmal doubles, and then in the escalating violence of her hallucinations which include bleeding wounds, sexual encounters, 'demonic' portraits that come to life, horrific deformities/metamorphosis, and murder/suicide. With the highly kinetic (and almost exclusively) handheld camerawork that fluidly moves with Nina as she dances and traverses her everyday life—sometimes following behind her, sometimes in front; sometimes catching up with, encircling, and swirling all about her, and occasionally embodying her point-of-view— the viewer is encouraged to feel more connected to her world as they are touched, increasingly uncomfortably, by the disorienting and claustrophobic experience of her unstable and paranoid subjectivity. In variation from 'objective' formal norms, then, Nina's subjectivity is thus expressed even when she is seen in the frame (and not just in point-of-view shots) because the *film itself* mirrors and brings close Nina's physical, emotional, and psychological experience/crisis. Stylistic decisions are thereby based on the immersion in her increasingly disturbed mind, decisions which, whilst undoubtedly playing with traditional identification, serve to draw the viewer in as they are implicated in the subjective 'feel' of the shots and the psychosis of the film itself. Nina's audition for the role of Black Swan near the beginning of the film is an exemplary illustration of this, and although only 43 seconds long, is a crucial sequence for the way it both introduces and prefigures the action of the film.

Having auditioned the White Swan to perfection, Nina is directed by Thomas (Vincent Cassel) to dance Odile's (the Black Swan's) coda. As she turns and walks towards her starting position, the camera also turns and follows her from behind, capturing a close-up of the back of her head, hair pulled back into a perfect ballet bun. As it catches up with her, revealing a close-up of her side profile, she 'senses' that she is being watched, looks out from the corner of her eye, takes an audibly sharp intake of breath and turns her head. Just at this moment the film cuts to a close-up of Veronica (Ksenia Solo), her fellow dancer and rival for the part, who inclines her head slightly to one side as she glares back at the camera/Nina with a cold, malicious, and defiantly superior expression in her unblinking eyes. The camera then cuts back to a close-up of Nina looking back, then turning away and casting her eyes down to the ground in side profile, anxiously taking another sharp intake of breath as she clenches her jaw. The sounds of her footsteps and anxious breathing amplify the sense of her 'aloneness' in this harsh and hostile environment. Neither fellow dancers nor director are rooting for her, doubting that she can and hoping that she won't embody the sensuality and freedom of the Black Swan.

As she gets to her position and turns toward the maestro, another close-up of the back of her head bowed towards the floor reinforces her anxiety and isolation, as well as heightening the (perhaps paranoid) sense that she is always being watched and spoken about from *behind* her back and by those who are close to her. Indeed, there are numerous shots like this throughout the film that follow her in close-up and from behind as she walks through forbidding hallways, corridors, and subways. Therefore, in what is an interesting duality of expression, camerawork is able to both objectify Nina as it breathes down her neck, and simultaneously express the *feeling* of her paranoid subjectivity.[1] This is because whilst the camera is always *close to* and *motivated by* her movements, it is neither (strictly) subjective, nor exactly objective, but somewhere between these. And because of this, it can potentially both draw the viewer in and distance them from Nina's experience, making her a subject/object. This cinematographic split not only reflects the film's theme of doubling, but also highlights what Ann Cooper Albright refers to as the 'fascinating double moment' in the performance of dance, 'in which performing bodies are both objects of the representation and subjects of their own experience. [...] [And] [t]he ambiguity of this situation creates the possibility of an interesting slippage of viewing priorities.'[2] Moreover, it visualises the way in which Nina's interiority threatens to separate her self from the exterior world, just as a severe mental illness might.

As Steven Shaviro hints in his blog on *Black Swan*, this expressive ambiguity offers a version of cinematic free indirect discourse.[3] Adapted from the literary term by Pier Paolo Pasolini in his essay on 'The "Cinema of

Poetry,"' this device identifies a style of cinematography that 'is, simply, the immersion of the filmmaker in the mind of the character and then the adoption on the part of the filmmaker not only of the psychology of his character but also of his language.'[4] In the case of cinema, this is the language of images. Although the sequences that follow Nina from behind are not *strictly* point-of-view shots, they do, as I have argued above, express a subjective sense of her separation and paranoia, whilst simultaneously forcing an awareness of the formal qualities of the film itself. As Pasolini argues, then, this poetic device 'has the common characteristic of producing films with a *double nature*,' which in turn creates an irresolvable ambiguity that can be divisive.[5] For example, Katherine Fusco argues that *Black Swan*'s cinematography 'emphasises the voyeuristic act of looking at Nina ... encourag[ing] examination, not empathy,'[6] whereas Mark Fisher believes that '[m]uch of the film's power derives from its lack of proper perspective: we are always inside Nina's paranoid schizophrenia, just as we are inside the madness of Carole (Catherine Deneuve) in Polanski's *Repulsion*.'[7] However, what is infinitely more interesting than either perspective being 'right' or 'wrong' is the unnerving *effect* of this cinematographic 'queerness.' Whether objectifying Nina or expressing her psychology, or both, the unrelenting intensity of the camerawork builds up a tone of unease and anxiety which can, in turn, push the viewer into feeling consistently 'on the edge' throughout their filmic experience, just as Nina is in the diegesis of the film.

OVERWHELMING PROXIMITY

With the back of her head in close-up as she faces the maestro, Nina clears her throat and the film cuts to a medium-long-shot of the studio: placing her in the right-hand corner of the frame stretching her feet whilst fellow ballet dancers/auditionees are seated against a vertical, mirrored wall behind her—except for Veronica who is standing, and is, significantly, dressed all in black. Not only does this contrast with the soft pink, grey, and white shades of Nina's attire, but along with her attitude, also further enhances the sense that Veronica is more suited to the role of the Black Swan. Thomas is also standing in front of the horizontal mirrored wall in front of Nina, and due to his mirror reflections both behind and to the (screen) left of him, he is tripled in this shot, accentuating Nina's objectness as she is literally surrounded by his critical panoptic gaze.

Nina nods at the maestro, the music begins, and the film cuts to a close-up of her (visibly sweaty) side profile anxiously looking in the direction that she will move into. The camera then travels with her in medium close-up as she pirouettes in a diagonal phrase across the studio, cutting to a close-up of her foot rising onto pointe—the amplified sound of which expresses the tremendous (and painful) effort it takes to appear weightless. A cut to a medium-close-up of Thomas shows him watching, negatively shaking his head from side to side with his finger on his lip. Reflected in the mirror behind him is a double mirror image of Veronica 'standing' out, once again hinting at her suitability for the role as Thomas expresses his dissatisfaction with Nina's Black Swan. As he shouts out 'not so controlled, seduce us' there is a cut to a medium shot of Nina pirouetting past him, and for a split second the doubled mirror reflections of Thomas, Veronica, and a seated woman are visible. Not only does this reflect the film's theme of doubling, of exploring (multifaceted) identity and of not knowing who you are, but it also suggests that Nina, at this point, is not in touch with her dark side/double, because her reflection is not visible as she dances past the mirror—as indeed it should be and as it was when auditioning Odette, the White Swan. This could perhaps be attributed to an oversight in post-production, where the digital removal of the camera operator's reflection has also caused the erasure of Nina's, since they were moving in synch, at pace, and in such close proximity. However, due to the film's attention to detail as well as its play with doubling throughout, it seems more likely to be a deliberate device used to highlight Nina's inadequacy at this split second in the film.

The constant motion of the dynamic camera cuts back to Thomas shouting 'Not just the Prince, but the court,' then back to a medium-close-up of Nina repeatedly pirouetting as Thomas can be heard shouting 'The audience, the entire world, come on.' At this point there is a momentary reprieve as the camera cuts to a static long shot of the studio as Nina presents her *fouettés en tournant*, with Thomas shouting, 'Your *fouettées* are like a spider spinning a web.'[8] Then the last few moments of this already intense sequence intensify, as images blur in and out and frenetic editing cuts between close-ups of Nina's anxious, wide-eyed expression as she spins, dizzying 360-degree camera rotations that are a whirl of exposed brick wall and harsh light, and medium close-ups of Thomas shouting, before blurring out again and into the same whirl of wall and light, and then cutting back to close-ups of Nina spinning. Throughout, Thomas is shouting, 'Attack it. Attack it. Come on,' as well as visually expressing his displeasure and audibly sighing in disappointment. This dizzying and pressured sequence is repeated until the sound of the door being opened distracts Nina, and in one of the whirling rotations the camera briefly focuses in on a figure at the door, which, *only* when viewed in slow-motion is clearly Natalie Portman playing the 'dark double' of herself/Nina, with her hair loose and dressed all in black. Indeed, the film delights in playing with these uncanny tricks of the eye, and this face-changing motif, along with the doppelganger and the split personality motifs, run throughout the film. This all works to play (visual) mind games with the viewer, so that when combined with the delirious effect of the dancing camera, we, like Nina, become increasingly confused as to what in the images we have seen is 'real' and what isn't, or whether we even saw it at all.[9] We can thus potentially begin to feel as confused and (emotionally) unstable as she does.

The camera then proceeds to blur out again, continuing to rotate until cutting back to a shaky handheld close-up of Nina as she stumbles out of the frame, gasping. We then cut to a close-up of her legs and hands as she struggles to regain control, cut back to her face turning to look and then to a short blurry whip around to a medium long shot that reveals that it is in fact Lily who has entered the studio, late. Although also dressed all in black with a black bag, her hair is in a bun, differentiating her from the 'dark' figure that momentarily flashed onto the screen. Therefore, through the subjectivity of the camerawork, it is clear that Nina sees in and projects onto Lily a version/the opposite of herself that she wishes she could be, but hasn't allowed herself to be, yet. The arrival of Lily has, then, literally 'opened the door' to Nina's repressed Black Swan, and this doubling further mirrors the rivalry between Odette and Odile: the Black and White Swan of the ballet.

The relentless 'closeness' of the camera to Nina in this sequence is a technique that is used throughout the film, effecting a claustrophobic and oppressive quality due to the sense of there being no separate, outside world, but only the world as it exists in connection to her, in her mind. And the small, insular, and tightly framed space of the ballet studio, just like the apartment she shares with her mother, her bedroom within it, Beth/Nina's dressing room, Thomas's office, and the numerous bathrooms she locks herself into, all work to exacerbate this sense of her confinement. Nina *is* the ballerina in the music box by her bed, trapped within the restrictive space of her arrested development and her obsessive-compulsive drive for perfection.[10] In order to become the Black Swan she has to break out of this imprisoning desire to please others (her mother, Thomas, her audience), because only then will she find *her own* pleasure and release. However, the abundance of mirrors in *all* of these spaces implies that there is no way out, that she is trapped in and surrounded by her own (narcissistic) reflections and doubles, by her desire to be other, and by the constant surveillance from all angles. So just as Nina cannot escape the intensity of her own internal (as well as physical) struggle, neither can the viewer, since the repeated close-ups put her emotions and presence, as well as the pressure of Veronica's competitiveness and Thomas's displeasure, literally 'in our face.' Through denying its viewers any comforting objective distance in this way, the spatial relationship established between film and viewer is one of stifling proximity. Not only does this viscerally express the 'closing in' of Nina's world/psychosis, but it also effectively mirrors the relationship that she has with her mother—with its absence of appropriate individual, emotional, and physical boundaries. And since, as Merleau-Ponty writes, '[d]istance is what distinguishes [a] loose and approximate grip from the *complete grip which is proximity*,'[11] *Black Swan* has the ability (and is clearly attempting) to completely overwhelm the viewer. This is because cinematography, sound, mise-en-scène, and performance all work together to elicit in the viewer the same kinds of feelings Nina experiences as her psychosis begins to take hold, potentially deepening their bodily and emotional connection to, and empathy with, her experience. Through this sensorial assault, it is as if the viewer is being constructed as Nina's (extradiegetic) double. And not unlike psychosis *and* ballet, there is nothing subtle or comfortable about this incredibly over-the-top and melodramatic visual language that pummels its unreal realism into the audience.[12]

Vertiginous Intertextuality and the Prefiguration of Doom

The whirling camera rotations that express Nina's dizzying perspective as she spins draw the viewer into the sensation of the movement by inducing a similarly vertiginous experience; and the blurring in and out of Thomas shouting renders palpable the pressure she is under. This affective camerawork is directly taken from a sequence in Powell and Pressburger's ballet film, *The Red Shoes* (1948), highlighting the intertextuality between the films and thus allowing director Darren Aronofsky and Matthew Libatique (the director of photography) to pay homage to this classic of

British cinema and of dance film. The subjective whirls in *The Red Shoes* do not occur in the famous 15-minute ballet sequence of the film's name, but in an earlier matinee performance of none other than *Lac des Cygnes*, or *Swan Lake*, just as this sequence from *Black Swan* occurs at the beginning of the film and not in Nina's opening night performance. Both are composed of a multiplicity of shots and are exceptionally short, with *The Red Shoes* sequence lasting only 28 seconds. However, as is also the case for Nina's audition, this sequence is crucial for the way it both introduces and prefigures the action of the film.

As a medium close-up moving shot of Vicky Page (Moira Shearer) pirouetting cuts to her perspective, the theatre turns round in a blur through a series of whip pans over the audience that alternate with shots of her ecstatic face. That is until a subjective whirl flashes past the impresario of the Ballet Company in the audience, Lermontov (Anton Walbrook), cutting to a long shot of Vicky holding her pose in order to cut back to a medium close-up of him watching. Like Thomas, he observes 'his' dancer critically: with one eyebrow raised, a cold expression in his eyes, and his hands clenched and touching/covering part of his closed mouth as everybody else in the audience applauds. The camera then cuts back to an extreme close-up of Vicky, and there is something about her heavily made-up face and wide-eyed, wild expression that offers a frightening glimpse of madness/horror—a generic element that Aronofsky will push to an extreme in *Black Swan*. The whiteness of her powdered face connotes (and foreshadows) her death, whilst the scarlet red around her painted eyes and lips prefigure her starring role in *The Red Shoes* as well as accentuating the passion/madness of her desire to dance as well as please Lermontov on the one hand, and Julian (her husband) on the other. The ecstasy conveyed on her face whilst dancing thus contrasts with the fear and panic of being (emotionally) divided, and it is this conflict that will ultimately lead to her suicide. The ecstatic sensation of and obsessive compulsion to dance and to attain perfection is therefore shown to be deadly.

Consequently, *Black Swan*'s reference to this film 13 minutes in is foreboding. And whilst Nina bears a close resemblance to Vicky in that they share a compulsive desire to attain perfection in their dancing, are dominated by a manipulative director, and are both, albeit in different ways, split in two, Vicky at least expresses her rapturous joy when dancing. In contrast, Nina's inner anguish is permanently etched onto her face (until her transformation at the end). This detail accentuates the already overwhelming sense of anxiety created through cinematography and sound, and *Black Swan* is undeniably a much 'darker' film, as reflected in the monochrome palette compared to the glorious Technicolor of *The Red Shoes*. In terms of prefiguring the action and thereby acting as a (phenomenologically felt) microcosm of the whole film, this audition sequence shows that Nina is already under intense (psychological) pressure even before she is given the role(s). The shaky handheld camera that captures her stumbling out of the frame as she is distracted by the entrance of Lily/her dark side, elicits in the viewer her growing sense of instability and nervousness, just as the grainy texture of the film stock reflects her ever-diminishing grip on reality. The feverish pace of the editing combined with the speed of filming and intricate detail of the sequence enacts a compulsive drive that doesn't allow the viewer to catch their breath, almost as if they have just performed the audition themselves. More importantly, this drive mirrors the film's/Nina's unrelenting acceleration into full-blown horror/psychosis, as she begins to hallucinate, 'becomes' her dark double, and then ultimately stumbles out of the frame/the ballet/her life/her mind as her compulsion to attain perfection destroys her. It is, then, as Maya Deren argues, the emotional integrity of the body of the film that 'recreate[s] through filmic means—editing rhythms, camera attitudes and movements etc.—the sense and spirit of,' in this case, Nina's physical as well as emotional/psychological experience, thereby prefiguring the action of the film.[13]

An Intense Auditory/Bodily Experience

The first indication that this ballet film has a 'dark side' occurs right at the beginning in the title sequence. After 20 seconds of the opening of Tchaikovsky's 'Swan Theme,' a reversed whoosh of wind/breath comes in. This fades into a sinister, distorted laughter that then dissipates into a low-end throbbing sound before returning to the score. All of this coincides with the appearance of the title, *Black Swan*, and comes just before the film opens onto Nina's dream of dancing the White Swan. With both the reverse reverb and sinister laughter signalling an eerie sense of demonic/otherworldly possession, a daunting and unsettling undertone to her dream/the film is established before it even begins, with the low-end throbbing adding a sense of unnerving anxiety. Variations of this darkly dissonant insertion will be repeated and adapted throughout in order to indicate Nina's paranoid hallucinations, as well as marking the moments in which we catch a glimpse of her inner black swan. This provides a POV audio that supports the subjective feel of the cinematography and thereby allows me to enter Nina's unstable headspace acoustically. However, despite the unsettling effect of these kinds of acoustic conventions of horror, it is the gruesome sounds of her bodily injuries (or her slow and terrifying metamorphosis) that for me provide the real 'horror.' This is because whether diegetically 'real' or imagined, these visceral sounds/images directly address my body, inviting me to experience the same sensations through their textural qualities. And because of this visceral immediacy and direct address, *Black Swan* fits perfectly within the categories of what Linda Williams calls 'body genres,' since 'the success of these genres is often measured by the degree to which the audience sensation mimics what is seen on the screen.'[14]

Straight after the opening dream sequence, a visual and auditory close-up of Nina's neck and feet cracking is nauseatingly intense. Like the dissonant insertion in the title sequence, this immediately establishes the 'politics' of the film, which is less concerned with the ethereal, dream-like, and distanced portrayal of ballet dancing, and more interested in overpowering the viewer with the affective intensity of its underlying brutality. Like Nina, I do not feel in control of the images I see/hear but am rather subjected to them, and this physical/emotional vulnerability counters any (illusory) sense of power and mastery over the image that classical film spectatorship might provide.

Having returned home from her disastrous audition, Nina begins to obsess over her pirouettes by practicing in front of a mirror, and as the camera cuts to a close-up of her foot rising onto *pointe*, the film briefly slows down in order to exaggerate the disturbing crunching sounds as she spins and grinds into the floorboards. The force and tension of what sounds like wood being twisted to the point of snapping is actually painful to hear/see, because it effects a sense of the agony of this unnatural load-bearing, as well as sounding as a metaphor for Nina herself, who also begins to crack and give way under the pressure. This is, however, nothing compared to the even more exaggerated and squirm-inducing sound of her toenail splitting, which is more gruesome than the actual image itself. Similarly, whilst being debuted as the new Swan Queen at a black-tie fundraiser for the ballet company, Nina fixates on a tear in her cuticle and, after a cut to the toilet, tears away a long strip of skin from her finger. It is not only the texture but also the length of this fleshy ripping sound that makes it particularly horrific in its attack, and despite it being signalled as one of Nina's hallucinations, is rooted in a kind of everyday pain that many of us have actually experienced, thus evoking body memories that contribute to an overwhelming feeling of physical revulsion and pain. Furthermore, Nina's pulling at this wound reflects the incessant pressure that she is under as the pain of her psychiatric instability gradually becomes uncontainable, threatening to sabotage the image of 'exquisite' perfection that Thomas demands she project.

However, the most disgusting/captivating sound/image for me comes towards the end of the film during Nina's horrific transformation/hallucination, as bristles violently tear through the bubbling skin of her animated rash. As she pulls out what proves to be a black feather from her back, the drawn out squelching sound/image is *so* affecting I feel as if I am pulling it from my own body, perfectly illustrating how the texture of a film's sound design can communicate 'feeling' through its close association with the sense of touch. And whilst the touch of this sequence is quite literally repulsive, her viscerally marked and suffering body certainly captures my attention, thereby destabilising the pain/pleasure dichotomy. Moreover, because the 'realistic' texture of these sounds endows them with a greater sense of metamorphosis than do the images alone, it also breaks down ontological distinctions between human and animal. This perhaps helps to explain why I find this scene so disgusting, since the morph, as Vivian Sobchack writes, taps into 'novel—and specifically historical—concretions of contemporary confusions, fears, and desires,'[15] particularly concerning notions of self-identity and contagion. And when considering how hair, in particular, is so overdetermined with (gendered) meanings and associations, and how our dominant western culture has become 'especially obsessive about denying the hairiness of women, who remove it from legs, upper lip, chest, and armpits, and… from the pubic region also,'[16] it is no surprise that despite my proud feminism and rejection of these constructed, ideological norms, I have nonetheless learnt and internalised this specifically gendered 'horror.'

Therefore, this sound/image also collapses other boundaries founded on gender and disfigurement/beauty, which reflect the kind of bodily transformations many women go through every month, when hormones connected to the menstrual cycle can produce extra/excessive hair growth. Despite being a common occurrence, the undeniable cultural taboo and disgust with hairy women can deeply affect a woman's self-confidence, and, in extreme cases, her mental health. This, then, brings the horror *as well* as the fascination and freedom that Nina's final metamorphosis provides even closer, because it is only during this final process that we see her 'let go' of her need for control, of concealing and plucking, in order to embrace and enjoy the sensuality and 'freedom' of her (hairy) embodiment. To quote Sobchack again, Nina's uncanny morphing thus 'generates our physical and cultural "double"—some radically other "familiar" whose visible image [...] not only "reflects" us but also "renders" and "clarifies" us.'[17]

Although not directly connected to her body, the final examples of visual and auditory close-ups that I want to consider are of Nina breaking in a new pair of *pointe* shoes towards the beginning of the film. This is because the amplified and ritualistic sounds of taking them out of the plastic, pulling and thwacking them apart, sewing on the ribbon, plastering up sore and swollen feet, and scoring the soles with scissors, all presage the mutilation and fragmentation of Nina's body/mind. Just as the shoes are smashed and flattened in order to conform to the shape of her feet, Nina is similarly 'broken' in order to fit the role of the Black Swan. In contrast to this auditory violence is the sensuous sound/image of putting on the shoes and tying the satin ribbon around the fine and delicate material of her tights. Indeed, the texture of this sound gives me a *feel* of the fabric as if against my own skin, offering a momentary and luxurious flash of pleasure. However, because this is followed by the squirm-inducing twisting/manipulating sound of her feet rising onto *pointe*, as well as the fact that I have just seen the battered and deformed reality of what is hidden beneath, I am not seduced by its elegance. Rather, I am again reminded of the central metaphor of the film: that however enticing and 'beautiful' ballet/Nina appears to be on the outside; beneath this veneer is a great deal of (physical, emotional, and psychological) pain and horror. In this way, sound unveils the problems inherent within 'ideal' images, and the extent to which they can be destructive to a woman's body/mind, working to subvert the image of the female ballet dancer as an ideal of embodied femininity. Yet this reading is undoubtedly complicated due to the 'unstable woman' being such a familiar trope in cinema, historically representing *woman in general* rather than disability. Indeed, the most significant development in the treatment of women in film during the 1980s, was, as Molly Haskell asserts, 'the crazy women... an endlessly expanding category of neurotics, murderers, *femmes fatales*, vamps, punks, misfits, and free-floating loonies whose very existence was an affront, not only to the old, sexist definitions of pliant women (or even categorisable psychotics), but also to the upbeat rhetoric of the women's movement.'[18] With this in mind, it is difficult to see Nina as representing mental disability in any serious way—particularly when *most* of the female characters in the film (except for Lily, who might not be 'real'), are also mentally unstable.

AN 'INFERNAL VISION OF PATRIARCHY': GRATIFYING (OR SUBVERTING) THE MALE GAZE?[19]

Black Swan is undoubtedly influenced by stereotypes of gender and lesbianism. With its constant references to mirrors and reflections, female archetypes, individuation, and transfiguration, it has an undeniably heavy allegorical hand, and indeed, Amber Jacobs goes so far as to argue that it is anti-feminist, 'proceed[ing] as if feminist film theory never happened.'[20] Therefore, it is impossible *not* to look at this film through a feminist lens, since the body is not simply an issue in phenomenology and epistemology, but also a theoretical location for debates about power and ideology. In the next section I will explore its aestheticisation of female madness, and the fetishisation of melodramatic, hysterical, and tragic femininity through the trope of the ballet dancer. It is, unfortunately, still too often the case that '[w]hile the mad men of contemporary cinema are often represented as active heroes struggling against psychiatric adversity, mad women are more typically represented as the passive victims of their disordered psyches.'[21]

Mirrors and reflecting surfaces are omnipresent throughout the film, reflecting back at Nina the desired yet repressed adult/dancer she wishes she could be, and is pressured into as well as held back from being. Many of her hallucinations occur when she is locked in a bathroom looking into a mirror, since it is one of the rare places in which Nina escapes the gaze of others, and thus offers her a private space in which her internal battles may be fought with her 'darkly' seductive, dangerous, and even vicious self. This recurring and 'worn-out visual cliché'[22] thereby highlights her increasingly fractured state of mind, her unstable and split subjectivity, and the centrality of the gaze. This is not only in terms of Nina's '*to-be-looked-at-ness*,'[23] but also in her own construction and projection of a specific image, an illusory ideal that marks the internalisation of her 'panoptical male connoisseur.'[24] In this way Nina reproduces the terms and pleasures of this male fantasy, because her obsession with the disjuncture between her 'one true original' (White Swan) 'self' and the aesthetic ideal of dark perfection to which she aspires, perpetually alienates her from her own subjective and material experience. Therefore, instead of showing identity as something that we *do* rather than something that *we are*, there is an overwhelming sense that she has to choose either/or, black or white, virgin or whore identity, as reflected in the film's black and white chiaroscuro. Like the camera that often follows her closely from behind, Nina is thus always on the 'outside,' obsessively scrutinising herself and thereby fuelling her own psychosis. For this reason, and although the causes of mental illness are complex and varying, it may be easy for some viewers to blame her for her own narcissistic self-absorption rather than acknowledge the overarching social and cultural factors that undoubtedly play a part. This highlights how the definition, judgement, and punishment of 'madness' can be seen as powerful tools that help maintain patriarchal (and heterosexual) hegemony.

In this way, mirrors/the film can be seen as instruments of control, because in fighting and literally shattering her own multi-faceted image in order to become the Black Swan, Nina/the film can be seen to undermine the (queer) understanding and celebration of identity as multiple, flexible, dynamic, and volatile in favour of a discourse of normalised dichotomous identities. The film can thus be read as the story of her sacrifice to the age-old archetype of the duplicated woman, to the patriarchal definitions of female 'beauty' and 'perfection,' how underneath this painted perfection is the horror of monstrous femininity, and to the enduring idea that women do not really exist at all, only for the sake of others.[25] Indeed, Nina's guilt-inducing and self-sacrificial mother, Erica, embodies yet another female archetype: the monstrously terrifying (and terrified) despotic mother, who only 'lives' vicariously through her daughter.[26] Having been ousted from her role as the company's prima ballerina and replaced by a much younger Nina, a suicidal Beth (Winona Ryder) speaks volumes about interchangeable female identity and aging when she (sarcastically) advises Nina to 'enjoy the moment,' and then later repeats the words 'I am nothing.' In a ballet world full of interchangeable doppelgangers all competing for Thomas's attention and approval, as well as for the same principal parts, it is undoubtedly a struggle to define who you are when you are merely one of many performing moves that are by and for somebody else. And Thomas's advice before her opening night performance is for Nina to 'lose' herself. Therefore, Amber Jacobs's exasperated dismissal of the film's 'fixed take on femininity' is certainly understandable, since '[t]he mirrors crudely hammer this point home; the infinite image of the reflected,

homogeneous bodies and faces of the ballerinas represents a construction of femininity that has no life outside the terms of the mirror/gaze
of the male symbolic.'[27]

Indeed, the idea that women are irrational, abject commodities who are
quite literally 'nothing' until they are selected/objectified by the dominant and controlling gaze of the male 'bearer of the look,'[28] is perfectly
expressed early on. Coming just after a scene set in the dressing room, in
which myriad mirror reflections highlight the striking similarities between
the female dancers as some of them gossip unkindly and competitively
about Beth's age, the film cuts to the daily company ballet barre class.
Moving in among the closely situated dancers, the camera establishes an
intimate sense of people hard at work as it moves between close-ups of
legs and feet, as well as panning up dancers' bodies to medium close-ups
of their faces and arms. This is heightened by the warmth and encourage-
ment of the ballet mistress who also walks among the dancers, smiling
and counting them in, saying 'good,' telling Nina that she is 'beautiful
as always,' and directing her to 'relax.' Therefore, when the film cuts to
a high-angled long shot looking down onto the studio, and the back
of Thomas's head comes into view, a very different spatial relationship
purposefully establishes his dominance before we even know who he is.
With a cut to a low angled shot looking up at him as he crosses his arms,
observes, objectifies, and judges, there is no mistaking his authority, which
is compounded by the ballet mistress as she acknowledges his presence,
claps her hands, and directs the pianist to stop. There is then a decided
shift in tone as dancers anxiously remove layers of clothing in order to
improve the display of their 'to-be-looked-at-ness.' It is only Lily, the new
addition to the company, who finds this behaviour strange, as expressed
by her puzzled, critical expression and her failure to remove any clothes.
Thomas then makes a motion with his hand, the lesson resumes, and he
walks down in among the dancers, recounting the tragic story of Swan
Lake as he scrutinises the female dancers at close range whilst tapping
many of them on the shoulder. As if playing ruthless mind games with
his 'subordinates,' he finishes his monologue by advising 'all the soloists
I tapped, go to your scheduled rehearsals this afternoon, and for the *girls*
I didn't tap, meet me in the principal studio at 5:00 pm.' A series of cuts
between the latter reveal their pleasure, and in the case of Veronica, her
sense of triumph in being selected to audition for the Swan Queen by this
'brilliant' man.

A COMPLEX NEGOTIATION BETWEEN
MISOGYNY AND FEMINISM

In so many respects, then, this scene is a textbook demonstration of the male gaze, as women who appear to lack a core identity are infantilised and dismembered under a misogynistic lens—and what is worse, are grateful for it! Importantly, however, this is complicated both by Lily's reaction to Thomas, and the way in which he is introduced as repellently egotistical and cruel. At the exact moment he explains how the Swan Queen desires her freedom, 'but only true love can break the spell,' he brazenly gazes into the mirror at his own reflection, strokes his hair, and thus identifies himself with the role of heroic 'rescuer.' This doubling serves to reveal how he uses his position as artistic director to live out his own exploitative, male fantasies, and a cut to Lily rolling her eyes reflects back a resistant viewers' sense of disapproval and exasperation with his dominating and manipulative will to power and mastery. It is moments like these that insert a subtle form of feminist politics into a film intended for mainstream exhibition, and I therefore have to *also* agree with Mark Fisher when he writes that Thomas is 'an almost parodically phallic artistic director,'[29] who selects Nina because she is so obviously vulnerable and in need of 'liberating' (from the confinement of her arrested development). However, whilst she is undoubtedly in need of psychological help, it is certainly not the kind of sexual harassment and humiliation that Thomas has to offer under the guise/excuse of tutelage, which only adds to her stress by exacerbating her anxiety.[30] In one scene, disappointed and frustrated with Nina's rehearsal, he even asks David/The Prince (Benjamin Millepied) in front of her, 'Honestly, would you fuck that girl?' thus reflecting back the kind of scopophilic pleasure and power that viewers may get from watching and judging the sexual worth of a female object based on the way that she moves. He then answers his own question with, 'No, no one would,' before going on to *kindly* demonstrate the necessary passion and sensuality he is looking for by forcing her to kiss him and groping her body in her most intimate places. As if humiliating an obviously vulnerable person's inexperience was not enough, what is particularly sadistic about this scene is that at the moment Nina appears to respond and actually enjoy this sexual contact, he walks away, asserting that it was him seducing her and that it needs to be the other way around.

Furthermore, it is abundantly clear that he is encouraging her to access her darker impulses and push herself to her limits not for altruistic reasons, but for his own selfish ends and with no regard for the devastating consequences that will entail. Thus, he does not see Nina as a real person, twisting her to fit his own image and loving only the reflection of himself that he sees in her. Nina is merely a commodity, groomed to replace the 'worn out' Beth and continue to sell his ballet company until she, too, wears out and/or is used up.[31] Business is business. This is shown in his acknowledgement to Nina that Beth's accident was an attempted suicide, driven by the 'dark impulse' that made 'her so thrilling to watch, so dangerous, even perfect at times,' knowing full well how Nina obsesses over perfection, and thus encouraging her to sacrifice herself to the medium and satisfy his impossible demands no matter what the cost. Having discovered that Lily has been made her alternate later on in the film, Nina tearfully approaches Thomas for reassurance but he only exacerbates her insecurity and paranoia by confirming that 'there is always an alternate' and that 'everyone in the world wants your place.' And finally, the theme of substituting one woman for another is cemented right at the end of the film when he calls Nina 'my little princess'—exactly the same name that he used to call Beth and will no doubt call the next in a long line of 'sweet girls.'

In Lily's succinct words, then, Thomas is a 'prick.' So if cinema is a mirror, then as well as reflecting and gratifying the male gaze, *Black Swan* can *also* be seen as 'a black mirror held up to patriarchy.'[32] Despite its 'boy-friendly thriller structure,'[33] it is a female-centric film with four major female roles, confronting many of the significant issues facing young girls and women in a way that few mainstream films dare. It touches upon the impossible nature of (arrogantly egotistical) male expectation; the ways in which (patriarchal/ballet) culture is constitutive in numerous ways of girls' and women's pathologised bodies, subjectivities, experiences, and practices; society's disdain for and unfair treatment of aging women; the damage that the internalisation of patriarchy has done to female friendship and competition; the mother/daughter relationship; sexual harassment in the workplace; and the pursuit of 'perfection.' In exploring the complex and contradictory mix of Nina's repression, desire, guilt, and achievement, *Black Swan* also addresses the ways in which women have been taught to fear our own power and abilities, believing that if we fully exercise both we risk destroying ourselves, and those close to us. It raises the question of whether we can maintain our integrity *and* be successful, or do we have to morph into something that is demonised and desired (by patriarchy) in order to fiercely go after what it is that we want? Alternatively, can we reconcile these contradictions by transcending this enduringly and deeply entrenched archetypal good/bad girl tug of war?

Reinvigorating and Exploiting Lesbian Clichés?

As with so many popular narrative films, it is impossible not to return to the fact that *Black Swan* is simultaneously interesting and found wanting in quite complex ways, and this continuous oscillation between potential progressiveness and regressive presentation is mirrored in the emotional tonality and rhythm of the sound design. Sometimes really quiet and at other times so loud it hurts, these abrupt shifts in pitch go to extremes then pull you back, which perfectly reflects the (patriarchal/feminist) dynamics of the film. Therefore, I cannot write about the contradictions within the text that offer up these feminist spaces of politics and desire, without considering the arguably cynical and gratuitous inclusion of the 2-minute softcore lesbian sex scene. Indeed, in an interview in the American magazine, *Entertainment Weekly*, Natalie Portman says: 'Everyone was so worried about who was going to want to see this movie... I remember them being like, "How do you get guys to a ballet movie? How do you get girls to a thriller?" And the answer is a lesbian scene... Everyone wants to see that.'[34]

Of most interest is the point at which a close-up of Nina's open-mouthed expression of pleasure cuts to a close-up from her perspective, as she looks down at Lily's head between her legs. As 'Lily' looks back up at her, her face morphs into Nina's, and an abrupt burst of kinetic syncopation expresses Nina's panic as she springs up in horror. As the camera cuts back to a close-up of Lily, now with her rightful face, the music changes to soft, romantic strings as she comforts Nina and eases her back down. Then both the music and Nina build to their climax, as Lily continues to perform oral sex on her. Throughout this scene, there is a conspicuous (and unpleasantly disturbing) juicy, slushing sound of fluid, layered with an uncanny twisting, manipulating sound as Lily's tattooed wings move about her shoulder blades. There is also an insect-like sound that merges with wings flapping as parts of Nina's skin become animated and goose-fleshed, and all of this is interspersed with Nina's gasps and moans of pleasure, until it goes quiet for a few seconds of peace after her orgasm. Then the sound of mournful strings come back in as a medium close-up of Lily, with a mirror directly behind her in the background, shows her sit up, wipe her mouth and say 'sweet girl,' the *exact* words that Nina's mother uses to refer to her daughter. A cut looking down onto Nina's panic coincides with the crashing chords that then build to the second (horror) climax of the scene, as Lily once again turns into Nina, grabs the pillow and smothers Nina as the screen goes black and the soundtrack goes silent.

Combining the body genres of pornography and horror with the viscerally disturbing sound effects and emotionally impactful music, this scene undoubtedly aims to incite a physical response in the viewer. And with its acceptably feminine, conventionally attractive Hollywood stars and standard lesbian porn clichés, it is no doubt particularly titillating for the kind of heterosexual male gaze that fantasises about (a stereotypical kind of) lesbian sex. Therefore, as Portman indicates above, lesbianism offers the 'spice' that will transform the film into a more sellable commodity, and both reveals and represses/exploits lesbian desire and representation at the same time. The switching of Lily's face to Nina's can be seen to support Freud's contention that lesbians are 'plainly seeking themselves as a love object.'[35] Which is further corroborated through the suggestion that this entire scene is hallucinogenic and masturbatory. Therefore, in accordance with Lacan's reformulation of Freud's work in *Feminine Sexuality*, Nina's sexual attraction to Lily is grounded in her desire to *be* her, connoting a narcissistic and pre-Oedipal desire that relegates lesbianism to immaturity.[36] Indeed, there is plenty of evidence in the text to support this theory of her arrested development, as she constantly projects a sexualised image of herself onto other women, has an overbearing and protective mother, and has thus failed to successfully complete her psychosexual development by fully transferring her desire/identification from the mother/self to the (absent) 'Other' father/man. Furthermore, her mother/lover/self/other literally smothers her in this scene, in front of a mirror. This psychoanalytic theory of lesbian psychosis thereby promotes the patriarchal, heterosexist, and homophobic assumption that lesbianism is a 'phase' that should be outgrown, and a desire based only on gender dysfunction rather than autonomous desire. Therefore, because the sex scene is represented as a natural consequence of Nina's neurosis/psychosis, and no 'real' lesbians are involved, any subversion that it may have posed to hetero-patriarchy is dissolved, and what is left is a 'safe' male fantasy.

It is, then, clearly understandable why this scene has evoked mistrust and cynicism, since it is, as ever, a patriarchal institution (Hollywood) that benefits from institutionalised lesbian verisimilitudes. However, what is once again interesting is the contradictory way in which it is designed to both repel and gratify, as highlighted by the David Cronenberg-esque body-horror sound effects, as well as Nina's own horrified and appalled reaction to her own apparent narcissism. Moreover, as much as the indeterminacy of their encounter being 'real' or not may well strengthen male fantasy, it can also be seen 'as a knowing joke on the desires of the [heterosexual] male audience, giving them what they want but at the same time making it disturbing, uncanny and only an embarrassing wet dream!'[37] Indeed, although in no way do I believe him to be representative of *all* heterosexual male viewers, Mark Fisher argues that: 'A heterosexual male viewer coming to *Black Swan* looking for titillation would surely be deeply disappointed. The film shows a female body too destabilised by anxiety and delirium to be the object of a masturbatory male gaze.'[38]

Yet apart from these considerations of the male gaze, and regardless of whether it is yet another case of assimilationist visibility (at the expense of a marginalised invisibility), this scene *does* represent a woman's fantasy about another woman—who happens to be flattered by the idea, if not the reality. A mainstream indie-Hollywood film undoubtedly increases the visibility of and discussion about queer/lesbian desire in a space in which lesbianism still remains relatively invisible, propagating a more fluid conception of human sexuality. It will therefore have resonance in different ways for different audiences, and as my previous MA (audience) research into lesbian viewing (dis)pleasure in (un)friendly popular cinema suggests, lesbians are not a homogeneous mass who respond to the politics of representation in the same way, so no doubt there will be some who will derive just as much visual pleasure from this scene as the next 'guy.' And these will not necessarily be just lesbian/bi/queer-identified women either, as highlighted by Portman's comment above. For this reason, Amber Jacobs's assertion that '[i]t functions entirely for the pleasure of the heterosexual male spectator [and] absolutely precludes any other kind of desire,'[39] seems somewhat reactionary in its dismissal of the contradictions within the text that reflect the same contradictions within the dominant ideologies of the day. However, to further the sense of contradiction, as a lesbian/queer/feminist viewer myself, I tend to agree with her whilst simultaneously acknowledging the fact that 'our' response cannot speak for all women.

CONCLUSION: A FEMINIST PHENOMENOLOGICAL ASSAULT

Whilst *Black Swan*'s cinematic excess can thus be potentially 'maddening,' it can also be completely and viscerally overwhelming, and it is this way-over-the-top, hysterical, conflicted, and intense tone that differentiates the politics of this popular dance film from avant-garde feminist film. For example, whilst *Meshes of the Afternoon* (Maya Deren, 1943/59) and *Tides* (Amy Greenfield, 1982) also privilege embodied experience, immersion, and connection, they do so by giving viewers the time and space in which to enter into their 'depths,' creatively imagining alternatives to patriarchal thinking and reality (despite being considerably shorter films). This is achieved through their use of rhythm, time (particularly slow motion), space, and repetition, which drastically contrasts to the violent immediacy of *Black Swan*'s exploration of the power structures that have given rise to Nina's psychosis, without necessarily confirming them. This perhaps addresses the wider context of our cultural fascination with and Hollywood's need to sell experiences of immediacy, in order to compete with an increasingly digital media landscape which aims to provide unmediated visual and aural experiences. However, this is not meant as a value judgement because they are different forms of filmmaking, and the avant-garde has always worked against the predominant cultural forms of its day. Instead, the point of this comparison is to show how this independent Hollywood film is undoubtedly a hybrid form that incorporates and assimilates different filmmaking practices and genres, whilst retaining its allegiance to representational practices. This undoubtedly creates the contradictions that are so deeply embedded within *Black Swan*, as the affective elements of the film are compromised by the ideological elements, which are themselves contradictory—making it impossible to fully yield to the progressive potential that can be read into it.

NOTES

1. The sound is also crucial in establishing this sense of Nina's subjective experience, and is explored in depth below.
2. Ann Cooper Albright, *Choreographing Difference: The Body and Identity in Contemporary Dance* (Middletown, Connecticut: Wesleyan University Press, 1997), 13.
3. Steven Shaviro's weblog is called 'The Pinocchio Theory,' and his full review of *Black Swan* can be found at http://www.shaviro. com/Blog/?p=975
4. Pier Paolo Pasolini, 'The "Cinema of Poetry"' [1965] in *Heretical Empiricism*, trans. Ben Lawton and Louise K Barnett (Washington: New Academia, 2005), 167–86; 175. Free indirect discourse/ speech is a literary device favored by modernist writers such as James Joyce and Virginia Woolf, in which a third-person narration contains the essence of first-person direct speech.
5. Pasolini, 182.

6. Katherine Fusco, 'The Actress Experience: Cruel Knowing and the Death of the Picture Personality in *Black Swan* and *The Girlfriend Experience*,' *Camera Obscura*, 82 (2013) 28:1, 1–35; 21.

7. Mark Fisher and Amber Jacobs, 'Debating *Black Swan*: Gender and Horror,' *Film Quarterly* (2011) 65:1, 58–62.

8. The *fouettés en tournant* is a movement in classical ballet where the dancer is momentarily on flat foot with the supporting knee bent, with the whipping motion of the other 'working' leg enabling her to spin around. This working leg pulls back in to touch the supporting knee as she rises up onto pointe on the supporting foot. Being able to consecutively perform 32 of these is considered a bravura step by the ballerina.

9. The film also plays aural tricks on the viewer. For example, an eerie, mocking reverb/dissonance helps the viewer to adopt Nina's fear and paranoia, and is particularly associated with Lily. However, there are moments that imply Lily is in fact perfectly nice and innocent in her dealings with Nina, and that her coveting the role of the Swan Queen is all in Nina's mind.

10. This makes the close-up of this broken figure, torso-less and missing a leg, but still turning to the twinkling of the *Swan Theme*, all the more disturbing, since it comes directly after Nina's violent hallucination/transformation and collapse the night before her opening performance. Despite Nina's psychological and emotional fragmentation, the show must go on.

11. Maurice Merleau-Ponty, *Phenomenology of Perception* [1962], trans. Colin Smith (London: Routledge, 1989), 261, my emphasis.

12. Further contributing to this fevered pitch of the film's visual language is the dark, moody lighting and imagery that underscore Nina's inner psychological disintegration. The muted, monotone palette of blacks, whites, pinks, and greens, and the overt symbolism of these colours are demonstrated in the gradual darkening of her ballet clothes from the whites and pinks of her innocence, to shades of grey, and, finally, to the black that personifies the release of her dark side/swan. The extreme pinkness of her bedroom filled with pink teddies and childish trinkets represents her arrested development, and the green walls of the apartment's narrow hallway underscore the competitive, envious, and claustrophobic nature of the relationship between mother and daughter, also reflected in her relationship with other dancers.

13. Maya Deren, *Essential Deren. Collected Writings on Film by Maya Deren*, ed. Bruce R. McPherson (Kingston, New York: Documentext, 2005), 230.
14. Linda Williams, 'Film Bodies: Gender, Genre and Excess,' *Film Quarterly* 44 (1991) (4): 2–13; 4.
15. Vivian Sobchack, 'Introduction' and '"At the Still Point of the Turning World" Meta-Morphing and Meta-Stasis' in Vivian Sobchack, ed., *Meta Morphing. Visual Transformation and the Culture of Quick-Change* (Minneapolis & London: University of Minnesota Press, 2000), xi–xxiii and 131–58.
16. William Ian Miller, *The Anatomy of Disgust* (Cambridge, Mass, & London: Harvard University Press, 1997), 57.
17. Sobchack, xii.
18. Molly Haskell, *From Reverence to Rape: The Treatment of Women in the Movies*, 2nd edn (Chicago & London: The University of Chicago Press, 1987), 373.
19. Fisher and Jacobs, 59.
20. Fisher and Jacobs, 60.
21. Stephen Harper, *Madness, Power and the Media. Class, Gender and Race in Popular Representations of Mental Distress* (Basingstoke & New York: Palgrave Macmillan, 2009), 77.
22. Fisher and Jacobs, 60.
23. Laura Mulvey, 'Visual Pleasure and Narrative Cinema,' [1975] in Sue Thornham, ed., *Feminist Film Theory. A Reader* (Edinburgh: Edinburgh University Press, 1999), 58–69; 63, original emphasis.
24. Sandra Lee Bartky, 'Foucault, Femininity, and the Modernization of Patriarchal Power,' in Irene Diamond and Lee Quinby, eds., *Feminism and Foucault: Reflections on Resistance* (Boston: Northeastern University Press, 1988) 61–86; 72.
25. The trope of the duplicated woman is largely a male fantasy that has inspired too many cinematic doubles to mention.
26. Through wielding her power over her daughter by picking on her Achilles' heel: her rash/skin, as well as dressing/undressing, manicuring, constantly calling, feeding her cake from her fingers, and even watching her sleep, the relationship between Erica and Nina is shown to be disturbingly intimate, suffocating, and strained. This then implies that Nina's trauma has been born and created from her mother's own mental instability, from which she needs to be 'rescued' by the invariably absent father figure/phallic director.

As Barbara Creed explores in her 1986 essay on 'Horror and the Monstrous-Feminine: An Imaginary Abjection,' this pathological construction of the monstrous mother 'reveals a great deal about male desires and fears but tells us nothing about feminine desire in relation to the horrific' (70). Erica thus contributes to the horror of the film precisely because she is a typical Freudian nightmare, threatening to devour her daughter with her needs as well as mould her into a version of herself. Whilst there may well be ballet/stage mothers like her, this cinematic trope reveals the enduring ways in which mothers continue to be categorised, idealised, and demonised, and how this individualising of her 'monstrosity' works to absolve both the audience and society of any responsibility. This is because it fails to set her actions within a larger cultural and social framework, which might, for example, consider how abandoning her attachment to her daughter is made more difficult by patriarchy's placing of the responsibility for childrearing on the mother. Neither does it offer an explanation for her controlling behaviour. Indeed, one only need think of the sheer number of cinematic monstrous mothers, as compared to their counterparts, demonic fathers, in order to understand how this cinematic trope works to 'shore up the symbolic order by constructing the feminine as an imaginary "other" which must be repressed and controlled in order to secure and protect the social order' (70). To cite just a few examples of these cinematic monstrosities: there is the classic dead mum in *Psycho*, the religiously-fanatical and abusive mum in *Carrie* (1976), the vain and self-absorbed (biographical) mum in *Mommy Dearest* (1981), the frighteningly abusive mum in *Precious* (2009), and the terrifying matriarch of a crime family in *Animal Kingdom* (2010). See Barbara Creed's essay at http://www.johnmenick.com/wp-content/uploads/creed.pdf
27. Fisher and Jacobs, 60.
28. Mulvey, 61.
29. Fisher and Jacobs, 59.
30. In a chapter on "Women's Mental Health Research," Gayle Y. Iwamasa and Audrey K. Bangi write that: 'Although some may not feel that sexual harassment is at the same level as domestic violence or rape, it still has profound psychological effects on its victims. Certainly, domestic violence and rape are severe physical assaults on women, and may even cause death. However, sexual

harassment may lead women to feel trapped and psychologically immobile' (279). Therefore, Thomas' fantasy of liberating Nina may only serve to further her imprisonment. See Gayle Y. Iwamasa and Audrey K Bangi, 'Women's Mental Health Research. History, Current Status, and Future Directions,' in Jeffery Scott Milo and Gayle Y. Iwamasa, eds., *Culturally Diverse Mental Health. The Challenges of Research and Resistance* (New York & Hove: Brunner-Routledge, 2003), 251–68.

31. A telling exchange between Nina and a male admirer (in the club scene) reveals the extent to which she has learnt and internalised this self-negation, as she answers the question of who she is with 'I'm a dancer,' rather than giving her name.

32. Fisher and Jacobs, 59.

33. Lisa Mullen, "Review: *Black Swan*," *Sight & Sound* 21:2 (2011), 49–50.

34. *Entertainment Weekly*'s feature cover story, 'Natalie's Dark Victory,' 31 December 2010, 32.

35. Lynda Hart, *Fatal Women: Lesbian Sexuality and the Mark of Aggression* (London: Routledge, 1994), 18.

36. Jacques Lacan, *Feminine Sexuality,* ed. by Juliet Mitchell & Jacqueline Rose, trans. Jacqueline Rose (New York and London: W.W. Norton, 1982).

37. Steen Christiansen, 'Body Refractions. Darren Aronofsky's *Black Swan*,' akademisk 3 (2011): 306–15. See http://www.academia.edu/2671366/Body_Refractions_Darren_Aronofskys_Black_Swan

38. Fisher and Jacobs, 61.

39. Fisher and Jacobs, 60.

PART II

Movement Beyond the I/Eye

The most renowned of cameras, the Hollywood lens, began filming dance from perspectives such as Busby Berkeley with his ultimate kaleidoscopic vision for dancing bodies while Fred Astaire insisted on a full-body shot, always. And although mainstream film has progressed beyond these early forays into dance representation, there continue to be unexplored pockets of physical motion that find better welcome in the Independent Film Industry. So, what happens when this I/eye in the camera unmoors itself from the politics of Hollywood cinematography to focus on what such institutions have historically either refused to see or misrepresented in stereotypical ways? Sparling would answer 'the electric body': the nude form on stage as a mechanism of artistic movement rather than a throwback to more static examples of the nude in other arts practices. Pruska-Oldenhof wonders what happens with a multiple I/eye in a camera that tries unsuccessfully to capture dancing forms, allowing these bodies to escape the gaze and evoke absent presences that overflow singular subject positions altogether.

CHAPTER 5

Loïe Fuller and the Poetics of Light, Colour, and Rhythm: Some Thoughts on the Making of *fugitive l(i)ght*

Izabella Pruska-Oldenhof

It is often difficult to describe a fast-moving object or a person that begins to move even faster and slip away from the eye's grasp as soon as our gaze puts any pressure on it while trying to pierce through it and fix, by means of description, its mobile state. Furthermore, it becomes even more impossible to pursue an understanding of a being whose hide and seek game continually tries to subvert the pursuing subject's stable position— a position that an ego concocts for a subject—thus pulling the ego-rug from underneath the subject's feet and forcing her erect scopic stance to fall crumbling down into the simple play of a child whose rapid eye-I movements, filled with wonder and adventure, are the only way to catch a quick glimpse of this perpetually fleeing scintillating enigma. Such was the case with both my research on Loïe Fuller (1869–1928) and with the film project inspired by her *Serpentine Dance*, which I titled *fugitive l(i)ght*. During the course of my search in 2004 for film documentations of Loïe Fuller performing her *Serpentine Dance*, I came to a realization, paradoxically after actually locating one that appeared and was deemed authentic, that perhaps Fuller intended her dance performance to be impossible to locate, place or fix on film as 'the performance' by 'the' Loïe.[1] Fuller's

I. Pruska-Oldenhof (✉)
School of Image Arts Communication and Culture, and Documentary Media at Ryerson University, Toronto, Ontario, Canada

© The Editor(s) (if applicable) and The Author(s) 2016
T.D. Arendell, R. Barnes (eds.), *Dance's Duet with the Camera*,
DOI 10.1057/978-1-137-59610-9_5

97

performance presents itself to us by means of its absence, only as an evocation, meaning she slips through the gaps of the numerous representations of her dance fixed into poetic and aesthetic objects, and through several films that document her *Serpentine Dance* performed by her imitators. She meets us at the threshold of the visible and the invisible, thus making herself and her performance (in)visible to us through its palpitating playful rhythm expressed as a field of energy resonating within the spectator.

In addition, my initial suspicion of Loïe Fuller's purposeful subversion of the control of the author/maker and the playful ambiguity and multiplicity of her persona was confirmed after having carefully and playfully read her biography, *Fifteen Years of a Dancer's Life*, and, most importantly, after having closely studied various texts and aesthetic renditions of Fuller's performances by several artists and poets of the same period (lithographs by Henri de Toulouse-Lautrec, drawings of James Abbott McNeill Whistler, posters by Jules Chéret, futurist manifesto of dance by Filippo Thommaso Marinetti, and texts by Stéphane Mallarmé). Many of these artists whose works I have examined have personally known Loïe Fuller, while others have probably not even heard of her, but, nevertheless, their aesthetic approach and interests displayed a striking resemblance to Fuller's. In this essay I would like to focus on one particular artist in relation to Loïe Fuller's work, whose oeuvre, I believe, shares the highest degree of common aesthetic concerns with that of Fuller, and whose writings on her have provided me with much needed guidance on the poetics of her performance and a way to imaginatively engage it in my film *fugitive l(i)ght*. This artist is Stéphane Mallarmé.

The goal of this chapter is to demonstrate the lasting relevance and importance of ideas on the notion of the subject/author position as unstable and always in flux, first introduced over one hundred years ago, by drawing attention to the connections between the work of Loïe Fuller and the writings of Stéphane Mallarmé (1880s), subsequently to the resurgence of those ideas in Julia Kristeva's theory of the 'subject in process/on trial' (1960s), and, of course, to my own film project *fugitive l(i)ght* (2004). Particular focus will be drawn to the position of an artist and the self, which already at the dawn of the twentieth century began to disappear/dissolve by means of its actual multiplication through art practice. The play on the visible and the invisible, or the presence and the absence of the author/I-eye, will be explored in connection to the destabilizing of the power position of the author's I-eye, as well as that of the spectator's, prompted by Fuller's work and shared with Mallarmé, and later reintroduced by Kristeva. Resuscitating these "notions" might be the way to set into motion the I-eye, and hopefully dig into the darkness of indefinable spatial depth, deep beneath the surfaces of the visibles, where the dynamism and mobility of energy can only be viscerally experienced through rhythm that multiplies and destabilizes the I-eye, along with its unified and focused piercing gaze which crystalizes matter into illuminations for the sheer delight of the viscerally bereft mind.

Loïe Fuller was a woman who literally became an overnight sensation by taking Paris of the 1890s by storm with her lightning dances.[2] Her spectacular *Serpentine Dance*, with its radiance of colored effects, possible only with electric light, revolutionized both traditional dance choreography and theatrical stage design (13). Most importantly, she exploded the boundaries between the popular forms of entertainment, the vaudeville with its skirt dancers, and the high art institutions, such as the theatres and the operas, by luring her mesmerized audiences, as if under a hypnotic spell, into the undulating chimera of visions and sensations. 'The possibilities of color in motion, of glowing, undulating excitement was the magic that Loïe created in her manipulation of turbulent yards of shimmering fabric' (13), and it was this magic that permitted her to unify, or actually level, the hierarchical differences between the classes. Furthermore, she inspired both poets and artists, and thus became 'the creation of the fantasies of others' (15), whose radiant dance and multiplying persona was depicted in art objects and poems 'more often than any other woman of her time.'[3] '[S]he served as a symbol of the symbolist movement' and 'she became the personification of Art Nouveau' (4). But who actually was this woman? And why is she of interest to us today, after over one hundred years of silence?

BIOGRAPHICAL NOTES ON FULLER

Loïe Fuller was born as Marie Louise Fuller in January 1862 in Fullersburg near Chicago, Illinois. She was a daughter of Reuben Fuller and Delilah Eaton who moved to Chicago when Loïe was two and opened a boardinghouse.[4] Her father was 'a first-rate fiddler and graceful dancer' (4) and her mother remained by Loïe's side encouraging her daughter's theatrical career, both as a faithful companion and a watchful parent. Fuller had two brothers, one younger and one older. Incidentally, as Elizabeth Coffman points out, in 1896 when Loïe Fuller was offered a chance to make a film with Thomas Edison she claimed that she sent her sister instead, when in fact she never had a sister.[5] This brings us, of course, to her natural ability to act, a talent and a profession, which she rarely left on stage but instead lived through its multiple manifestations in her dance as well as in her personal life. She was first and foremost an actress, a comedian to be more precise, who performed on vaudeville stage in various plays and in between the dance numbers of the skirt dancers. She had made her acting debut at two when she recited a verse from a prayer to an audience at a Sunday school. The audience was more amused than shocked by her performance and burst into laughter when 'too small to walk down the steps, she slid down, bumpety-bump.'[6] Indeed, she appeared to be a naturally born comedian and unfortunately this image haunted her career, partly because in reality her physical appearance was far from what one would then, and even now, expect in a dancer or a dramatic actor, she was 'a rather chubby woman with a fairly plain face... turned-up nose, big blue eyes, and light reddish brown hair'[7] and because she was also not formally trained in dance but instead was a dance innovator. Nevertheless, her stage design techniques and her introduction of open form or improvisation to dance performance paved the way for other, formally trained dancers, such as Isadora Duncan and Josephine Baker, both who made it into the modern dance history books as revolutionaries of dance. As Richard and Marcia Current point out, Loïe Fuller was 'something of a paradox,' in part because the posters and the art objects depicting her dance as a 'tall and lovely sylph' (4) and a graceful dancer, were at odds with her living body.

However, I would like to suggest that this paradox lies precisely at the core of Fuller's creation, and had much in common with the ideas introduced in the 1880s by the Symbolists, in particular those of Stéphane Mallarmé, but I will get to that later. She experienced years of struggle in vaudeville theatres, first as an actress and later as a dancer, where she in fact endured humiliation inflicted by managers who literally laughed in her face when she asked to perform as a dancer.[8] These experiences permitted her to become quite familiar with the power of the gaze and what was required from an actress or a dancer to fulfill its desires, and subsequently what would overturn it and shatter it into pieces. Therefore, this paradox of Loïe prompted the polyvocality and multiplicity of her art creation as well as of her persona. She became the force that broke all the visibly and the invisibly lived boundaries, which separated classes, by bringing her audiences to a hybrid of vaudeville spectacle/theatre of the high brow, and disciplines by eliding and sliding in between while appropriating 'the metaphors and methods of both high art and science.'[9] According to Tom Gunning, the hypnotic quality of Fuller's dance, through its rapid movements and bursts of colored light, fascinated the public and instead of being 'a barrier to reception, its abstraction possessed an immediate sensual attraction that cut across classes and required no previous training or initiation to appreciate.'[10] Most importantly, this form of dance and visual spectacle on stage freed her body, and I will argue also that of future generations of women, by paving the way for the impossibility of the gaze to truly fix, depict, or represent her as Loïe Fuller, but always as someone-something else: the nymph, the lily, the butterfly, the snake... the imitator.

SERPENTINE DANCE

One might question why her work is of importance to us today, especially since much of feminist discourse has identified the power positions of the masculine gaze and some even point to ways of potentially subverting it. Nevertheless, all one needs to do is to turn on the television or go to the cinema or even walk past a store display to realize that despite all this intellectual discourse, not much has been put into practice, and the power of the stifling gaze has a frozen hold on women, and in fact defines for us what it means to be 'one.' The ideas Fuller introduced and explored over one hundred years ago we are still living through and experiencing with our bodies today. Perhaps that is why she slips into the works I discuss, unknowingly to the artist, and asserts her (in)visible presence to the maker. According to Elizabeth Coffman, Fuller's dance was a dance of empowerment at the time when motion and visual spectacle, coupled with erotic display, fascinated the public. Coffman insists on the importance of seeing Fuller as a 'maker of an assertive female dance style... [Her work's] "aberrance" only outlines the undoing of a certain categorical distinctiveness, and does not... condemn her movement style to the rubbish heap of historical neglect.'[11] Answering my question about Fuller's invisibility in cinema, Coffman states: 'The fact that Fuller's name has not been identified with early film history testifies to how dominant film culture has privileged the more predictable vaudeville striptease versions of female performance and the more accessible (but much later) avant-garde work of Maya Deren.'[12] It is perhaps not surprising why in the recent years a handful of makers have stumbled on the roots of their disciples, film and dance, and have come into contact with Fuller's work and are currently re(acting) to it while permitting Fuller to cont(act) the viewers through today's makers' creations. I have here in mind three of them, ironically all women: Amy Greenfield (film and video maker), Jessica Sparling (dancer and choreographer), and myself.

And how did I stumble on the roots of my discipline, on that *fugitive l(i)ght* which slips its luminous rays on the screen of cinema? Where else but at the cinema? In February 2001 when I was in the midst of the production of a dance film titled *Double Ellipse/∞*—which has repeatedly been put on hold, first in Summer 2001, then in Spring 2005—I saw a film by Bruce Elder titled *Crack Brutal Grief* (2000). This film was certainly far from an inspiration of a subject matter for my project; however, Elder's use of found imagery that was solely obtained from the World Wide Web and its manipulation has certainly impacted my way of working with hybrid film forms. Nevertheless, it was in this film by Elder where I saw for several seconds a sequence of Annabelle Whitford Moore performing the *Butterfly Dance*. I thought that this sequence would be very appropriate for my dance film project, because the dancer created double elliptical movements with her dress: the figure eight when upright and infinity when on the side. I searched for this footage but could not find Annabelle's dance anywhere on the internet. Instead, I came across a different footage, one of a dancer named Crissie Sheridan performing the *Serpentine Dance* in 1897 for Thomas Edison. Frustrated and determined to find the *Butterfly Dance*, I kept searching for Annabelle but kept on finding other dancers performing what I now know as variations on the *Serpentine Dance* of Fuller. They included: Ameta (a French imitator of Fuller, probably filmed by the Lumière Brothers), and three other women dancers who were filmed by Edison, but the date was not always indicated on those films. In the end, the project was put on hold until later, when I had hoped to revisit the project again and finally finish it—wishful thinking!

Of course, just like any project, this project put up a fight, and in despair I decided to start off slow by playing around with the found footage of Crissie Sheridan performing the *Serpentine Dance*. This footage is originally in black and white, and in it Sheridan appears and disappears while moving the white fabric against the black background. I imported this video file into Adobe After Effects, a video compositing program where imagination is the limit—and certainly it is, since one feels that there are no boundaries and begins to sink into the infinite void of the virtual world of possibilities. I began to systematically move from the top to the bottom of the long list of effects, applying each one and waiting to see what happens. Finally, I came across one, the simplest one, the most aesthetically pleasing and conceptually fitting. This effect separates light into the six colors of the light spectrum: yellow and blue, magenta and green, and cyan and red. Here I found what I was searching for or perhaps what it, the footage, was searching for and directed me towards. I set up a system of fives, and created the first sequence based on splitting the white light into six colors and overlapping them as layers by controlling their luminosity and the type of transparency. The fives were based on the size of the actual clip (100–500 percent of the original size), and the duration of the clip (100–500 percent of the original speed of the clip). When superimposed, these sequences took on a life of their own, moving rhythmically, as if with a pulse of their own, and creating color variations unrestrained by my intention. I waited in anticipation to see what eye adventure they would direct me to next. After seeing this footage literally unfold on its own in front of my eyes, I decided to search for more footage of the *Serpentine Dance* and create a whole film using only this footage. At this point, because of my previous searches, I knew that there must be more of them out there, caught in the World Wide Web waiting to be retrieved by me and brought into their new existence. Incidentally, I came across a web site that outlined the history of the *Serpentine Dance*, noting Loïe Fuller as its originator and describing her colorful luminous performances. At that point I realized that I was unknowingly, unconsciously, tapping into something beyond my control and was literally at my wit's end. Through my playfulness with the found footage of Crissie Sheridan, who was performing Fuller's *Serpentine Dance*, I actually began to recreate, by introducing color and multiple layers, what would appear to have been Fuller's actual live performance of the 1890s but in 2004, by permitting it—rather than me in my director's chair—to direct its course. Indeed, Loïe Fuller slipped into this project, without me even knowing it, and asserted her (in) visible presence through the filmed performances of her imitators, where she continuously slips in through cracks of these existing representations as rhythm and flees before becoming moored by any of them.

FUGITIVE L(I)GHT

Fugitive l(i)ght was indeed a self-directing project, one that was directing and instructing me rather than me forcing its course of being. In the fall of 2004, after returning to this project, I once again realized that while working on it, with it, I was being guided by some(thing)/one other than my conscious self, and this otherness only surfaced when I removed myself from the creative act, loosened the grip of my conscious hold on the project, and relied on chance-based operations to guide the film. The more I permitted my insight-seeking gaze to immerse itself and dissolve its grip within the rhythmic folding and unfolding of the dress, the veils, the flower petals of the system-chance derived sequence, the more I-eye got lost and the more I was capable of attuning myself and actively see-ing; sea-ing among its own rhythms. *fugitive l(i)ght* is composed of four blocks of system-chance derived sequences. The first one is based on fives and uses the Crissie Sheridan footage. The second is composed of the forwards and backwards of a *Serpentine Dance* sequence performed by an unknown dancer and shot by Edison. This sequence is mostly red, white and black. The third sequence is composed again of Crissie Sheridan's footage and it is mostly black with colored outlines of the fabric and face. In this sequence, I create multiple rhythmic superimpositions of a very short section from the original performance by Sheridan. Through these appearing and disappearing rhythmic pulsations of the original image, various new images are evoked, rather than being represented, as the light and color begin to wander into one's I-eye: birds, volcanoes, tornadoes, swirls, and so on. Towards the film's end, I introduce Annabelle Whitford Moore, the dancer with whom I originally began my search but could not find. Using this sequence I will try to recreate the tongues of fire, which comprise the final sequence; the final sequence is inspired by the *Fire Dance* of Fuller. By inverting the white dancing body of Annabelle into black and superimposing it on her other white and colored moving bodies in this sequence, these moving bodies of light act as if fighting for their existence as their encroaching dark shadow strives to extinguish them. The presence of the shadow was yet another playful, unconscious, response to a system in this final sequence, a system with a slightly looser structure based on multiplying the body of Annabelle. To some extent the final sequence might resemble the *Dance of Death*, which I guess might be quite appropriate for the final sequence and fitting for a project which in some ways explores the notions of being, in both its metaphysical and ontological sense.

The loosening of the conscious grip of the intellect by means of a sys-tem permitted me, or actually forced me, to go with the flow of the proj-ect. It also became a very practical solution to my obsession with trying to desperately find 'the footage' of Loïe Fuller performing her dance, which I was convinced must exist somewhere but which I was able to finally locate only about a month ago, at an archive in New York's public library. This sequence, which I am still not 100 percent certain is 'the' Loïe Fuller, is woven into the final sequence of my film. I should also mention that the system used in each one of the four film blocks creates the underlying foundation of each block, into which I loosely weave myself, by rhythmically intercutting and superimposing fragments of other *Serpentine Dance* sequences as a response to the called-forth experience. In addition, many of the colors and forms created by means of using the system preceded my acquaintance with the posters and other imagery depicting Fuller's dance, which was in particular the case with the first sequence. Later, after being more exposed to the representations of Fuller, I used them as a rough guide in choosing color schemes, although often the system itself would unveil other patterns and color combinations that I was not considering at the time but were still present, in some way or other, amidst these representations.

The music in *fugitive l(i)ght* will be composed entirely using an LP recording of Richard Wagner's opera, *Ride of the Valkyries = Die Walküre* (1856, first performed 1870). According to a number of sources, including that of Richard and Marcia Current, certainly the most rigorously researched book on Fuller, she originally performed her *Fire Dance* to the music from this opera, and used it as a source for rhythmic structuring of her dance. However, later she turned to other composers such as Léo Delibes whose music provided the mood for her dances.[13] I thought that using Wagner's opera might be quite fitting for two reasons: one, Fuller performed her dances to it; and two, because he, like Fuller, was one of the first artists who aimed at breaking beyond the boundaries of a discipline and introducing interdisciplinary practice. He coined the term 'total work of art,' also known as *Gesamtkünstwerk*, and envisioned the opera as a manifestation of this concept. Despite all the relevant conceptual underpinnings of Wagner's work, his *Ride of the Valkyries* will be treated in a similar manner to the visuals of the film, incorporating the tonal, rhythmic and textured qualities rendered by the LP recording. The music for the soundtrack is composed by my brother, Oskar Pruski.

The title *fugitive l(i)ght* attempts to conjure up the notion of Loïe Fuller's performative being, both on the stage and in real life, and of course in this film; as a multiplying moving light and as a persona with multiple I's, constantly fleeing fixed positioning and conscious determinations. In her biography *Fifteen Years of a Dancer's Life* in a chapter titled 'My Dances and the Children' she included a five-stanza poem by a little boy, around eight years old, composed for Fuller based on his experience of her performance. It is in this poem that I arrived at the words that form the title for this film.

> Pale vision
> A l'horizon
> En ce lieu sombre
> Fugitive ombre ...[14]

Hence, 'Fugitive ombre,' which actually means 'fugitive shadow,' became *fugitive l(i)ght*, which I felt was more in line with the nature of Fuller's performances and with the instability or mobility of her position as an author, her ego. This was the only poem included in her biography, and I am quite skeptical about it being written by an eight-year-old youngster. Nevertheless, it must have been important to her, for her to include it in her biography, and knowing that she had a tendency to make up 'fantastic tales' about her life while creating 'her own myth,'[15] I would not be surprised if it was either composed by her or somebody else, but was a notion she wanted communicated to the reader of her biography. Most importantly, this title is supposed to suggest the loosening of the grip of the author/maker over their creation, by means of their unmoored, mobile and multiple I, which I tried to engage by locking up my ego temporarily in a cage of a system—in 'John's cage' as Brakhage called it in reference to John Cage's chance operations.[16]

LOÏE FULLER'S MYSTERIOUS IMAGE

To further elaborate on Loïe Fuller's myth-making abilities, and the advancing of her multiple-mobile I, it might be quite valuable to examine the accounts of children's responses to her in the same chapter of her biography, written of course through the lens of Loïe. In this chapter she provides various accounts of them being disillusioned with her real-life appearance after first seeing her perform on stage. According to Fuller, several of the well-to-do Parisian parents, as well as the middle class, would bring their children back stage after Fuller's performance to meet her in person (142). To the astonishment of parents, their children, in disbelief that the same lady performed the dances on stage and appears on the posters, would ironically deem Loïe Fuller an impostor. One little girl, according to Fuller, responded as follows: 'No, no. That isn't her. I don't want to see her. This one here is a fat lady, and it was a fairy I saw dancing' (141–2). Another little girl, Princess Marie of Roumania's daughter, exclaimed: 'You don't fool me. This woman is telling fibs' (145) after previously calling her a butterfly and an angel. In both instances she wanted to 'avoid disillusioning these children' (146) and with tears in her eyes she would reply to the first little girl 'I hear the fairy whispering in my ear that she would like to dance for you all the time' (142), thus acting as if a mediator between the fairy, butterfly, angel Loïe Fuller and the 'fat lady' Fuller. However, I would like to draw your attention to a very peculiar thing in this chapter, one that becomes visible only when read in between the lines of her prose. She appears to be oscillating between at least two subject positions when describing her dances in this chapter. One is the reflective position on her dances as an art critic, the second responding to her dance through the I-eyes of a child, and the third being as if a silent voice of the 'ideal' Loïe Fuller echoing through the other two positions. What is important is that in the first two of these positions she is seeing herself through the eyes of another, being outside of herself and watching herself dance, as if being uncoupled from the 'I.' The following passage is an example of the 'critic-Loïe ideal' combination, she writes: 'From the unearthly appearance of my dances, caused by the light and the mingling of color, they ought particularly to appeal to the young, making them believe that the being flitting about there before them among the shadows and flashes of light belongs to the unreal world which holds sway in their lives' (137). The next passage demonstrates her combination of the 'child's eye-Loïe ideal':

> … [The child] must have supposed that she was going to be taken into some celestial place. She looked round with restless eyes, surveying the bare walls, the uncarpeted floor, and seemed to be waiting to see the ceiling or the flooring open suddenly and permit an entrance into Loïe Fuller's kingdom.
>
> Suddenly a folding screen was drawn and a young woman came forward, who looked tired and in whose appearance there was nothing supernatural. With arms outstretched she advanced smiling. (141)

I would also like to draw your attention to the words she chose to describe herself and her surroundings, 'kingdom': 'the being flitting about [that] belongs to the unreal world,' 'celestial place,' 'a young woman… in whose appearance was nothing supernatural' and of course in this last one implying the 'supernatural' being. Many of these words describe her as an otherworldly creature; in fact, she also calls herself in this chapter that 'extraordinary creature' and 'out of this world' (137, 141). Perhaps tired of the struggle of living in a body that the western culture of the 1890s would not permit the spotlight of dance stage or serious theatrical roles, she presents us with her ideal world, a 'kingdom,' through her multiple and otherworldly being.

STÉPHANE MALLARMÉ

Nevertheless, it is quite evident, especially in the second passage, that Fuller enjoyed the elisions and constant sliding of the subject positions. Just like in her dance performances, where she would move between different shapes, physically transforming her bodily appearance, in language she slid with her words in between positions, in between the lines, evoking 'la Loïe' only momentarily, in passing, in flight, in motion. This finally brings us to Stéphane Mallarmé. It is certainly not a coincidence that Loïe Fuller can be found in the pages of this poet, who called her 'a phantom in the Ballet' and her dances 'the theatrical form of poetry *par excellence*,'[17] as both of them appear to have shared similar ideas in regards to the role/position of an artist/author in art practice. Incidentally, as Mary Ann Caws points out, Mallarmé enjoyed writing using many different voices and under 'multiple pseudonyms (of both genders): Madame de Ponty, Mademoiselle Satin, Olympia le négresse, le Chef de Bouche de chez Brabant, and the redoubtable yet unspecified IX.'[18] This release, or liberation, from the unified position of the 'one' subject/author, 'the Stéphane Mallarmé,' is not dissimilar from Fuller's multiple I's: embodied though her imposters, her multiplying dance and her actor-self.

In 1886, six years prior to Fuller's arrival in Paris, Mallarmé wrote an essay titled *Crisis in Poetry*, which comprised the oeuvre of Symbolist manifestos, along with the writings of James Abbott McNeill Whistler, Oscar Wilde, Pierre-Louis (also known as Maurice Denis), Jean Moréas, Odilon Redon and several other artists. In this essay he explicitly states that for a poem to come to its being the artist/poet must vanish as the intentional voice of the I and leave the job to words themselves:

> The pure work implies the disappearance of the poet as speaker, yielding his initiative to words, which are mobilized by the shock of their differences; they light up with reciprocal reflections like a virtual stream of fireworks over jewels, restoring perceptible breath to the former lyric impulse, or the enthusiastic personal directing of the sentence.

...

What good is the marvel of transposing a fact of nature into its almost complete and *vibratory* disappearance with the play of the word, however, unless there comes forth from it, without the bother of a nearby or concrete reminder, the *pure notion*.[19]

Indeed, it is by directing attention to language, to the words themselves, and allowing the collisions of words to form new constellations of meaning, which are severed from representations and not predetermined by conscious reasoning, that permit something other to slip in, past the immobile I-eye of the author, and thus attune the old lyrical style to the new rhythm, the new (in)pulse. However, the goal of his approach is not to send the reader into a nebula of abstract and arbitrary language through the 'play' of language, but to release the reader from fixed conceptual thinking, rendered by immobile representations, by setting the I-eye in motion, in search for 'the pure notion.' What Mallarmé was after was not a representation, a fixed (re)presentation of the world for the absolute comprehension of the I-eye, but instead for an evocation, an analogy, a suggestion, a momentary and fleeting whisper that refuses stasis and draws the I-eye into its rhythmic pulses of being/non-being. He writes: 'I say: a flower! And outside the oblivion to which my voice relegates any shape, insofar as it is something other than the calyx, there arises musically, as the very idea and delicate, the one absent from every bouquet.'[20] The embodiment of this idea of the 'flower!' became Loïe Fuller, six years later, who through her dances (her lilies, fires, snakes and butterflies) rhythmically evoked Mallarmé's 'flower!' As Gunning noted 'this Chicago dancer... provided the Symbolists with the most vivid embodiment of the ideal their new aesthetic pursued.... The symbol as the radiating center of unending transformation.'[21] Indeed through the style of her dance with its ever-changing evocations of nature—flowing with the movement, always slipping from the grasp of the gaze and reason—she was capable of accomplishing with her body what the Symbolist poets aimed at with language.

THE DANCER AS POET

In his essay on Loïe Fuller, Gunning draws our attention to another 1886 essay by Mallarmé: this one is on ballet, where Mallarmé 'seemed to have dreamed of a form of dance like Fuller's even before he saw her.'[22] Indeed, several of the passages in this essay sound as if they were literal descriptions of Loïe Fuller. When I read it for the first time I was a little puzzled, and even confused, because on the one hand I knew that he was writing about various ballerinas, and naturally made references to point-shoes and the exposed legs of the dancer, but on the other hand, he wrote about the rhythmic style of dance, its transforming quality, and even mentioned veils. One can certainly imagine that this could become quite confusing and send readers on the wrong track, but who knows perhaps this state of confusion or dispersal of the reader was his intent, which would not be inconsistent with his mischievous playfulness. For Mallarmé a performing dancer, through her ever transforming and suggestive movements, takes on a non-human quality, a kind of supernatural quality if you will, thus becoming a poem herself. He writes:

> ...the dancer is *not a woman who dances* for these combined reasons: *she is not a woman*, but a metaphor summing up one of the elementary aspects of our form—sword, cup, flower, etc.; and *that she does not dance*, suggesting, through the miracle of shortcuts and bounds, with a corporal writing what it would take paragraphs of prose, in dialogue and description, to express: she is a poem set free of any scribe's apparatus.[23]

One certainly gets a sense of Mallarmé's revolutionary ideas on dance in this passage, in fact reaching even further into the future of dance, well after Loïe Fuller, and announcing another American dancer Martha Graham (1920s) for whom dance was an expression of the most primal emotions rather than a story, a narrative. The dancer in this passage uses her body as a writer would a pen, by means of her expressive 'corporal writing' all the while impressing her being into the lived space of the viewer and creating a body-time/body-space poetry. Furthermore, this passage suggests that the creation of meanings, however fleeting, in this poetry lies in the hands of the reader, spectator, who being presented with the ever-changing visions of the poem/dance flows with them, thus permitting her/his mind, by means of visceral engagement, to create constellations of previously unknown meanings. Recalling his 'flower!' to the reader, he concludes this essay:

> ...the Flower, first, of your poetic instinct, expecting that nothing else will provide the revelation in its true light of thousands of latent imaginations: then, through some steps whose secret her smile seems to transmit, she gives to you unhesitating, through the one last veil which will always remain, exposing your concepts, silently writing your vision in the form of a Sign, the sign that she herself is. (113)

This last sentence of his essay, in particular such phrases as 'the one last veil,' 'the revelation in its true light of thousands of latent imaginations' and 'the sign that she herself is,' are as if prophetic descriptions of Fuller, whom at least six years later he had fully inscribed into another essay titled *Another Dance Study: Settings and the Ballet.*

This essay, I believe, is one of the finest examples that demonstrates Mallarmé's poetic ideas put into practice through Fuller's dance. Furthermore, this essay touches on the notion of threat, a kind of menacing quality of art that perpetually threatens the stability of the I-eye and which, through the course of this essay, reveals itself as the latent goal of both Mallarmé and Fuller. Unlike the previous essay on the ballet dancers, where the dancer did not pose any threat to the I-eye of the subject in the audience, partly because of her still fully graspable body that only would momentarily take the spectator into the poetry of her movement, in this essay the dancer is described as if an embodiment of a menace, the perpetual threat to the I-eye, which veils itself with beautiful 'phantasmagoric' images. It is this menacing, 'fearsome,' in 'rage,' and 'furious' quality that looms over Fuller's dance and produces a poetics of movement that Mallarmé recognizes as 'the theatrical form of *poetry par excellence.*'[24] He writes:

> In the fearsome bath of the materials swoons—radiant and cold—the interpreter who illustrates many gyratory themes towards which stretches a thread in full bloom: an unfolding, like giant petals or butterflies.... Its fusion with the fast-moving nuances, constantly transforming their phantasmagoric mixture of air and water, typical of dusks and caves, like swiftly changing passions—delight, grief, rage; to set them in motion, diluted with all their prismatic violence, we need the vertigo of a soul that seems to have been placed in the air through some kind of artifice.
>
> ...
>
> ...there appears like a snowflake, blown from where? furious, the dancer.... The décor lies—latent in the orchestra—a treasure for the imagination; only to escape from it, dazzlingly, according to the gaze that dispenses the representer here and there from all idea of footlights. Well this transition from sounds to tissue... is, uniquely, the spell exerted by Loïe Fuller, who instinctively, with exaggeration, uses the retreats of her skirt—her wing—to create a place. The enchantress creates the atmosphere, draws it to her and returns to it, through a palpitating silence of crepe de Chine. (114–5)

The looming menace to the I-eye in both of these passages that Mallarmé sketches out for us is a weave of two particular forms of threat, which surface through the play of his words: one, the threat of the mobile danc-ing body that aims at dispersing the I-eye into the infinity of its transfor-mations through the excess of the visibles; two, the threat of death or non-being through the constant allusions to objects/events resisting the grasp of a gaze, the invisibles.

The first form of threat, the threat of excess visibility conjured up by means of the mobile body, is the most prevalent in the first paragraph; however, both forms of threat exist in each paragraph and phrase. This threat particularly presents itself through such phrases as 'fearsome bath of materials swoons' where 'bath' suggests excess or an immersion in some form of substance, and 'many gyratory themes towards which stretches a thread in full bloom' where 'gyration' implies a form of constant move-ment which through the excess of this perpetual motion will force some-thing to burst into 'full bloom' or burst into nothingness. And more directly and literally in these two sentences, 'Its fusion with the fast-moving nuances, constantly transforming their phantasmagoric mixture' and 'like swiftly changing passions—delight, grief, rage; to set them in motion, diluted with all their prismatic violence' both implying excess through the notions of 'fusion' and 'passions' that result in dispersal or refraction of the uniform I-eye through 'phantasmagoria' and 'prismatic violence.' The second threat, the threat prompted by the lack of visibles, is quite evident in the second paragraph, in particular in the phrase that alludes to the orchestra pit, a grave?, which is always darkened and barely invisible to the audience: 'The décor lies—latent in the orchestra—a treasure for the imagination.' The orchestra pit is where the heart of Fuller's performance is hidden, the electric colored lights, where the eye of the viewer cannot reach but where only the imagination can wonder. One can also read this quote as a reference to the origin, the origin of being—our being and that of Fuller's dance—where no-thing was, was visible, which is also inter-twined with death, where no-thing will be, will stay forever foreclosed for us and invisible. The same notion of threat, the one prompted by the lack of the visibles, is also present in the last two sentences: 'the spell exerted by Loïe Fuller, who… uses the retreats of her skirt—her wing—to create a place. The enchantress creates the atmosphere, draws it to her and returns to it, through a palpitating silence of crepe de Chine.' The notion of spell is an allusion to a hypnotic spell where the I-eye becomes disengaged from the lived-now and floats somewhere in between the words of hypnotist or the visions of spectacle and her/his own body. In this case the audi-ence is floating, moving, in this in-between space created by the rhythmic, and repetitive, motions of Fuller's wing-skirt. Fuller creates through her body 'the atmosphere,' a kind of aura, into which she disappears and from which she reappears again, once again playing with the notions of birth and death or the pre-natal state.

The last part of Mallarmé's sentence, in the preceding paragraph, 'through a palpitating silence of crepe de Chine,' can be read as a rhythmic oscillation between the looming presence of invisibility, 'silence' or death, and the presence of life force through the visibles or the audibles of 'palpitation.' This threatening quality to Fuller's dance, and of Mallarmé's prose, is aimed at expanding and re-engaging the mobility of the subject, the I-eye, through a different kind of gaze: 'the gaze that dispenses the representer [I-eye] here and there from all idea of footlights.'[25] The notion of the dispersal of the I-eye appears to have been synonymous for Mallarmé with the expansion of being, of going beyond the self. This quality was the goal of Mallarmé's poetic texts, which I have previously outlined in reference to his Symbolist manifesto, and he also identified it in Fuller's dance which he stated in another part of this essay: 'That a woman should link the flight of clothes with a powerful or vast dance to the point of lifting them, infinitely high, like the expansion of her own being.'[26] Interestingly, the same idea of expansion of the subject, of its excess and its subsequent dispersion, is picked up nearly seventy years later and worked out by Julia Kristeva in her *Revolution in Poetic Language*.

JULIA KRISTEVA'S OPPOSING DRIVES: REVISING SPECULAR MODALITIES

Kristeva's dissertation, which was later published as a book,[27] introduces the term 'subject in process/on trial' as a response to the poetic texts of Stéphane Mallarmé, Lautremont, and Antonin Artaud. This peculiar subject position/disposition, which she identified as most prominent in the avant-garde texts, is based on the perpetual oscillations between the two opposing poles of a dyad; 'the semiotic' and 'the symbolic' modalities of the signifying process. However, the mobility prompted through this oscillation between these two modalities forces the subject to dispense with the extremism of 'either/or,' that fixes the subject into immobility, and thus thrusts the I-eye into an unstable position of the other, the third of a dyad, which is always in question and on trial while fighting for its existence. According to Kristeva there are two modalities that comprise the signifying process and which determine the type of discourse:

the semiotic and the symbolic. The semiotic modality is pre-subjective, thus pre-Oedipal and prior to the mirror stage. It is present in the form of energy charges and discharges of the psychical drives in the physical/ psychological body of the subject. Kristeva notes: 'Discrete quantities of energy move through the body of the subject who is not yet constituted as such and, in the course of his development, they are arranged according to the various constraints imposed on this body—always involved in a semiotic process—by family and social structures.'[28] These constraints of the 'family and social structures' comprise the symbolic modality, the social body, which is first introduced in the mirror stage and becomes fully realized with the acquisition of language and upon the entrance into the Oedipal stage, where the newly formed subject meets the symbolic 'law of the father.' Furthermore, both of these modalities are always, and must always, be present in the subject, however the degree of their presence might vary. The subject is produced through the dialectic process of both of these modalities; the oscillations between the two opposing poles. What prompts this dialectic process? And what is at the root of movement, be it social or psychical? It is a space called 'the *chora*.'

The *chora* belongs to the semiotic modality and is formed by the pulses and stases of the psychical drives, which like energy surge through the body. It is 'a-subjective,' 'a-familial,' 'a-filial,' 'a-social' and precedes, while at the same time being the condition of, the social/symbolic body.[29] According to Kristeva 'the *chora* is not yet a position that represents something for someone... nor is it a position that represents someone for another position... the *chora* precedes and underlies figuration and thus specularization, and is analogous only to vocal or kinetic rhythm... nourishing and maternal.'[30] Furthermore, it is a 'pulsional network... *the mobile-receptacle site of the process*, which takes the place of the unitary subject.'[31] According to Kristeva, poetic language, in particular that of the avant-garde poets such us Mallarmé, by means of its close affinity with the semiotic modality, because of its emphasis on rhythm rather than denotation or representation, 'puts the subject in process/on trial through a network of marks and semiotic facilitations. But the moment it stops being mere instinctual glossolalia and becomes part of the linguistic order, poetry meets up with denotation and enunciation—verisimilitude and the subject—and, through them, the social.'[32] In other words, poetic language as much as it privileges the disruption of the 'unitary subject' by means of the semiotic, the maternal, and the rhythmic 'pulsions' of the *chora*, nevertheless still needs to meet up with 'the law of the father,' 'the symbolic' dimension of the process of signification and of the subject, in order for meaning, however disrupted and irruptive, to come forth; to flower!

Kristeva's semiotic weave of art (poetic language) and ontology of the subject, an ontology predicated on the existential crisis of 'the subject in process/on trial,' helps us understand the relationship between the process of art making and the subject position. Whether the I-eye is 'caged' or 'multiplied' or egocentrically shines through the work, ultimately the artwork always relates and makes visible the often invisible subject, who hides behind its existence. However, this subject has to stay always in terror, in motion, on trial, in question, for the work of art to originate by moving out and beyond, or below and before, the ordering rigidity of the symbolic. The importance of Loïe Fuller's dances and Stéphane Mallarmé's poetic language lies precisely in their aim at loosening of the grip of the unitary subject, the I-eye, of both the maker and the reader/spectator, over their creations and permitting the work to slip in and out with its rhythmic multiplicity beyond the conscious grasping of the gaze and the intellect. By setting the I-eye in motion and in question, both of these artists not only addressed aesthetic issues of art at the turn of last century but also drew our attention to the social realm, by means of shattering the existing boundaries. Most importantly, they unveiled to us the indivisibility of art practice from the social existence through the twists and turns of the subject in crisis, fighting for its existence while oscillating between both the social and physical/psychological bodies.

Perhaps the question one has to ask oneself is whether the project started by the Symbolists, in particular Stéphane Mallarmé, where the speaking poet has disappeared or withdrawn into invisibility, and continued by Loïe Fuller, through her multiplying persona and dances, was specific only to that period of Modernity and whether it is still pertinent to us today? After all, *fugitive l(i)ght* would have been inconceivable otherwise, if it was not for something that prompted me to momentarily suspend my I-eye, to loosen the fixing grip of my intellect, in order to open up towards that something other; the other who met me in midst of her (un)veiling motions.

Notes

1. Richard Nelson Current and Marcia Ewing Current, *Loïe Fuller: Goddess of Light* (Boston: Northeastern University Press, 1997), 70.
2. Margaret Haile Harris, *Loïe Fuller: Magician of Light* (Richmond: The Virginia Museum, 1979), 13.

3. Current and Current, 4.
4. Current and Current, 4.
5. Elizabeth Coffman, 'Women in Motion: Loïe Fuller and the "Interpenetration" of Art and Science,' *Camera Obscura* 17:1 (2002): 101.
6. Current and Current, 8.
7. Current and Current, 4, 6.
8. Loïe Fuller, *Fifteen Years of a Dancer's Life: With Some Account of her Distinguished Friends*, Introduction by Anatole France (Boston: Small Maynard and Company, 1913), 35.
9. Coffman, 77.
10. Tom Gunning, 'Loïe Fuller and the Art of Motion: Body, Light, Electricity, and the Origins of Cinema.' In: *Camera Obscura, Camera Lucida: Essays in Honor of Annette Michelson*, ed. Richard Allen and Malcolm Turvey (Amsterdam: Amsterdam University Press, 2003), 84.
11. Coffman, 88.
12. Coffman, 78.
13. Current and Current, 100.
14. Marx in Fuller, 147.
15. Current and Current, 6.
16. Stan Brakhage, *Metaphors on Vision*, edited and with introduction by P. Adams Sitney (New York: Film Culture, 1963), 18.
17. Stéphane Mallarmé, 'Crisis in Poetry (1886b).' In: *Manifesto: A Century of Isms*, ed. Mary Ann Caws (Lincoln: University of Nebraska Press, 2001), 114.
18. Mary Ann Caws, ed. Introduction to *Mallarmé in Prose*, by Mary Ann Caws (New York: New Directions, 2001), 1.
19. Stéphane Mallarmé, 'Crisis in Poetry (1886b).' In: *Manifesto: A Century of Isms*, ed. Mary Ann Caws (Lincoln: University of Nebraska Press, 2001), 114–6. Caws2: 25, my italics.
20. Mallarmé, *Crisis in Poetry*. 114–6.
21. Gunning, 79–80.
22. Gunning, 81.
23. Stéphane Mallarmé, 'Another Dance Study: Settings and the Ballet (1886a).' In: *Mallarmé in Prose*, edited by Mary Ann Caws and translated by Rosemary Lloyd and Mary Ann Caws (New York: New Directions, 2001), 109.
24. Mallarmé, *Crisis in Poetry*, 114.

25. Mallarmé, *Crisis in Poetry*, 114.
26. Mallarmé, *Crisis in Poetry*, 114.
27. Julia Kristeva, *Revolution in Poetic Language*, translated by Margaret Waller and introduction by Leon S. Roudiez (New York: Columbia University Press, 1984).
28. Kristeva, *Revolution in Poetic Language*, 25.
29. Julia Kristeva, 'The Subject in Process.' In: *The Tel Quel Reader*, ed. Patrick French and Roland François Lack (London and New York: Routledge, 1998), 134–5.
30. Kristeva, *Revolution in Poetic Language*, 26.
31. Kristeva, 'The Subject in Process,' 134.
32. Kristeva, *Revolution in Poetic Language*, 58.

CHAPTER 6

Naked Came I/Eye: Lights, Camera and the Ultimate Spectacle

Peter Sparling

The naked body, though the most commonly shared 'fact' of existence, is also the most scripted, inscribed, censored, and/or 'performed' spectacle. Nakedness and degrees of nakedness occupy our attention in our private, everyday etiquettes and insinuate themselves into the worlds of media, fashion and performance. The body's relative degrees of nakedness signify for the eye of the beholder a set of templates, traditions and acceptable or transgressive social norms. These templates evolve to provide each culture with its (often voyeuristic) means of performing the body while defining boundaries of public/private. The traditions of western concert dance have offered a certain protected space and aesthetic rationale for the stripped-down body on stage. What kind of status is this aestheticized body granted once it is performed, edited and produced as screen art?

In studying recent screendances I have made in which I embody, videotape and edit my own improvisational dance performance—alternating anterior and posterior facings of my naked body—I hope to address this and other related questions. Do the camera and editing allow for greater objectification, and/or a fusion of corporeal and idealized aesthetic orientations with twentieth-century theories of opticality and traditions of Modern Dance... such that the naked dancing body aligns itself more with Modernity

P. Sparling (✉)
University of Michigan, Ann Arbor School of Music, Theatre & Dance
Department of Dance, Ann Arbor, Michigan, USA

© The Editor(s) (if applicable) and The Author(s) 2016   119
T.D. Arendell, R. Barnes (eds.), *Dance's Duet with the Camera*,
DOI 10.1057/978-1-137-59610-9_6

and a poetics of dance rather than coming off as an embarrassing display of narcissism, exhibitionism or soft porn? Do the aesthetic and choreographic choices made in the act of video self-portraiture—and in the relationship to the camera and to an imagined audience—re-claim the gaze as the creator's own and guard him against accusations that he is merely making a spectacle of himself? Or is the point to make a spectacle of the body? Indeed, what IS spectacle and its relationship to the artist/creator's body?[1]

DEVANT AND *DERRIÈRE*

Two studies for the screen, *DEVANT* and *DERRIÈRE*, feature the two facings—front and back—of the naked male form. *DERRIÈRE* is described as follows for submissions to festivals:

> This mock-serious study of the backside of dance exposes to the camera the typically unseen facet of the dancer's body. By showing the flip side of the usual frontal facing of the performing body, DERRIÈRE celebrates the hidden mechanics of the dancer's instrument as it engages in modes ranging from lyrical or highly emotive to spasmodic and wildly disjointed.

Is this man making a spectacle of his buttocks, or is he making art? Do editing devices, formatting and effects tell us something either way? (Do the curators of international video festivals make the final call?) What about the creator's own high intentions as a professor and working artist who embraces a certain poetics of modern dance?

Considering the artist's intentionality is largely out of fashion among academic circles, except that, in this case, the body as spectacle on video has a very difficult time hiding its intentions. As the ghost of Martha Graham's physician father reminds us constantly, 'Movement never lies.' Perhaps with camera and editing—particularly when the naked dancer is subject—this well-worn admonition is given new meaning for the realm of screendance and its potential for not only intimate exposure, revelation and truth-saying but for masterly disguise, deconstruction and recontextualization.

SCREENDANCE AS SPECTACLE

Adding, then, the variables of camera work and editing to those of the dancing itself, we might contemplate a newly calibrated set of aesthetic considerations for the screendance as spectacle. It's less a matter of addition or translation from the stage and more one of intertextual or inter-disciplinary alchemy for the screen. Isolating first the aspect of movement, the body is stripped of everything in the void of the video studio's black box, with no costume or ornamentation, no setting other than carefully designed artificial lighting, we are left alone with a highly trained (albeit aging) dancer's naked body, groomed in a certain mode of movement presentation deemed 'artistic.'

Laurence Louppe, in her treatise *Poetics of Contemporary Dance*, identifies the 'tools' of contemporary dance movement in terms of body, breath, weight, flow, space, time, invention, style and composition.[2] Can this movement poetics override the fact of nakedness as a distraction to the making of art? I certainly expect that of my improvisational performance in *DERRIÈRE*, designed to embody four different contrasting dynamic modes. As performer, I aspire to art as spectacle through a mature virtuosity—a skillful modulation of my Humphrey-Limon roots in rhythm, design, dynamics, motivation, fall-rebound, with a generous dose of Grahamesque contraction-release and evocative contortions, spasms, and contourings—all within an overarching time/space/force continuum, re-affirming movement for movement's sake.

To this groomed production of improvisational movement I add the calculated play of light on muscle and flesh, captured and rendered so that the body is both the canvas and the generator of movement colorations, gestures and utterances that animate the frame. The camera frames and creates this movement picture, anticipating, through editing and projection, the rectangular plane of the screen. This plane, one step removed from the proscenium frame, framed photograph or painting, provides objective distance, a more remote positioning for viewing, and perhaps further license to artfully arrange and display the spectacle. We are also provided the opticality of the privileged camera eye's invasive intimacy and ability to define multiple points of view, to move towards, away from, and around the subject. And finally, a vast array of effects, transitions, and re-stagings are applied in editing, during which the moving picture is digitally re-choreographed, re-positioned, multiplied, and altered in its timing and relationship to a succession of other images or episodes.

This distancing and objectification in the editing process of composition for the screen comes as a welcome relief for the solo artist familiar with performing original material on stage and for live audiences. Becoming arbiter of his own moving image while sitting at the computer places him literally in the driver's seat.

VIDEO POSTCARDS

In *Upon Viewing Picasso's Nude Self-Portraits*, from a set of a dozen or so daily studies or 'Videocartepostales' I made while on sabbatical in Paris in 2007, the camera remains static, and an in-camera slow-motion effect is employed that stretches a 12-inch improvisation to 48 inches. The nude figure is cast in various painterly, poster art or photographic templates, disguising and/or highlighting the moving image in discreet rectangles. The music of Satie provides yet another frame.

In *Photoformance I: Long Lie Down*, made for projections onto an architectural installation, the borders between the human figure, abstraction, and anthropomorphism are crossed and blurred in an amalgam of photographic imagery and editing. First connecting by cross-dissolves then overlaying photographer Ernestine Ruben's still sequences of the slowly moving naked figure with a series of images of reflected light that Ruben calls 'Dancing Veils,' the overlays are treated or developed with various colorization effects. Projected onto two walls of a museum gallery and onto the undulating structure by architect Monica Ponce de Leon, the moving imagery is distributed across many surfaces—both opaque and translucent—to orchestrate a hallucinatory journey of the body in gradual recline, hovering between two worlds, before coming to final rest.

As we watch these works on the screen, the video self-portraits register as more than narcissistic indulgence. Indeed, like similar works by other artists featuring the nude figure as medium, they aspire towards and extend a dream of Modernism in dance that is and has always been made problematic by the fact of the human body. This dancing image embodies the thorny tension between corporeality and the idealized in aesthetic appreciation. The body and its humanity, its idiosyncrasies, its genitalia, its emotive or mimetic tendencies, get in the way of the process of refining, abstracting, and purifying down to what Clement Greenberg might argue were the essentials of the medium.

This leads us to the argument for twentieth-century Modernism and the quest for the utopian abstract, freed from the burden of history—or encountering it head-on, and then moving beyond. Beyond illusion, representation, sign, symbolism, narrative... Art theorist T.J. Clark, in his *Farewell to an Idea: Episodes from a History of Modernism*, traces this ill-starred quest through Cézanne's nudes, Cubism's distorted illusionism, Malevich's Suprematist purification rituals to Jackson Pollock's densely woven canvases. Referring specifically to Pollock's work between 1947 and 1950, Clark describes the Modernist idea as containing 'contraries of nature and anti-nature, skeleton and script, thicket and palimpsest, depiction and inscription, infinity and confinement, entanglement and paper-thinness, dissonance and totality.'[3] These are qualities embodied in the improvisational scrawls of *DEVANT/DERRIÈRE* or in the distortions of *Self-Portrait* or *Photoformance*. Call it distortion or a blurring of boundaries between the representational and abstract, this sacrifice of the recognizable human form for the dynamic tension between a more purely sculptural morphology and the negative space it inhabits is essential in the shift of our attentions from the live studio to the computer's flat screen.

To further explain the complex relationships involved in Modernism, Clark seeks an alternative to a doomed, Foucauldian loop in which he imagines the Modernist experiment as trapped in the futile search for an Other to bourgeois experience while constantly being re-absorbed into and re-created as a response to that same bourgeois world. In seeking Modernism's emergence to some kind of authentic dialogue, Clark cites Mikhail Bakhtin from his 'Discourse in the Novel':

> Discourse lives, as it were, beyond itself, in a living impulse toward the object; and it is in relation to this overall movement of construction—this continual opening of discourse toward its objects, this effort to tie word to world, this wish for agreement and grounding—that the possibility of truth arises.[4]

This speaks of the reaching of videotaped dancer's movement towards the camera, to engage the collective of all audiences he has ever danced for that is imagined as contained in the camera's singular eye. Replacing 'word' with 'movement' in Bakhtin's text, the argument would continue as follows:

> The [movement], breaking through to its own meaning and its own expression across an environment full of alien [movements] and variously evaluating accents, harmonizing with some of the elements in this environment and striking a dissonance with others, is able, in this dialogized process, to shape its own stylistic profile and tone.[5]

An excellent backdrop for *DEVANT* is Clark's essay on 'Freud's Cézanne' in which he contrasts the *naked* vs the *nude*, and positions sexuality not as performance but as a kind of fate. He compares and contrasts the two large-scale Cézanne 'Bathers,' both found in museums in Philadelphia. He sees the Barnes Bathers as archeological, more corporeal, moving back to 'naked' bodies, to 'sensations, sights, shocks, touches,'[6] a materialization of (Freudian) fantasy, depicting transgressive acts, or 'seeing the unspeakable and paying the price.'[7] By contrast, the 'nude' Bathers in the Philadelphia Museum of Art, 'stands on its [a]esthetic dignity.'[8] It is more discreetly posed in relationship to its setting; it is an idealized, highly symmetrical, cathedral-like arrangement.

DOUBLE LIFE

Straddling the two modes of naked/nude, performance/fate in the act of dancing for the camera and 'pictorializing' it for the screen, the dancing figure in DEVANT ranges from engaging in a spontaneous visceral 'wrestling match' with himself that obeys no laws of visualization, to a more calculated, flattened or frontal presentation of the forms he knows only too well from decades of performing for both audiences and the studio mirror. This double life is further negotiated by the presence of the camera as outside eye. In viewing DEVANT, we notice in particular the addition of close-up follow-shots, juxtapositions in scale of figure, and the opticality and presence of the camera's roving eye as it scans the moving body. Also, the overlay of the piano score by Ravel alters its register and tone, providing a more reflective point of view and a yearning quality to highlight the writhing viscerality of the dancer's improvisations.

Clark's words on Cézanne's nude solo bathers resonate particularly well with dance made for the screen and contained within its frame:

> ...—no body, however singular and strongly bounded, occupies just one space. The parts of a body, and the movements and positions of those parts, generate different and incompatible imaginings of their surroundings—different scales, different degrees of empathy and identification, different intuitions of distance and proximity—which simply cannot (ever) be brought to the point of totalization. Because in the case of bodies, *we are* what fills, or reaches out to, the space another body occupies; and the space gets multiplied by our imagined acts, by the plurality of our own experience of our body getting beyond us.[9]

And finally, with particular relevance to the doubled-up overlays of full-figure frames and their own close-up follow shots that fill *DEVANT*, Clark then attempts a rationale for the bizarre image of a bather whose buttocks appear receding upstage where her forward-facing slumped shoulders should be:

> I take the double figure in the Philadelphia picture to sum up two basic conditions of knowledge and representation as Cézanne came to understand them. First, that our representation of bodies—our own and other people's—just is some such process of interchange and duplication, of unstoppable weird empathy, of our somehow putting an internal sense of what being in the body feels like into our picture of how another body looks. (Of course, this empathy informs our looking at everything: it is just that looking specifically at the body makes the odd and uncontrollable nature of the process declare itself. The weirdness of the Bathers, to repeat my previous point, is what they most deeply have to say about what seeing the body is like. The double figure is the emblem of that.[10]

So, am I performing the ultimate twenty-first-century spectacle? One embodying its own history, 'dressed' in it—its movement templates, traditions, stylistic habits—yet free of them in an exalted state of mindful improvisation for the camera in the cloistered privacy of a black-box video studio? Am I asserting my own *empire of ecstasy*, to borrow the title from Karl Toepfer's examination of German body culture 1910–1935. Toepfer seeks in photographic imagery of the time proof of an emerging 'modern body' radiating freedom and power, and a transgressive energy, by:

> ...situating the body within the pure white (black) zone that contains no contaminating sign of the past, no attachments to history. The modern body is, one might say, the context, the determining power of the space it chooses to inhabit: perception of the body determines the identity of the world, the reality external to the self. This decontextualization of the body implies that the more naked the body becomes, the more the body dominates perception, [and] the more the body assumes an abstract identity.[11]

In closing, we observe that, in this ecstatic, exposed zone, the body becomes more visual, the eye more visceral. By way of video and screendance, audiences, practitioners and scholars in our field are primed to confront and celebrate the ultimate spectacle of the dancing body, whether naked, nude or costumed: one that re-engages us with every issue inherent in the Modernist idea in high art and moves us forward to a kinesthetically and aesthetically charged space—a space contained by the frame of camera and screen, and endowing new meaning to Walt Whitman's vision for the body electric.

NOTES

1. Examples of his work including those discussed here are best viewed at www.petersparling.com
2. Laurence Louppe, *Poetics of Contemporary Dance*, trans. Sally Gardner (Alton, Hampshire: Dance Books, 1997).
3. T.J. Clark, *Farewell to an Idea: Episodes from a History of Modernism* (New Haven and London: Yale University Press, 1999), 314.
4. Clark, 314.
5. Clark, 316.
6. Clark, 151.
7. Clark, 150.
8. Clark, 152.
9. Clark, 157.
10. Clark, 157.
11. Karl Toepfer, *Empire of Ecstasy: Nudity and Movement in German Body Culture, 1910–1935* (Berkeley and Los Angeles: University of California Press, 1997), 1.

PART III

Querying Praxis

When dance and moving projected images intersect, what do those intersections create—and why? In this section, two practitioners making dances combined with moving images discuss their own work in mixed media production. These narratives about process, application—and, in a very real sense, making theory visible—provide an opening and a lens(!) for us to view and understand the working and workings of creating a mixed media performance piece. Choreographer-filmmaker Heather Coker draws on Eisenstein's classic film theory and McLuhan's 1960s postmodernist parsing of television as the starting point for her discussion about the difference between live dance and video. Choreographer Ruth Barnes looks at promenade performance in the round. What does one see—and why? The focus is on notions of proximity and distance, whether physical or emotional, and creating an environment in which the audience and performers are equally visible to each other. Questions arise about where the spectator's gaze lands, who is controlling whose gaze, and how the gaze functions in this particular configuration of the environment.

CHAPTER 7

Theoretical Duet

Telory D. Arendell and Ruth Barnes

Telory D. Arendell   Ruth Barnes and I have co-edited this collection of essays in order to explore the dynamics of live versus filmed dance, in a number of different combinations. We hope to begin this discussion with a grounding in recent film theory about space, time, body, perspective, dimension, and the like in relation to both live and filmed dance. As dance writer and archivist for Merce Cunningham, David Vaughan observes, 'One of the most obvious differences between dance as seen on the stage and on television or film screen is that in the former the spectator is free to choose where to direct his attention, while on the screen the viewpoint is that of the camera, controlled by the director.'[1] So, does this difference limit screen dance in ways that make it a less viable mode of presenting dance? Possibly. And yet, if the choreographer and film director are the same person, this characteristic might fall under the purview of such a hybrid artist as a way to focus audience attention on particular movement.

T.D. Arendell (✉) • R. Barnes
Missouri State University, Springfield, MO, USA

© The Editor(s) (if applicable) and The Author(s) 2016   129
T.D. Arendell, R. Barnes (eds.), *Dance's Duet with the Camera*,
DOI 10.1057/978-1-137-59610-9_7

Ruth Barnes   Also, for more linear narrative works, and for choreographers and/or film directors who believe it is the responsibility of the creator to direct the spectator's eye and attention, dance on screen—large or small—is arguably a *more* viable mode for presenting dance. This seems to be about the philosophical stance of the choreographer and/or director.

TDA   And what about the viewing politics involved in using filmed work (either live or prerecorded) as part of live dance? There will always be a visual draw to bodies in motion on screen. This is especially true in a live performance that competes heavily with live dancers, for more recent generations whose eyes have been preconditioned in first-world environments to rely on technology as the most direct means of communication, entertainment, identity development, and personal voice. Does either live dance or bodies prerecorded or simultaneously filmed with live-feed video necessarily favor kinesthetic sense over visual sense? Admittedly, live dancing bodies with no video mediation continue to offer the strongest sense of experiential kinesthesia for audience members at the level of body weight, length of movement, physical sound, and perceptual proportion. And a given strength of filmed dance is the choreographer/videographer's ability to play with each of these elements in ways that are only possible on screen.

RB   Yes, but on the other hand, performance scholar Philip Auslander points out that projected images overpower live performers—he theorizes that this is the case in mixed media performance, rock concerts, and in lectures that include projected images.

TDA   But is screen dance automatically flat, displaying a lack of depth and perspective? Surely the noticeable depth and weight of live dancers is fairly difficult to capture realistically on screen.

RB   As technology improves, the 'sense of weight' becomes more perceivable. HD and high resolution video create an increasingly crisp and realistic image than with earlier technologies.

TDA   Three-dimensionality is clearly what a two-dimensional screen version of dance compromises or sacrifices to some extent. One could argue that 3D film is the best way to present realistic capture of live dance without making these sacrifices, and yet there are also those who warn that 3D film will never make it to a high enough level of technological resolution to allow bodies to appear in equally tangible form to their live performance counterparts. Using an idea from Ray Zone, Philip Sandifer claims that '"3D images present a heightened realism—a visual allure so powerful that they can easily overwhelm the story and subvert the narrative." ...And although some films are able to transcend, ignore, or take advantage of this grammar, in the end that grammar is a grammar of allure, based not on narrative or story, and certainly not on immersive realism. ... the technology is designed not to create a compelling narrative experience, but rather simply to create a compelling spectacle.'[2]

RB   How does this apply to non-linear narrative, or to 'abstract' dance or theatre? Looking at Wim Wenders's *Pina*, where the choreography is more imagistic than narrative, where metaphor and free association (for choreographer, performers and spectator) are arguably more prominent than linear story development, does the 3D image not enhance the experience by giving the viewer a heightened kinesthetic sense?

TDA   Yes, possibly 3D gives viewers a fuller sense of physical presence and movement that aids an imagistic rather than narrative meaning structure.

RB   Also, Sandifer says that 'Rather than being immersive, 3D film is profoundly bound up in an act of spectatorship whereby the theater, instead of disappearing, is even more conspicuously visible.'[3] If the spectator becomes more aware of her/his environment/location, how does that affect his/her perception of the film/performance? Is this a distancing, or a broadening or enlarging of the experience? Does this make the experience more kinesthetic? How does this relate to mixed media work?

TDA   I have a tendency to go directly to more immersive viewing environments like Virtual Reality for this sort of experiential knowledge. And it may well be that the future of 3D filming has more promise in Virtual Reality environs than on film screens. Somehow, VR seems to stand on its own grounds better because instead of trying to take the viewer to the screen, it takes the screen to the viewer. Full immersion as viewer in VR means that the actual viewing body is surrounded by a three-dimensional reality that the lived-in body interacts with all the time.

RB   Returning to Sandifer: he also provides us with the notion that 'While non-3D film and perspectival drawing have developed a complex rhetoric beyond their initial myths of immersive realism, 3D film continues to cling to a demo phase in which it is marveled at as an act of vision instead of as a communicative form. The reason for this is closely tied to the essential difference between 3D film and traditional film in terms of their relationships to the traditional understanding of perspectival vision that has been dominant since the Renaissance.'[4] Does this create yet another—or a deeper—removal from the performance? In other words, one of the differences between live and filmed/videotaped dance is the spectator perceives the latter as flat, and is less kinesthetically engaged than when watching a live performance. So, if 3D film more closely relates to a perspectival model, does that mean that it replaces the kinesthetic response associated with live performance?

TDA   Again, I think it's about immersion as the viewer. In non-digital models, the frame is of extreme import for the apparatus of viewing. Our only way of entering the perspectival frame of a painting is by taking the parameters of the frame as our truest givens. We experience the fixed-point perspective in the painting only because we ourselves as viewers are fully outside of its frame. I believe that 3D film still assumes a frame, whereas VR is less about framing and more about putting viewers in control of the viewing apparatus.

RB   But if the frame is the entire theatre, the sense of being *in* the film is, indeed, heightened in 3D film, and the sense of the frame itself probably dissolves—unlike the frame of a picture, which is always visible (even for unframed paintings: the edge of the painting is within sight; whereas, in a theatre, the walls are all around the spectator and not necessarily visible). My experience with Virtual Reality is in three forms. The first is in telematics performance, in which the 'frame' is multiple: the location which one actually occupies, the location(s) where the partner performer(s) are, the screens on which one sees the distant partner(s), and the internet—invisible but omnipresent, and the facilitator of the event. Another form of VR is motion capture; the deconstruction and reconstruction of the live body creates numerous visual effects, whether replicating the body or using a living being (human or animal) as a means of creating another form. My other experience of VR is that it is comparable to a game—and in games—some VR is most likely happening in the player's head: taking on a 'skin' or a 'second life.'

TDA So, maybe it all comes down to viewer positioning, and as Sandifer tells us, 'Film, then can be said to follow a conceptual tradition that can be traced back to Albertian perspective. A key element of that tradition is that the relationship between the viewer's eye and the origin point of the image is variable. Central to this is the framed Albertian window, in film provided by the screen on which the image is projected. The screen serves as a border between the diegetic space and the theatre, which is merely a collection of seats organized around the screen to facilitate seeing it. The window serves not merely as the medium that holds the image, but as the delineation between the necessarily structured space of the image and the variable space of the viewer.'[5]

RB So, if 3D film bursts through (or, disrupts?) the theatrical 'fourth wall,' does it replace live performance, and query Walter Benjamin's actor's aura?

TDA I don't think that 3D will ever replace live performance. I believe there is more potential for the experience of live performance within VR, I just am not sure how that can be translated into dance as a lived VR experience. There is bound to be more aura in VR than 3D will ever reach, no?

RB   This seems incredibly conceptual to me—and relates to some postmodernist work of the 1960s. For example: a member of the Judson Dance Theatre famously disrupted the notion of 'performance' by booking a venue, sending out announcements, having the audience ushered in and... not showing up to perform. VR also seems more closely related to, and present in, video games, telematic performance and SnapChat than to live performance.

TDA   How does the space/time continuum change in each medium? In live dance, perspective merges space and time in ways that allow each movement to cover the ground and take the time bodies performing such motion require for its completion. Dance film takes its own liberties with both time and space in relation to bodies on screen, calling into question the very notion of perspective, and perhaps returns us to much earlier theoretical discussions about perspectival painting. As suggested by Sandifer, 'The very act of painting creates a spatial and temporal schism between the object that is painted and the painting. Simply put, the painting stands in place of the object it depicts... The painting becomes an act of seeing that exists separate from the observer and the observed object—a pure act of vision. Thus the painting preserves itself when it is moved away from its artist and subject, and even, to an extent, from its viewer.'[6]

RB   This relates directly to Benjamin's discussion of the actor's presence: while film reproduces the performance and enables a much wider audience the possibility of seeing it, what is lacking is the actor's (or, in our discussion, the dancer's) aura and authenticity: 'For aura is tied to his (*sic*) presence; there can be no replica of it. The aura, which on the stage emanates... cannot be separated for the spectators from that of the actor. However, the singularity of the shot... is that the camera is substituted for the public. Consequently, the aura that envelops the actor vanishes.'[7] Likewise, John Berger, in his dialog with Susan Sontag, notes that, 'What the camera does... and what the eye in itself can never do, is to fix the appearance of [an] event... The camera saves a set of appearances from the otherwise inevitable suppression of further appearances. It holds them unchanging.'[8] Thus, for live and filmed/videotaped performance, the very relationship to time is different: the former embraces ephemerality and the individual spectator's kinesthetic response; the latter seeks to create permanence and uniformity of response throughout its audience.

TDA   So, what happens when we put live and taped bodies on stage together? What does the simultaneity of live moving body and recorded image create? And is this ever an equal duet? There will always be a call to presence in live performance that seems faded or somehow lost in filmic duplication of these bodies.

RB   Or, if the projections are larger than life, they can overwhelm the live bodies—or create an environment in/through which the live bodies navigate.

TDA   But there is also a possibility that presence itself is unrepeatable, inimitable in any form other than live bodies. So when present bodies appear alongside their filmic other, who ghosts whom in this simultaneous space? As Hélène Cixous writes, 'We are faced, then, with a text and its hesitating shadow, and their double escapade.'[9] So, is the live dancer always a hesitating shadow when played next to the filmed body, especially if the film image overwhelms the live body? There is arguably more presence in the live body, and yet the power of this live-ness may somehow fail to override the projected proximity of filmed bodies. The closeness of a camera's gaze to the dancer's body will always have the tendency to trump other elements of live performance that connect viewers to performers such as body heat, sound of breath, and weight of motion. The camera body promises an intimacy here that the live body cannot match. And yet, both mediums depend on body and motion for their very existence.

RB   Also, do impact and perception necessarily depend on image *size*? Or, is it more about intimacy and detail?

TDA   Well, yes, size of image paired with the camera's close-up attention to detail that we cannot see from a dance/theatre audience setting makes this difference. And where does aura or presence go on screen? If, as Benjamin argues, a live dancer's aura is both ephemeral and unrepeatable, what does this tell us about the potential folly of trying to capture dance on film? Does not film dance rely on a repeatability of dancing forms, and, if so, does this mark it as false or inauthentic in some way? Short of pointing to Philip Auslander's prolific theorization on the subject of simulacra inherent in film of any sort, we could perhaps invite a discussion of how simulacra in contemporary existence is often sold as a more real reality. Following Sandifer's line of thought cited earlier, is dance film inherently non-narrative? Most of our authors would thoroughly contradict this notion, particularly Cara Hagan, who feels that movement of any kind, filmed or live, presents a vocabulary and narrative of its own that may or may not be independent of verbal story equivalents.

RB   Rather than 'non-narrative' we should say 'non-linear narrative.' There has always been something intrinsically violent or nostalgic about dance and screen work—either because of the warping of time, or because of something that has to do with socioeconomic distribution.

TDA   In light of all these considerations, we should definitely mention Douglas Rosenberg's 2012 Oxford University Press book, *Screendance: Inscribing the Ephemeral Image.* This text suggests that screendance itself represents an amalgamation of videodance ('actual production or method of inscription'), filmdance (work is part of material culture), dance for camera (dance is simultaneously privileged and in service to the camera), and in being so, screendance 'codifies a particular space of representation' and meaning.[10] Does placing screen prior to dance in this neologism automatically privilege film over dance? In other words, does the term 'screendance' automatically set up a power dynamic between film and dance that the term 'dance film' avoids? Or, as one might assume, does the order of concepts in the terminology dictate whose art form gains greater prominence and import in the duet between the two. Our own collection tries as hard as it can to give equal import to both sides. Without creating yet another neologism to reflect this equality, we present a range of practitioners and scholars whose praxis takes both sides of this equation into full account.

RB   Yes, absolutely—also, which word comes first used to indicate the focus of the work. Thus, dance/video and video/dance (with or without the/) are, in fact, different genres, with different emphases, points of view and—undoubtedly—different politics.

TDA   Rosenberg also suggests that, 'The raw data of the dancing body is stitched together in the editing process of either film or video, resulting in an *impossible* body.'[11] What we would like to point out here is that even the designation of the body's motion in dance relegates this body to a more primitive location of 'raw data' rather than what Rosenberg potentially assumes film to be: far more sophisticated and refined in his lexicon. He goes on to name the camera as 'a carnivorous image-prosthetic device' and in so doing inevitably implicates filmed versions of the dancing body as both devoured and disabled by the camera's colonization of raw material. Perhaps he does not see how this language reinscribes film as male, dance as female, with the socio-economic implications usually implied in such analogies.

RB   However, for Freudians, isn't it the female (vagina) who devours the male (penis)? Wouldn't this make the camera in this scenario female and the dancer male? Hmm... perhaps relegating this filming apparatus to separate body parts or genders is not so useful or even pertinent. And, where (and whose) is the gaze?

TDA   Well, Rosenberg strives to let film 'recorporealize the fragmented and disjointed bits of dance captured on film... into a cohesive whole' in order to tell a story with these collected images. So, who is allowed to piece body fragments back together in the name of screen choreography? The dancer, the choreographer, or the filmmaker? And what is the gender breakdown in this arrangement?[12]

RB   Are we talking about the body itself—the dancer—or about the choreographic body—or, about the body as culture? Aside from very close-up shots, the editor could take parts of the dancing (not the dancer), reorder them, and create a different piece.

TDA   Film often relegates the raw material of dancers' bodies to just one of many various visual elements, recorporealizing such bodies at the film editor's command. Does this editing re-inscribe the dancing body to a space of voiceless existence, all in the name of screendance? Perhaps, but if choreographer and filmmaker are either in a partnership or are housed in one individual, this may not be the case. For our contribution to this conversation, we wish to call attention to the ways in which language frames this discussion in highly gendered and somewhat hierarchical ways. Even within the uses of both practical experience and theoretical scholarship there exist an undeniable competition and a latent assumption that phenomenology is the closest that theatre and dance writers have come to theorizing praxis. Our own collection includes writers who span this continuum of theory and practice in ways that approach this duet as one danced by equal participants in every sense of this union. This is our conscious choice, and also a way to include more varied voices.

NOTES

1. David Vaughn, 'The Collaboration of Merce Cunningham and Charles Atlas,' in Richard Kostelanetz, ed. *Merce Cunningham: Dancing in Space and Time* (London: Dance Books, 1992), 153.
2. Philip Sandifer, 'Out of the Screen and Into the Theater: 3D Film as Demo,' *Cinema Journal* 5.3 (Spring 2011): 62–78; 78 includes quote from Ray Zone.
3. Sandifer, 69.
4. Sandifer, 64.
5. Sandifer, 66–7.
6. Sandifer, 66–7.
7. Walter Benjamin, 'The Work of Art in the Age of Mechanical Reproduction,' trans. Harry Zohn, in *Illuminations: Walter Benjamin, Essays and Reflections*, ed. Hannah Arendt (New York: Schocken Books, 1968), 229.
8. John Berger, 'The Uses of Photography,' *About Looking* (New York: Pantheon Books, 1980), 50–1.

9. Hélène Cixous, 'Fictions and Its Phantoms: A Reading of Freud's *Das Unheimliche* (The Uncanny)' in *New Literary History* 7:3 (1976): 525.
10. Douglas Rosenberg, *Screendance: Inscribing the Ephemeral Image* (New York: Oxford University Press, 2012), 3.
11. Rosenberg, 10.
12. Rosenberg, 158.

CHAPTER 8

Wrestling the Beast... and Not Getting Too Much Blood on Your Skirt: Integration of Live Performance and Video Projection

Heather Coker

This is an offering of personal considerations that surface when I face the daunting challenge of integrating moving pictures with live dance.[1] There is reluctance in my voice as I describe the use of video projection[2] in live performance as a 'struggle.' With any collaboration, great effort is made putting together two ideas or two mediums that do not usually fit together. One medium requires electricity, technical apparatus, and darkness to be seen and the other requires nothing more than a live body. Regardless of how cinematic a dance might be, or how dance-like a film might be, translating meaning across mediums creates anguish and sometimes pain. What may be quite discreet in one medium can read as explicit and vulgar in the other. Ushering the imagined vision into manifest material conjures technical, theoretical and design considerations calling to question artistic intention. As a choreographer and filmmaker my personal plight has been to integrate the two mediums, thereby demonstrating my belief, through practical application, that the two do belong together.

H. Coker (✉)
Freelance Choreographer-Filmmaker and Casting Associate,
Los Angeles, California, US

© The Editor(s) (if applicable) and The Author(s) 2016
T.D. Arendell, R. Barnes (eds.), *Dance's Duet with the Camera*,
DOI 10.1057/978-1-137-59610-9_8

141

LIVE PERFORMANCE AND PROJECTED PERFORMANCE

My education in both mediums began in the context of mainstream, classical dance making and filmmaking: ballet and Hollywood. Unfortunately, neither ballet nor Hollywood supports the current vision I have for conveying the visual and kinesthetic expressions of my imagination. The use of film and dance in the conventions of Hollywood and ballet are steeped in fantasy and illusion. My practice focuses on revealing the fabrication of moments and contrived circumstances in search of the honesty of an idea.

I locate myself as a modern dancer whose choreography recalls postmodern, modern, jazz, and ballet training, with quotations of pedestrian movement and arrested moments of the body in sport. The words 'experimental film' and 'personal narrative' are terms that elucidate my aesthetic as a filmmaker. Two years previously, my idea of integrating dance and film involved only making dance film, which is to say, choreographing movement and camera to exist as a stand-alone work without integration of a live performing body. Departing from the convention of dance film in isolation, I am now investigating how these two unequal mediums, live performance and video projection, can sit side by side in a theater without one making the other subservient.

My current investigation questions what is 'real' when a live body and a projected image are juxtaposed. As always, the question within the question is how am I, the director, constructing the audience's perception of the 'real.' My present work, a piece titled *Pretty Good for a Girl*, is the case study upon which this writing is based. *Pretty Good for a Girl* involves the integration of two mediums, dance and video, within the situation of a live performance. The entire piece consists of a single dancer and two sites of video projection. The video is projected onto screens that are made of non-traditional materials like painted cardboard panels mounted to rolling frames (that are positioned as a single staggered screen) and a sheet of frame-less, draped polymuslin. At times, the live performer's body is placed in front of the projection surface and serves as yet another canvas. The elements are few and simple to isolate allowing for examination of the struggle when integrating video projection with live performance.

Separate... Together... Separate Again...
Piecing Together the Whole

I see the integration of video projection within stage design as a study in the confluence of three simultaneous elements: live dance composition, video composition, and stage composition. For the purposes of this piece of writing, live dance composition pertains to the dance choreography presented as live performance. Video composition includes the content and structure of moving images as they are put together for video projection. On a practical and theoretical level, video takes its cues from film composition, as film is the first format of moving images. Stage composition relates to the overall stage picture. It is the thoughtful arrangement of bodies, objects and images in the context of the three-dimensional stage space. It is my experience that the choreographer is in constant pursuit of balancing the three elements with the intention of directing the audience's perception of the whole piece. I write from the perspective of a choreographer-filmmaker who is both perplexed by and enamored of the potency of the transmission of meaning when the medium of live performance is integrated with the medium of video (projection). When I make work, I no longer distinguish between dance and video as two separate mediums. Instead, I share tools across disciplines when I choreograph, write, shoot and edit. (For the purposes of elucidating how each medium is working, I must, at times, maintain them as two separate entities.)

Video wields the power of immediate clarity and specificity while a live human performer offers corporeal immediacy and identification. These characteristics are by no means an exhaustive catalog of attributes asserted with value judgment. Instead, they are quickly identifiable assets pertaining to each medium in isolation. These two elements, live performance and projected image, are no longer separate entities; their juxtaposition implies connection forming a third meaning. Essentially, this is a crude version of the definition of 'montage' (of theater and film) as posited by Soviet filmmaker and film theorist Sergei Eisenstein:

> ...in theatre an effect is achieved primarily through the physiological perception of an actually occurring fact..., in cinema it is made up of the juxtaposition and accumulation, in the audience's psyche, of associations that the film's purpose requires, associations that are aroused by the separate elements of the stated... fact, associations that produce, albeit tangentially, a similar (and often stronger) effect only when taken as a whole.[3]

The theory of montage in theater and film can be translated to live dance and video projection. Dance like theater and video like film is similar in environmental presentation and spatial application. Concerning *Pretty Good for a Girl*, the choreography of the live body and the projected video exist as two separate elements. When placed in near proximity, the two elements create a third meaning that could only be achieved by their two separate 'wholes' comprising the third and cumulative 'whole.' While the elements add up to a third 'whole' meaning, they also exist as individual parts that call attention to one another. In an effort to expose a medium's convention, a useful practice is to disturb it from its natural setting. Putting a live body next to video projection disrupts the medium from its own context and points up difference, as it exists in the company of the other. By merely placing the two mediums in the same stage space, the spectators, whether subliminally or consciously, are disallowed the comfort of knowing how their experience will be shaped according to the conventions of live dance theater or to that of cinema. Each medium bears a different contract calling for a different level of participation from the audience.

Stay Cool... Being 'Hot' Is Overrated

Is it a true statement that when given the choice to watch a live performer or video projected onto a screen that an audience's eye will gravitate toward the screen? I am unable to locate any research or statistic that supports this idea. Instead, I find that some theories of Marshall McLuhan, a famous philosopher of the 1960s whose writings on mass media and technology appropriately address the question. McLuhan categorized mediums as either 'hot' or 'cool.' He describes a 'hot medium' as one that commands one of the five senses with a dense amount, a 'high definition' of information. Movies achieve this over television, radio over telephone, and a book over spoken dialogue. With a 'cool medium,' less information is transmitted and more participation is required of the audience member to connect incomplete information. In the case of a 'hotter medium' of 'higher definition,' the density of visual information requires less participation from the audience member.[4] In a 'hotter' version of video, the visual information would be highly specific allowing no room for interpretation or abstraction. The style and structure employed would be according to popular iterations of filmmaking allowing for quick transmission of visual information leaving no time for the audience to 'think' about what is being shown.

> Intensity or high definition engenders specialism and fragmentation in living as in entertainment, which explains why any intense experience must be 'forgotten,' 'censored,' and reduced to a very cool state before it can be 'learned' or assimilated... For many people, this cooling system brings on a life-long state of psychic *rigor mortis*, or of somnambulism, particularly observable in periods of new technology.[5]

In essence, the hotter medium stimulates the eyes or ears to the point of stupor where the audience member is not given room to cogitate and derive any meaning other than that which is explicitly posited through the medium.

THE EFFECT OF THE SCREEN

If we were to compare video projection to live dance performance as visual mediums, video projection would be a much 'hotter' medium than live performance. Video is more explicit and able to give a closer view of the body in an instant while the live performer maintains a distance from the audience.[6] Video can privilege the audience with a different spatial and visual relationship to a body by changing angles and locations while a live performing body is restricted by gravity and location, to the backdrop of the theater. Video has facility to immediately focus the audience's attention to the exact idea while live dance tends to focus around an idea. Compared to video, live performance is the 'cooler' medium inviting participation from the audience to make cognitive leaps and connections.

It is important to point out that within each medium there exist 'hot' and 'cold' variations. When creating video content for a live performance, I shoot and organize the images in a 'cooler' way than I would for a stand-alone video work. With a video whose purpose is for the cinema alone (hotter version), I might use a narrative structure to convey the idea of the piece. Regardless of structure, I am aware that the audience is physically reading the stand-alone work differently, with eyes trained on the screen the entire time instead of roving from live performer to the screen and back. In the 'cooler' version of the video medium, more time can be given to an audience; they are invited to look at, around, and outside of the screen frame. Liberties can be taken with composition to disrupt the viewer and give them pause rather than lull them into visual consumption without participation. The seamless editing and smooth transitions of the 'hotter' version of the medium would be replaced by juggling two images together that would not normally go together or leaving an image on screen long past the necessary time needed to 'take it in.' The video element of *Pretty Good for a Girl* alternates from long takes of continuous action to frozen images and action in slow motion to looping of a continuous action. Editing together video in this 'cooler' manner relies on the audience's sensory participation and the duration of images to make meaning over time, rather than the 'hotter' version that allows the audience to sit idly by staring at the pretty pictures as they flash before the eyes at a shot every 3 seconds or less.[7]

Upon seeing a screen, a certain expectation is elicited in the audience member, an association with the broader occurrence of the kind of information and the convention by which it is disseminated on a television, movie or computer screen in everyday life. Hollywood is notorious for disseminating visual and aural information by a certain narrative structure that can excite, lull, or incite a myriad of emotions in its audience using provocative images and fast pacing. When a screen is present, the assumption is that information will be dispensed in the way we are trained to receive it. We are viewers literate in a consumer-driven mass medium by virtue of repetition through everyday exposure. As members of a visual culture, audiences, whether they know it or not, look for the message within the medium which will tell them how to process the visual information they are receiving. Whether film, television, or internet, we are receiving directives to buy products, programming, services, and occasionally, ideas. We are attuned to these messages perhaps on a subconscious, maybe even preverbal level, but ultimately, we are subservient to them as consumers of popular visual culture.

In the case of dance composition for live performance, there also live 'hotter' and 'cooler' variations within the medium. The 'hot' version would be a performance where one easily recognizable genre of dance is maintained for the duration. Let us think about a performance where classical ballet is on the bill and after intermission, a 'contemporary' dance piece occurs. The classical selection is the hotter of the two mediums because it is the explicit version of the medium, using a long-established vocabulary of movement. The audience's participation is low because they are able to quickly receive information via the familiar vocabulary (and scenic cues of classical ballet). The second piece on the bill, being a 'contemporary' dance selection, invites more room for interpretation through new vocabularies and experimental forms of movement. My understanding of contemporary dance is steeped in confusion by the fact that on some companies 'contemporary' reads as modernized story ballets set to mainstream music. For other companies, the dance resembles a balletic take on modern, postmodern or hip-hop vocabularies. My intention is not to distill 'contemporary' dance into two rigid containers, but to point out the hybrid nature of the genre. My point is that the modern-day story ballet with mainstream music and reimagining of historical choreography offers a crossover effect resulting in a hybrid form. Similarly, the vocabulary-crossing postmodern hip-hop ballet is a hybrid. Hybridity 'cools' off the live dance performance medium causing collision of form and culture, which raises questions about how the two or three intermingle. The audience is invited to participate more readily with the cooler medium contemplating the experimental nature of the hybrid.

When placed in close proximity and direct juxtaposition to a live body on stage, a video projection screen is taken out of its context and it can be repurposed for some function other than 'selling.' Its presence in contrast to the human body already critiques its usual placement in the world elevated above or on display in front of the human body. McLuhan writes, 'The hybrid or the meeting of two media is a moment of truth and revelation from which new form is born. The moment of the meeting of media is a moment of freedom and release from the ordinary trance and numbness imposed by them on our senses.'[8] The presence of a live body juxtaposed with a video projection screen complicates the audience's understanding of reality and authority. This complication can pass undetected by the audience as they perceive the piece as a 'whole.'

TRACKING THE BEAST

My overwhelming concern integrating video projection with live performance is that the live performer is in danger of being overshadowed by the video projection. My fears are validated by McLuhan's theory when the two are only compared in terms of medium dominance by way of 'hotness' and 'coolness.' McLuhan's position is useful when thinking, as a maker, about how to structure elements and develop vocabularies for a multi-media piece. What medium 'hotness' and 'coolness' does not account for is the immediacy of the live performing body over the 'recorded' video image that only exists as a past event, 'live' only at the time of the recording.

WHAT DOES 'LIVE' MEAN?

Music, media and technology theorist Philip Auslander defines 'live' as the 'performer and audience are physically and temporally co-present to one another.'[9] He asserts that new technologies invoke amendments to or qualifications of what is 'live.' 'Live broadcasts' and the disclaimer of a television show being 'recorded live' challenge his earlier definition of 'live.' 'Live broadcast falls short of the complete definition foregoing physical "co-presence" of performer and audience. "Recorded live" falls short of both but can be considered "live" if you consider that "presence or live-ness does not inhere in the thing; it results from our engagement with the thing."'[10] It is 'the act of consciousness that allows the audience to experience the virtual as "live."'[11] To reason this way would mean to take the 'whole' piece, live performer and video projection, as a cumulative 'live' event reflexively exhibiting equality between the elements. As a choreographer, this thinking is useful once all elements have been produced and it is the appropriate moment to consider timing and simultaneity of the elements. However, if you are an artist beginning a new work, thinking of the piece as a theoretical 'live' 'whole' forecloses rather than generates tangible material elements that can be examined and adjusted. I find continual questioning and redefining of loose terms a fruitful exercise to readjust my own perspective when making and editing work.

With McLuhan on one shoulder and Auslander on the other, I continue my plight marching into the creative unknown with three possible truths. (1) The live human holds more dominance for the reason that she has a tangible body while the video projection is light and shadow with its screen as the only tangible link to the 'real' world. (2) The visual weight of the screen is greater than that of the live human who is dwarfed by the size of the screen.[12] (3) The audience's eyes are attracted to the video screen over the live body because the medium is 'hotter' offering more explicit visual information at a faster pace than a live performing human can provide.

The artist must balance the mediums finding the appropriate spatial composition that will direct the audience's focus. Searching for a balance between screen and live performer is a struggle and at times a losing battle for the poor choreographer. The human on stage inherently carries some weight as the performer who wields authority by virtue of knowing the choreography of the piece. Her authority exists as the corporeal pencil inscribing the idea of the piece onto the blank page of the three-dimensional theater space. However integral her role as conveyor of the idea of the piece, when placed next to a projection screen, the human performer's authority and command of audience attention is in jeopardy. When threat of losing focus is imminent, how can the choreographer redistribute more of the scenic focus to the live performer?

FOCUS, TIMING AND CONTENT

When constructing work, the choreographer-filmmaker must isolate and examine the elements separately to gain perspective of the whole piece. I make decisions and edit my work consulting the following three categories: *Focus, Timing* and *Content*. Each aspect both informs and is causally affected by the other two. Much forethought and laboratory-like testing is necessary to develop an intended relationship of the three.[13]

FOCUS

Pretty Good for a Girl is a trio between one live performer and two screens located in different positions on stage. Each screen receives its own video signal, allowing for divergence or doubling of the image and simultaneity. The work of making the piece is rooted not only in choices, but also challenges of focus, timing and content.

'Focus' involves asking these questions: What is the intention for any given moment of this piece? Where do I want the audience to look? What do I want them to see? Is it important to give more focus to the screen? If so, which one? And if not, how do I give the live performer more dominance? Spatial and scenic design inform the positioning of the screens, the size and shape of the screens, the proximity of the live body to the screen, and whether the image supports, contrasts, or is muted in comparison to the live performer at any given moment.

If we hold Doris Humphrey's ideas on 'design' to be our own, then we know that the most dominant stage diagonal leads from upstage right to downstage left. The strongest fixed position on stage is center-center—unless there is a person or object downstage of center-center. Additionally, the corners of the stage are more potent than the neither-space you would traverse to reach center stage from the corners.[14]

SCENIC DESIGN

Inherently defeated by the size of the screens, the live performer in my piece vies for dominance from the start. Speaking logically, the way to balance a body with a screen would be to position the human in the most dominant stage position and the screen in the least visually dominant position. This is no small feat when the choreography moves the performer all around the stage deck, rarely allowing her to pause in any section of the stage. Without the ability or desire to, at all times, give dominance to the live performer, the choreographer must design intended moments of visual imbalance and transitions to shift focus from one medium to another. The point of integrating video would be lost if it only served as a backdrop to the live performer.

Unfortunately, scenic design is not as simple as placing the projection screen in the same, 'golden' position for every piece. Depending on the size and shape of the screen, the number of live performers, the content and use of the projected images, the screen is going to warrant a well-thought out position for each piece. Adding more screens to the mix adds to the complexity of the scenic picture and raises more questions. What content is designated to this screen and, to that one? What does the positioning of this screen with this content mean when placed in conjunction with the other screen(s)? Which screen is pulling more attention? How shall the video be timed to highlight certain content during simultaneous play? Where will the audience's eyes be drawn? How will you direct the audience's eyes to shift between the different mediums? At this point, I can only raise the questions that are helping me to find answers for my piece. Hopefully, the questions will be general enough to be useful for you to imagine your own imminent pressing or imagined future choreography of screens with live performer while reading.

TIMING

Pertaining to video, 'timing' relates to the duration of the images as they play on the screen and the pace at which they are edited together. In the case of multiple video projections, 'timing' is affected when considering simultaneity of play between screens and live performance. Each element is subject to its own relation to time; it can divide time differently, similarly or in exacting precision with the other element(s). Once orchestrated, the elements, as they are synchronized throughout the piece, contribute to the greater construction of the piece's timing and pacing. *Pretty Good for a Girl* works with repetition, freezing, and tripling images while the live element progresses in a relatively clock-time forward progression with arrested movement in specified moments. Initially I did not consciously realize that I am exploring time in similar ways with both the video and the live choreography. Perhaps I did not notice this because the live body never freezes when the video is frozen nor does the live choreography repeat while video repeats. My desire is to offset similar uses of timing across mediums with the intention of pushing the piece forward instead of stalling or grinding it into redundant circles.

The perception of time can be altered and is subject to manipulation with the use of creative spatial and scenic design. Video employs the use of special camera lenses to shape perspective and alter perception. Shooting video of a person moving toward the camera on a long (telephoto) lens gives the illusion that they are held in space not covering much distance. With a wide angle lens, a person moving at the same speed toward the camera will look as if they are moving with much more speed and covering more distance than with the long lens or a normal length lens.[15] Choreographic devices can speed, slow or suspend time and consequently, the perception of motion. Using theatrical convention the live performer can be carried forward or backward in narrative or linear time. She can retrograde, slow or fast-forward movement within human limitation. A blackout can occur and she can appear in another place on stage; however, she cannot actually defy time to get to that new post on the stage. A certain amount of time must pass in order for her to relocate herself in space.[16]

Video can disrupt the continuum of time and space from one cut to the next. The laws of physics and human nature do not apply to the medium but they are duplicated in ways to mimic 'real' life. Walter Murch writes,

> ...the visual reality we perceive is a continuous stream of linked images... film is actually being 'cut' twenty-four times a second. Each frame is a displacement from the previous one—it is just that in a continuous shot, the space/time displacement from frame to frame is small enough (twenty milliseconds) for the audience to see it as *motion within a context* rather than as twenty-four different contexts a second. On the other hand, when the visual displacement is great enough (as at the moment of the cut), we are forced to re-evaluate the new image as a *different context*: miraculously, most of the time we have no problem doing this.[17]

The live body in juxtaposition to the edited, never-changing images of light and shadow creates tension in the audience. The spectators' perception of time is divided between the two mediums' (live performance and video) individual construction of time and the audience's own sense of time as they watch the piece unfold. Painter, art critic and author, John Berger writes about how the camera changed people's perception of time. 'The camera showed that the notion of time passing was inseparable from the experience of the visual (except in paintings). What you saw depended upon where you were when. What you saw was relative to your position in time and space.'[18]

In most cases of video projection, the perception of time is a construction of the past (when the images were shot and edited together). The duration of the shot as it appears in its edited form constructs time as the 'present' moment, when the audience perceives the projected image. Within the 'present' of the audience's perception lies the ability of video to manipulate time in its own way. As the 'present' experience of the video occurs, video can flash back, forward, condense, extend, or freeze time. Meanwhile, the live performer is moving in and out of present moments that will eventually come to an end within the constraint of the performance itself. Her attention to time throughout the performance can exist at an entirely separate pace from the video. As the live dance fades from happening to just having happened, so does the projected image as it advances moment by moment forward toward the end of the piece. The way in which the two elements reach the end of the piece is unique to each medium's ability to manipulate time.

CONTENT

Video is always subjective, constructed subtly or not, from someone's point of view, just as dance has subjectivity and, an audience hopes, a point of view. The camera is only a machine; the camera operator is the person responsible for recording an image or a succession of images (in the case of motion pictures) from a particular angle, height, framing, and quality of motion. Similarly, a choreographer can temper the content of her dance choreography by concerning herself with these details.

While making live dances with video projection, I struggle to find the most useful way to cultivate content. One thought is that the mind needs to be divided to create live choreography and video elements separately. While in rough draft form, the elements are brought together to test the chemistry. In this rough draft form, each element is loose enough to be pliable and influenced by the other. Working with the elements together, the choreographer-filmmaker can find unexpected connections and address incongruencies until the piece is honed into a final draft. This way of working employs compartmentalization and has, in my last two works, resulted in an episodic structure. It could be that this process of working produces episodically structured work. Perhaps in a collaborative setting where I would only be responsible for one or the other of the elements (live choreography or video projection), the piece would be less segmented. The fragmentation of myself as the lone party responsible for multiple elements could be affecting the structure of the work.[19]

'Content' cannot be thought of in isolation from focus and timing; the three are intertwined. Related to the live body on stage, 'content' is crudely defined as the choreography of the body in space. The content of video projection relates to the chosen images and how they juxtapose with one another from shot to shot. The minutiae of the video projection then relates to the other corresponding elements as they unfold, both the choreography performed live and the content of the second projection to create multilayered meanings by forging several images into a predetermined order in time.

The coordination of video projection, choreography of the body, and the visual composition of the stage with the elements (screens, body(ies), set pieces, props) make up the overall stage picture. The job of the choreographer-filmmaker is, yes, to organize all of these elements but to do so with intention guiding their integration. Intention includes the artist's task of shaping the perception and experience of the audience. It goes beyond what the elements are doing to how the coordination of elements in this way affects the audience's perception of the 'whole.' It is the artist's hope to guide the audience into seeing all of the elements as a whole rather than gazing at the screen or softening the eyes on the live moving body. Instead, the invitation is for the audience to participate in the piece, make cognitive connections and activate sensory experience.

Soviet film theorist Rudolf Arnheim explains limitations of the mechanics of human vision as limited to acute visual perception of objects directly in front of the eye; however, he emphatically points to the ability of the human to turn his head and move his eyes to take in a room, for example, 'as a continuous field of vision... we visualize the entire room as an unbroken whole.'[20] The stage picture including live performer, projection screen(s) and all other elements of scenic design are possible to be taken in as a whole perceptually. It is always my hope that the audience stays engaged in seeing the 'whole' as the piece is occurring. While this 'whole' can be deconstructed to its smaller parts and retroactively dissimilated to the associations and counterpoints, as they exist, it is not a fruitful exercise for the audience to embark upon during a first viewing of the piece.

It is important to orchestrate the elements so that they are in conversation with one another. The danger of non-conversant elements is a disengaged audience. If this dilemma arises, I have learned first to address focus, then timing, and lastly content. I leave content as the last thing to alter or omit because the maker has gone through the process of living, breathing, creating and editing this piece. The visual or aural material that has made it through previous months of edits into the final draft of the piece stands to be a crucial element that will be missed if it is abandoned. My disclaimer is not to be too precious with any one thing but to constantly ask the nagging question of *every* 'thing': Does this (whatever it is), where it is positioned in time and space, in physical and cognitive juxtaposition to the other elements, serve the intention of the piece?

One medium should be used to help the other in forging meaning and deepening ideas by exercising the strengths of one to elevate the other. With video, showing anyone in close up assumes a certain privilege of intimacy, or invasion of privacy, depending on the tone of the piece. Mostly, when dance is filmed, the close up shows intricacy of movement or a facial expression, which could tell us how to feel about the movement. Or, it could just be a shot that occurred as the dancer moved through the frame. Audience members look for clues to understand a piece. They utilize the tools they have as viewers within a certain culture and attach their known language from mainstream visual culture to find either similarities or differences to extrapolate meaning from live performance with video projection.

Live dance performance can be quite abstract and self-referential where an audience member who is not a frequent patron of the performing arts could be denied access to the subtleties of the piece. If an artist is using video projection, she can do so in a manner that references the language of film (or visual culture) as a point of entry. Quick recognition can be used to convey information in a more elegant or immediate way than creating a new language for each piece. I will caution against reiterating the mainstream convention of one medium for the reason that it will sit in 'hot' contrast to the 'cooler' more challenging medium.

McLuhan writes, 'The serious artist is the only person able to encounter technology with impunity, just because he is an expert aware of the changes in sense perception.'[21] The interdisciplinary artist is the one who can not only sense the 'changes,' but who can understand the *why* behind the manipulation and redirect media and technology to shape her own message.

The problem is that many choreographers are not trained to shape a visual message through the medium of video. Choreographers' instincts as to the timing and composition of visual content are inherently heightened by their practice of composing bodies in (immediate) space. To a choreographer, I would say learn the language of filmmaking or find a fluent collaborator.

Intentions to Overcome the Beast

Pretty Good for a Girl may have few elements comprising its whole but it is no simple task creating these elements and situating them in relation to each other. The difficulty at the beginning of the process is steeped in questions of *what*. What is the content? What are the elements? What do I want them to do, describe or mean? Then, my concerns for timing and pacing emerge and lastly, I consider where to focus attention. The order of things shifts pertaining to which stage of the process I am involved in. At times, one question will spark a solution that coincidentally addresses two issues. I am making this sound too simple. Please know that this part of the process does not exist in a vacuum. At an early stage of development, I seek guidance from mentors and peers to determine how the elements are working. With their guidance I am able to tackle the final illusive ingredient: the audience's perception of the piece. This is a challenge almost as complex and varied as each audience member himself. In a feedback session, it is useful for me to hear whether my intention is apparent to the audience and what they think my intention is at any given moment.

Feedback on Audience Perceptions

The intention of a piece is evident to an audience when the choreographer answers her own nagging questions. Given that the artist has done her work calibrating focus, timing and content, the audience will sense that there is a driving force behind a piece and be more likely to participate in the dance of cognitive leaps and turns. Achieving willing audience participation depends upon the audience, but also on an artist's command of her skill set as a choreographer-filmmaker. After having examined the three elements: live dance composition, video composition, and resulting stage composition, I can now identify that my 'struggle' and greatest desire is to gain the audience's participation. You would now like for me to surrender the easy answer to the question: *How do you get an audience to participate?* If the aim is to gain audience cognitive participation, locate and maintain the 'coolest' possible version of the live performance and video mediums.

Make no mistake in understanding my position. I remain, cheek to concrete, in a headlock by the beast, trying to figure out the *when* and *how* of this piece. By now, I do know the *what*—live performance and video projection and my chosen vocabularies for each. With every decision, I am certain to call back into consideration focus, timing and content, ad nauseam. I do take comfort in knowing for what exactly I am struggling… about 20 minutes of your cognitive participation and consideration.

NOTES

1. The guidance and support I have received from David Roussève, Susan Foster and Aparna Sharma have shaped my current practice integrating live performance with video projection. I thank them for generosity with their time and imagination to discuss my work and mentor my artistic efforts.

2. My use of the word 'video' suffices for the word 'film' as I am speaking more to the distribution medium rather than the format that a work originates. Regardless of whether a project was shot on film or video, I am speaking of images as video projection because the signal is technically a 'video' signal. If I am speaking of the 'language of film,' the theory was born in an era predating video, and consequently, video follows the same compositional standards. Regardless of format, film or video, the practitioner is still referred to as 'filmmaker.' I delineate between dance film and video projection integrated with live performance to maintain the container by which each is held. For my purposes, dance film is constructed with the knowledge that it commands the audience's full attention. The pacing can be faster with less repetition and more variety of shots than video for projection when there is a concern for what is occurring outside of the 'frame.' The video projection is reliant upon the

live body to convey information that is left out of the video and vice versa.

3. Sergei M. Eisenstein, *Selected Works*, trans. Richard Taylor, Vol. 1: Writings 1922–1934 (London: BFI, 1988), 41.

4. Marshall McLuhan and Lewis Henry Lapham, *Understanding Media the Extensions of Man* (Cambridge: MIT Press, 1994), 40.

5. McLuhan and Lapham, 40.

6. McLuhan and Lapham, 39.

7. Not all stand-alone video work is a 'hotter' version of the medium; nor is its purpose to dull the mind. To see an extreme example, watch Derek Jarman's *Blue* (1993), a 79-minute film comprised of a completely blue screen for the duration as a soundtrack paints a portrait of the filmmaker's experiences with AIDS.

8. McLuhan and Lapham, 80–1.

9. Philip Auslander, 'Digital Liveness: Philip Auslander (us) about Digital Liveness in Historical, Philosophical Perspective,' *Digital Liveness: Philip Auslander (us) about Digital Liveness in Historical, Philosophical Perspective*, Proc. of Digital Liveness-Realtime, Desire and Sociability, Haus Der Kulturen Der Welt, Berlin, Transmediale, 28 Feb. 2011. Web. 30 Dec. 2011. See http://vimeo.com/20473967

10. Auslander.

11. Auslander.

12. I recall my first video production class when we studied from Herbert Zettl's *Sight, Sound, Motion: Applied Media Aesthetics*. I still reference the basic principles of composition and visual weight set forth in this book. Herbert Zettl, *Sight, Sound, Motion: Applied Media Aesthetics* (Belmont, CA: Wadsworth Pub., 1990), 131.

13. *Disclaimer on Sound:* This writing does not aim to under-serve sound design as a crucial element to the overall design of a piece. Instead, it maintains the position that sound design deserves its own exhaustive investigation and contemplation without being subsumed into a discussion on visual design of live performance and video projection. Nevertheless, the issue of sound will be raised intermittently as it cannot be divorced from the fiber of the design conversation. The synchronization of sound or the use of non-synchronous sound in live performance with video projection complicates the waters by adding a fourth layer contributing to the 'whole' (McLuhan has some interesting things to say about

synchronous and asynchronous sound, see McLuhan and Lapham, 386).

14. Doris Humphrey, *The Art of Making Dances*, ed. Barbara Pollack (New York: Grove, 1959), 75–8.

15. The normal lens I refer to is the 25 mm lens of a video camera. For a basic guide on how a camera works, composition, lighting and continuity, see Tom Schroeppel, *The Bare Bones Camera Course for Film and Video* (Tampa, FL: Tom Schroeppel, 2002), 12.

16. To read more about the human inability to defy time and space, read the section on 'Absence of the Space-Time Continuum' in Rudolf Arnheim, *Film as Art* (Berkeley: University of California Press, 1957), 20–1.

17. Walter Murch, *In the Blink of an Eye: a Perspective on Film Editing* (Los Angeles: Silman-James, 2001), 5–6.

18. John Berger, *Ways of Seeing* (London: British Broadcasting Corporation, 1972), 18.

19. It is useful for me to observe, reflect and report on my own choreographic experiences as I make work. I write throughout the process. This writing is usually informal and personal. Sometimes words or chunks of sentences will make their way into the work. Mostly the writing illuminates that which may seem obvious. To me, these simple thoughts are truths and they are gifts that make the work seem less overwhelming and more approachable. This is the truth I am sharing in this moment: *Process greatly affects product and practice affects performance.*

20. Arnheim, 17.

21. McLuhan and Lapham, 31.

CHAPTER 9

Turning Around the Gaze in the Age of Technological Proliferation; or, Things Are Seldom What They Seem

Ruth Barnes

The way you look at an object can affect how you see it… Cognitive 'illusions' rely on stored knowledge about the world (depth, rabbits, women) and are also under some degree of conscious control (we can generally reverse the perception at will)…[1]

In the summer of 2008, I began the initial phase of *Looking Outward/ Looking Inward*. This choreographic project encompasses original research and creative activity, with a focus on audience perception. To that end, I created *Homing/In*, a mixed media work designed for a variety of configurations. Here, I discuss some aspects of the first incarnation of *Homing/ In*. I focus in particular on aspects that demonstrate how that performance piece relates to relationship(s) of performers and spectators. *Homing/In* explores notions of distance and proximity, absence and presence, as well as questions of who is looking at whom in performance. The work presents perhaps not so much a reversal of the gaze as a proliferation of viewpoints made possible by the combination of live-feed video with dance. *Homing/ In* offers spectators the opportunity to change their vantage points while the piece unfolds.[2]

R. Barnes (✉)
Missouri State University, Springfield, MO, US

© The Editor(s) (if applicable) and The Author(s) 2016
T.D. Arendell, R. Barnes (eds.), *Dance's Duet with the Camera*,
DOI 10.1057/978-1-137-59610-9_9

159

WHICH MIXED MEDIA: AND WHY?

Mixed media performance's interdisciplinary collaborations create exciting artistic possibilities. My recent choreographic research has included video, thereby providing layering that complicates the spectator's experience and interpretations of the work. I do this for a variety of reasons. In its simplest application, mixed media is capable of showing the movement and choreography from multiple perspectives. Also, I sometimes aim to represent historical memory, or to create a temporal or spatial skew. In this last instance, my purpose in using projections is to bring the audience closer to the performance piece, in an emotional as well as a physical sense. We are, to a great extent, a televisual society—and, thus, more easily captivated by large projected images than by live performers. Also, due to their very size, projected images often dominate a stage space. They can be used to create an environment where live performers can appear out of the projections or disappear into them.

I wanted to study relationships between live dance and video and audience perception of mixed media work. *Homing/In* was a first phase of, and as the object in, a larger ongoing project, *Looking Outward/Looking Inward*. *Homing/In* combines live dance and aerial work with live-feed video. The piece explores the integration of dance and video projections in a space that is intersected diagonally by a translucent scrim. By focusing on physical distance and proximity through mixed media performance, I undertake:

1. To create a representation of notions of 'proximity,' 'distance,' 'intimacy,' 'remoteness,' 'privacy' and 'disclosure;'
2. Through that representation, query those notions; and
3. To investigate how changes in the performance environment impact spectators' and performers' perceptions of meaning, message, and metaphor.

In seeking to represent and emphasize remoteness, I used aerial work to heighten the discernment of distance. However, as the shift from the horizontal to the vertical cannot be equally visible from all angles, that discernment is variable. In any case, the question here is: how much do we ever really see? As of this writing, the overriding structure of *Homing/In* continues to transform as observations shape understanding, and as different venues become available for performances. The piece has become the basis for further choreographic research. Different spaces provide alternative configurations of the same or similar material. For example, a second version of *Homing/In*, without the video element, was presented on a proscenium stage. Removing that layer and having the audience on one side created a starker, sparer work that located audience and performers in their traditional western places. Much of the querying disappeared; the horizontal or vertical relationship between the dancers became the focal point.

SHIFTING OUTLOOKS

Mixed media work interests me for a number of reasons. The potential to change perspective, to represent temporal and spatial shifts through the mixing of media, and the possibility of layering are enticing. This play/ work creates ambiguity, which in turn leaves the performance open to interpretation. Because of an overabundance of visual input, the viewer notices, sifts through, selects, and ultimately decides how/if things and events relate—and what that relationship might mean. Hence, one could question Douglas Rosenberg, who theorizes on what he calls the 'privileged position' of the camera:

> ...in a darkened theater we have but one fixed point of view, that of where we sit. The language of cinema allows us to participate in a work from multiple points of view specifically because the camera, while recording an event, may wander at will.[3]

Rosenberg's preference for the camera comes, perhaps, from the videographer's assumption that the camera sees (and shows) all and everything. Whereas, in essence, the camera only presents one point of view: that of the camera operator, behind the lens. Then, through the editing process, we see the director and/or editor's perspective. Others, in fact, control the spectator's experience.

Depending on the field of vision and framing, the camera's point of view is even more limited than that of an audience member. A spectator can change vantage point (slightly), through a turn of the head, by scanning or panning with his/her eyes. A camera's close-up erases context; a long shot diminishes performers to a fraction of their real sizes. Choreographer Merce Cunningham's understanding of the camera's function is different from Rosenberg's. Cunningham speaks of what a dancer does, to compensate for the lens:

> [w]orking with dance in video requires a constant adjustment in terms of space, often on a small scale. A six-inch shift can seem large on the camera. This also can cause a displacement in the timing, requiring a change in rhythm, or the amplifying of a dance phrase, sometimes necessitating a cut or speed-up of the movement.[4]

Here again, the assumption is that the camera replaces the stationary spectator in a seat in a darkened room or theater. But, what if the spectator does *not* have a fixed place from which to view the performance? What if spectators are encouraged to move around the periphery of the space without being directed where to go? What if they improvise their relationship to the dancers, the screens and the musicians? What if spectators actively embody their decisions of what to look at by where they are in the space? What if the audience became a group of *flâneurs*?

The Observer and Ambiguity

Walter Benjamin theorized the *flâneur* is a member of the intelligentsia of Paris, a detached young man who contemplates and participates through observation. At once present and hidden, the *flâneur* is a prime example of Descartian mind/body split. Therefore, the *flâneur* is the ideal model for a study in presence and disappearance: of image, of body, of multi-perspective motion and its viewers.

In *The Arcades Project*, Benjamin devotes the letter M in his lexicon to the *flâneur*. Amidst Benjamin's own musings and theorizing we read citations from philosophers, journalists, poets, novelists and theorists that discuss this oh-so-Parisian being. Benjamin also presents the Marxist economic/political/sociological significance of the city *qua* city, and the development of public transportation. Unlike rubbernecks, who tend to lose themselves in the crowd (or become the crowd), *flâneurs* maintain a sense of individuality. They always know who and where they are. From Larousse, we learn the following:

> His eyes open, his ear ready, searching for something entirely different from what the crowd gathers to see. A word dropped by chance will reveal to him one of those character traits that cannot be invented and that must be drawn directly from life; those physiognomies so naively attentive will fur-

nish the painter with the expression he was dreaming of; a noise, significant to every other ear, will strike that of the musician and give him the cue for a harmonic combination; even for the thinker, the philosopher lost in his reverie, this external agitation is profitable: it stirs up his ideas as the storm stirs the waves of the sea.... Most men of genius were great *flâneurs*—but industrious, productive *flâneurs*...[sic].[5]

The *flâneur* is an excellent model for audience members, because of his active, albeit detached engagement with the goings-on. An outside observer, but not a daydreamer, the *flâneur*'s unique understanding generates new creativity. Such creativity is heightened in promenade performances.

In his chapter on the *flâneur*, Benjamin also touches on the phenomenon of perspective and layering. He cites Raymond Escholier, who in turn cites Odilon Redon's discussion of the ambiguity of the image. How we engage with ambiguity depends on our mental and/or emotional approach:

'The sense of mystery,' wrote Odilon Redon, who had learned the secret straight from da Vinci, 'comes from remaining always on the equivocal, with double and triple perspectives, or inklings of perspective (images within images)—forms that take shape and come into being according to the state of mind of the spectator. All things more suggestive just because they do appear.'[6]

This notion of an 'equivocal' state, of ambiguity, along with the practice of layering and creating multiple perspectives, presents the viewer with a conundrum. S/he has an object or event to investigate and observe. The *flâneur* takes her/his time exploring this terrain, always with the 'idea that the fruits of idleness are more precious than the fruits of labor.'[7] S/he is never rushed. After all, according to Benjamin: '...it was considered elegant to take a tortoise out walking.'[8]

The spectator, in his/her relationship to the work of art, theoretically becomes a voyeur or *flâneur*. By observing and taking the time to figure out meaning, the spectator looks for the essence or uniqueness of what is on display. In a promenade performance, the audience member's relationship to the work changes. Rather than remaining seated on the sidelines (literally), in this project the viewer becomes a sort of observer/participant, encouraged to walk around and find other vantage points. Also, we turned the notions of 'spectator' and 'object' around. In *Homing/*

In, the *performer's* gaze, as manifest through the surveillance lenses, presents an intriguing object for study. Rather than being merely observed, gazed upon, the performer's camera (close to her heart) captures her surroundings. The camera's gaze includes the spectators, and those images are projected in real time.[9]

OTHER POSSIBLE PERSPECTIVES

The promenade performance was the original configuration of *Homing/ In*. Several others have been conceived. One version is intended as an installation piece: a continuous loop performed over several hours, with the audience members entering and leaving whenever they wish. In this way, in a gallery or museum situation, the dance becomes a kind of moving sculpture, or a sidewalk café, where one can sit for hours, watching the world go by. In addition, an indeterminate structure could allow all the participants (dancers, musician, projectionist) to decide during the performances how the layering of the dance, music and video would shift throughout the evening. The repetitions of each of the elements would not necessarily have been synchronized with the repetitions of any of the others. In principle, different relationships between the elements would occur. The piece's meaning could change with each iteration.

Other subsequent (imagined) reconfigurations might include a number of possibilities:

1. Dancers and aerial equipment without video, a less layered event on a traditional western proscenium stage—this version was presented in High Point, NC, in September 2011.
2. The same choreographic material and prerecorded video, rearranged for a proscenium stage.
3. A single-front configuration with the audience at a distance from the dancers and the projected images, and with a different placement for the scrim.
4. Both dancers on the ground, that is, without the element of aerial dance.
5. A version with a third performer, a camera operator, replacing the surveillance equipment, providing a single alternative view of the choreography.

In most instances, projection surface and spatial configuration are elements integral to the work. They are part of the creative process. Their inclusion affects how the space is delineated and how a spectator might relate to the work. Another location for this work is the screen: a video/dance with footage captured throughout the process, edited for the web.

ILLUSION AND REALITY: INTERPRETING AND CREATING MEANING

Homing/In also relates to discussions of what 'presence' and 'absence' might mean. Benjamin, in his seminal 1936 essay, 'The Work of Art in the Age of Mechanical Reproduction,' addresses both the benefits and the issues/problems in works that are copies (that is, lithographs, books, recordings and film).[10] While extolling the value of making art and ideas available to the masses, the workers, the people, Benjamin discusses the difference between live and recorded (filmed) 'presence.' He comes to the conclusion that what is lacking in film is the actor's literal and figurative presence. Benjamin comes to the conclusion that what is lacking is the actor's *aura*. He thereby includes not just the physical, but also the metaphysical, in his argument. Today, one can posit that recent experiments in 'distance theatre' query Benjamin: is the video or laser projection of the actor/dancer truly less 'present' than the live performer? Is the Internet less real, less present, a location for performance than a physical place? Or, in the twenty-first century, do we now have a different understanding of what we mean by 'present' and 'absent'?

And then there is the eerie quality of the projections. In his much-read and discussed piece, *The Uncanny*, Sigmund Freud seeks definitions of 'uncanny' (*umheimlich*) events and explanations as to what even makes something uncanny. Literary theorist Robin Lydenberg, in her essay, 'Freud's Uncanny Narratives,' writes of '[t]he ambiguity of the uncanny as both familiar and unfamiliar,' noting that *heimlich* has contradictory meanings: its primary definition is 'familiar and agreeable;' but its secondary definition is 'concealed and kept out of sight.'[11] The notion of ambiguity leads Hélène Cixous to refer to Freud's essay as

...a commentary on uncertainty... The ensuing unfolding whose operation is contradictory is accomplished by the author's double: Hesitation. We are faced, then, with a text and its hesitating shadow, and their double escapade.'[12]

In other words, what we see is open to interpretation, based not only on what we see, but how we receive the image.

RECEPTION NEAR AND FAR

For the creation and original research period of *Homing/In* in the summer of 2008, Morag Deyes MBE, Artistic Director of Dance Base, Scotland's National Centre for Dance in Edinburgh, offered to be a partner for the project. Dance Base's Curator Funding matched a Missouri State University Faculty Summer Fellowship. Ms. Deyes provided a residency for my research/rehearsal period, including studio space for rehearsals. I also received support for performances, which were programmed as part of Dance Base's 2008 Edinburgh Festival Fringe activities. The creative team included Scottish dancers Kally Lloyd-Jones and Steinvor Palsson, and British composer Dmytro Morykit. I also invited Sheila MacDougall, a dancer and children's theatre director with experience in 'Viewpoints,'[13] to be my foil. Observing rehearsals and asking me questions, Sheila MacDougall enabled me to put my thoughts into words and define the focus of the work.

As previously noted, some questions for inquiry involve relationship. 'Relationship' in the first version of *Homing/In* is multiple: the dancers to each other, the projected image to the live dance, the dancers to the audience, the audience to the live movement and/or flat-screen image. Questions arise: What is distance? What is proximity? When (sometimes/always/never) is *Homing/In* intimate? When is the performance remote? Are 'proximity' and 'distance' merely physical? In other words, how does a performance, through physical proximity and distance, create and represent affective 'closeness' and 'remoteness'?

EARLIER WORKS: AND THE SPECTATOR'S GAZE

Another aspect of the project is shifting perspective. When I teach a dance technique class, I walk around the studio, to observe what the dancers are doing from all sides. This enables me to see everyone more clearly and to give corrections. Also, if I am in the process of choreographing a piece, by walking around it I see the movement from a variety of angles. I might find a more satisfying place from which to watch other than the place I had originally imagined as front, or facing the audience. I explored this roving eye in two earlier works. First, in the dance/video *Into the Glass,* taped in a studio in 2003, a stationary single shot tricks the spectator. The mirror creates a sense of depth in the 2D screen space, thereby framing the solo dancer in surprising ways: what we at first believe is the dancer turns out to be her reflection. The following year, I presented the mixed media work *On Reflection* as a promenade-performance-in-the-round. The audience's mobility reminded me of my teaching relationship to dancers in class. As stated above, changing vantage point to watch from other angles enables me to see the movement and/or the dancers more clearly. Some spectators expressed having experienced heightened sensory awareness, stating that the spatial organization and the invitation to walk around the piece generated a sense of intensified engagement. I therefore decided it would be interesting to present *Homing/In* at least once as a promenade-performance-in-the-round, to give the audience that same opportunity of seeing the movement from different vantage points, and to create additional layers and complexity in the performance.

THE PERFORMER'S GAZE

Another element that affects my choreographic research is my belief in the connectedness of the individual to the environment and, by extension, events in our global society. In 2008, in a worldwide atmosphere of increased security, I had been thinking a lot about surveillance, scanning, tracking, and searching. At the beginning of the year, I choreographed a quintet, entitled *Quicksilver. Homing/In* and *Quicksilver* overlapped in their querying of the relationship between spectator and performer. Also, some of the movement vocabulary from *Quicksilver* reappeared in *Homing/In,* although the notion of surveillance was represented differently. The duet uses mini-cams in an 'effect-free' studio: the sun provided the lighting and the studio has no masking or wings. The costumes for the quintet included LED headlights, and the piece was performed in lighting designer Mike Foster's hazy environment. Because of the headlights worn in *Quicksilver*, much of the time the dancers' faces were obscured to the spectators. At the same time, the dancers could see/observe/survey— spy on (!)—the spectators. Because the dancers could see the audience while the audience could not see the performers' faces, *Quicksilver* set up an unbalanced, non-habitual situation for a western theatre performance piece. This was not unlike one in which performers wear masks that obscure their natural physiognomies. The dancers in *Quicksilver* experienced an unfamiliar sensation of power. In the darkened house they could see the spectators, who could not entirely see them. However, the dancers' sense of power was dispelled when they noticed cell phones light up: text messaging was a more potent attention-grabber than their performance!

In *Homing/In*, the disruption of habitual western performance practice meant that spectators were visible to the dancers, as well as each other, for several reasons. Because of the environmental natural light, everyone in the room was equally visible. The performers and performing area were not marked by stage lighting, the costumes were simple rehearsal clothing, the 'set' consisted of the aerial apparatus and a free-standing rectangle of scrim, the audience could walk behind the musician, and all the video equipment was visible. Also, the mini-cams captured whatever was in the field—including the audience—in their somewhat random scanning of the studio space.

Camera Work

Until *Homing/In*, I had only used recorded footage in performance. This first configuration of *Homing/In* used live-feed video. Small, remote control surveillance cameras, placed on the dancers' sterna, captured the environment. The placement of the cameras was symbolic: they were close to the heart, recalling affect, or nostalgia for something 'missing.' Also, in European classical dance, the sternum is associated with the ego: in *Swan Lake*, the Prince pantomimes 'I swear' by touching his heart or sternum and gesturing to the heavens.

The data the cameras captured were routed through a VJ board, or switcher, which mixed the two streams in various ways. This image was then projected onto a semi-transparent scrim. The play between the 3D action and the 2D projections, as well as the possibility of seeing everyone in the room, challenged the spectators' attention. The piece as a whole presented multiple focal points and layers. How to decipher/decode meaning? Where to look? How much *can* we see?

One goal in this first phase of *Homing/In* was to establish, define and clarify relational possibilities. The dancers and I collaborated in the creation of movement and experimented with aerial apparatus (fabric panels and harness) as well as with video equipment. We explored the relationship between the two dancers—one always on the floor, one sometimes in the air. Other relationships presented themselves, including the relationship between the dancers and the projected images. In addition, the questions of how the dance and the music, the dancers and the musician, and, the audience and the performers relate were always considered. A scrim placed diagonally across part of the large studio space delineates skewed, asymmetrical areas in which the dancers move. This configuration creates the possibility of a layered visual image for the spectator: dancer, projected image, other dancer, spectator(s)—and, if seated in view of the wall of mirrors in the studio, the spectator can also see him/herself. The first performance of *Homing/In* took place in the same studio as our rehearsals.[14] During this promenade performance, audience members were invited to shift vantage points by wandering around the piece, while remaining on the periphery of the space (Fig. 9.1).

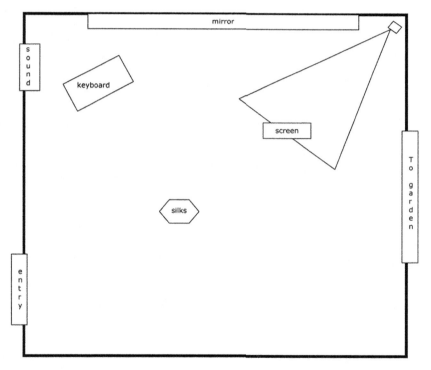

Fig. 9.1   Diagram for stage plan for *Homing/In* (2008) (NB- created by author so requires no acknowledgement)

REPRESENTATION AND RELATIONSHIP IN DANCE

The movement incorporates the notion of scanning (heads slowly turning with eyes frankly surveying the horizon) and also finding 'home' (a place that is familiar, or where one finds comfort, represented by nestling or holding). The movement's dynamics include slicing, piercing, off-kilter suspensions that encourage loss of balance and falls to the floor, and sustained stillness. The dancers explore the space with their extremities (hands, feet, and head reaching and slowly sweeping in an arc). They mirror or double each other with the shapes they make with their bodies. At the beginning of the piece, after an initial scanning of the space, one dancer performs a brief, lively solo that also uses pauses and broken phrasing. The goal with this solo was to recall how, on surveillance screens, we might jump from one image to another as we investigate each picture more closely. The second dancer enters and the two meet near the center of the space for a duet that explores extreme physical closeness. Proximity, spatial transposition (for example, one dancer dances standing while the other does the same movement supine) and unison work are the duet's principal themes.

In the next section of the dance, one dancer rises above the audience, using a harness and fabric panels. The aerial apparatus serves as a means of increasing spectators' perception of distance. It also creates an alternative location with a very different ambience from the studio's floor space. The aerial dancer performs a sequence of movement above the other dancer and the audience, and then invites her partner to join her in the fabric. There is a sense of both freedom and dominance. The aerial dancer appears protective as she opens the panels for the second figure. The cloth becomes a sort of cocoon, enveloping both dancers while we hear the music's most haunting motif. Breaking out of their casing, the dancers' arms slowly emerge. We then see their entire bodies again as one dancer slowly slides onto the floor, echoing the aerialist's shapes. Oddly, they both appear to be floating. A solo follows the descent back to the ground. We return to broken phrases with jumps and sustained balances, as if the dancer is testing a renewed encounter with the earth. She dances in the light of the projector, between the lens and the screen. Depending on her proximity to the light source, her shadow partially or totally blocks out the video image. The final duet segment comprises the most unison of the piece, using the dancers' placement in space to create more depth. Sometimes next to each other, sometimes on opposite sides of the room, they move individually and as a unit. They end in the same position and relationship as in the start of the beginning duet. The video images also come to rest, as the cameras are finally trained on the black of the dancers' attire.

SIMULTANEOUS CONTRADICTIONS: TRICKING THE GAZE

The play of live performer(s) and video image brings up questions of illusion and reality, of presence and absence, and of temporality. Another notion interrogated is the power the creator may derive from deciding what the viewer may see. The possibilities of *trompe l'oeil*, layering, creating hide-and-seek situations are rife. Choreographers use live-feed video as a means of either offering the spectator a different view of the dancer and the dance, or as a way of tricking the audience. A choreographer might confound the viewer through the use of images superimposed on live performers. Consider in particular the work of Philippe Decouflé (France) and Kathy Weis (New York). In several works, most notably *Shazam!*, Decouflé uses a layering of live performance, video, mirrors and shadow play to trick the audience's perception of what is happening. Weis uses video images in her performance pieces to create environments and also represent memory. In *Homing/In* and the extended project *Looking Outward/Looking Inward*, the use of surveillance cameras creates a layer of referential meaning. More questions arise: Who is watching whom, and to what end? Are the process and its result informational or voyeuristic? What is the difference between these two perspectives? The notion of terrorism has recently risen in prominence throughout the world. Governments track both citizens and foreigners in various ways. Facebook 'friends' stalk each other. Text messaging replaces face-to-face conversations... Are we becoming closer or more alien to each other (and, are we more alienated in ourselves)?

MORE QUESTIONS

What, then, will appear on the screen, and when? Is it what is in front of the spectator? Is it something else, somewhere else in (or outside) the room, which would not be seen without the projection? What does the screen add to (or take away from—disrupt) the liveliness of a live event? *Homing/In* upsets the expected balance between performers and audience, by incorporating live-feed video that includes the audience. My intention through the combination of live performance and projected images is to create a space in which the viewer becomes a truly active observer participant. Intrigued by duplicated or contrasting events, the *flâneur*-spectator can delve into layered and juxtaposed events by shifting vantage point and framing, and extrapolate a unique, creative meaning.

Notes

1. See http://www.world-mysteries.com/illusions/sci_illusions3.htm
2. For more information, see Ruth Barnes—Profile—Dance—Hatchfund—Artist Fundraising & Advocacy.webarchive.
3. Douglas Rosenberg, *Video Space: A Site for Choreography*. www.dvpg.net/essays.htmlr
4. Merce Cunningham, 'A Collaborative Process Between Music and Dance,' in *Merce Cunningham: Dancing in Space and Time*, ed. Richard Kostelanetz, (London: Dance Books, 1992), 138.
5. Walter Benjamin, *The Arcades Project*, trans. Howard Eiland and Kevin McLaughlin (Cambridge, MA and London: Belknap Press of Harvard University Press, 1999), 454.
6. Benjamin, 79.
7. Benjamin, 454.
8. Benjamin, 422.
9. Other instances of revealing the dancer's point of view include, for example, the dance video *Points in Space*, in which Merce Cunningham and Charles Atlas replaced one dancer with a camera, creating a dizzying effect for the viewer (our eyes do not, in fact, work the same way as what we see on video or film).
10. Walter Benjamin, 'The Work of Art in the Age of Mechanical Reproduction,' *The Arcades Project*, trans. Howard Eiland and Kevin McLaughlin (Cambridge, MA and London: Belknap Press of Harvard University Press, 1999), 217–42.
11. Robin Lydenberg, 'Freud's Uncanny Narratives,' *PMLA* 112 (1997): 1073.
12. Hélène Cixous, 'Fictions and Its Phantoms: A Reading of Freud's *Das Unheimliche* (The 'uncanny'),' *New Literary History* 7 (1976), 525.
13. 'Viewpoints' is a performance work methodology originally proposed by dancer/choreographer Mary Overlie. Actors/directors Anne Bogart and Tina Landau expanded on Overlie's principles, and later published *The Viewpoints Book* (Theatre Communications Group, 2005).
14. A video can be found at Homing/In Dress August 2008—YouTube. webarchive.

PART IV

Bodies, Spaces, Camera

This section of our text queries the film industry's tendency to fragment and splice dancing images in service of the larger picture. Different filmmakers have established varied approaches to capturing, sustaining, speed altering, and depth positioning dancing bodies. There is, after all, some movement sequencing that only exists as a physical possibility by means of filmic editing techniques. In many ways, this gets us back to the question of who's behind the camera. Whether the shots are about the alienation of movement with respect to gravity, surrounding environments, or multiple perspectives, film has the capacity to distort space/time dimensions with respect to physical movement that live dancers would never dare to attempt on stage. Fred Astaire in particular holds a highly valued place in dance film history as, among other things, the dancer who demanded that the camera follow him, not the other way around. His slight tilt off the vertical axis held viewers in anticipation of what the camera might have considered a wholly unorthodox relationship to the floor. Astaire's stipulation of full-body camera coverage, not just moving legs and feet or torso shots, raised the bar for a film industry just beginning to understand visualization of movement for movement's sake. While Kassel in this section generates ways in which film editing might enrich dance with use of unexpected angles, layered images, or coincidental configuration, Moore holds fast to the notion that either the camera needs to dance or the dancer but not necessarily both in contradiction with each other. Arendell locates Maya Deren's leaps in and out of camera frame as a visual dreamscape somewhere in between these two extremes, noticing a virtual flirtation between multiple selves and swiftly-shifting landscapes.

CHAPTER 10

Videodance: How Film Enriches the Dance

Angela Kassel

When I was still in my first year at Rotterdam's dance academy, I was already interested in videodance. At that time, it was not (as it now is) usual that every dance student would own a camera and computer with editing software. It was possible, however, to borrow these things from school, so I started to experiment with filming dance. I experienced how using the camera affected me as a dancer. I also discovered I could influence the outcome of the dance as a camera operator or by editing. Some years later I chose a more theoretical approach by enrolling at the University of Cologne for theater and film studies. This subject focuses separately on the two elements that are used to compose a videodance: the theatrical performance (in this case, dance) and film, a medium of moving pictures. I hereby introduce film as a more general consideration of the term *video*. In fact, videodance originally was bound to the material of video. Nowadays, the term videodance[1] is mostly used to name the product of a dancefilm with certain qualities no matter what material was used to produce it. At the end of my studies I made videodance the subject of my *magister* thesis, analyzing the way film affects dance in videodance. In this chapter I present some of this analysis.

A. Kassel (✉)
Director of Joymotion, Zollstock, Germany

© The Editor(s) (if applicable) and The Author(s) 2016
T.D. Arendell, R. Barnes (eds.), *Dance's Duet with the Camera*,
DOI 10.1057/978-1-137-59610-9_10

SPACE, TIME, BODY

In order to give this analysis a structure I use categories often referred to in research on (theater-)dance: space, time and body. Moreover, I add categories mainly referred to in film studies: perspective and editing/montage. I watched many videodance films[2] and selected the ones that were special in how they deal with one (or more) of these categories. This pool of films shows, in many different ways, how the medium of film can influence the *look* of dance. The original question for my research is: how does and how can film alter the presentation of dance?[3] Assuming that dance mainly comprises space, time, and the body, changes in one of these components cause changes in the dance. Film is able to make visible changes in space, time or the body. Thus, it provides dance the option of amplifying one or another of these components.

Amplifications of space, time, and the body affect both the viewer and the dancer performing in the videodance. Showing a movement in detail or to support the dynamics of the movement the spectator provides more kinesthetic involvement. The same can be said of editing techniques.[4] Also, film can make the dancer's abilities look phenomenal. Special perspectives or tricks make jumps look higher, movements quicker, than they are. On the other hand, this can function the other way around as well, sometimes taking away the impressiveness of the dancer's abilities and virtuosity. Seeing someone jump really high on stage is impressive because of the knowledge of how hard this is. Not everybody can do it. But in film everybody can appear able to do it: 'The aesthetic value of virtuosity is negated as the technology of television can enhance and extend the possible movement ranges of the body to such an extent that, on screen, it has no physical limitations.'[5]

In general, it can be said that videodance is an art form that produces a work of art that cannot be seen without either the dance or the film.[6] As such, videodance produces a new artwork out of two art forms. It merges dance with film. And, through this fusion, something is generated that could not have been achieved without either one or the other. Maya Deren, one of the first to experiment with video and dance, said that filmdance is 'a dance so related to the camera and cutting that it cannot be "performed" as a unit anywhere but in this particular film.'[7] As Sherril Dodds put it more than thirty years later, the original choreography is reworked 'specifically for the screen in order to create a new work in its own right.'[8] By using the camera, the possibilities of giving dance a form are extended. So, for example, filming a complete dance on stage from a frontal perspective, similar to the perspective of the audience, is not videodance. It is, rather, a documentation (or an archival video of a live performance) of the dance piece.[9]

To find a pleasing definition of videodance is hard. But, I have come to terms with the following: Videodance is a dance filmed in a way that extends and enriches the dance. Videodance exists in such a way that the dance cannot be seen in this form without filmic devices. In this essay, I will give some examples for the possibilities of changing the presentation and the *look* of the dance by using the film medium. These examples also include the categories of space, time, body, perspective and montage.

EDITING

Technically, film works as a row/connection of single pictures. Therefore, it can always be separated into these single pictures again. A cut can be made at every point, and images that don't belong together (that were not shot as a connected row of single pictures) can be combined. This can be used to put non-dance pictures in between the dance scenes. The effect this has is shown mostly in the arising of associations. For example, in *Divigations dans une chamber d'hôtel (Me and my choreographer in 63)* (2005) by Philippe Barcinski and Dainara Toffoli (choreography by Bruno Beltrão), or in *Shakti Rising* by Goar Sánchez (choreography by Julie Barnsley), non-dance scenes are mixed with dance scenes in a way that the non-dance scenes influence the perception of the dance scenes. In *Shakti Rising,* the non-dance scenes show pictures of war, including soldiers marching, bombed ruins of houses or a funeral. With this in mind, the viewer searches for a statement in the dance movements that relates to war. Because of the images of war framing them, non-specific dance movements seem to express grief and sorrow.

The possibilities of using this sort of editing are countless and easy to imagine. It is interesting to see how editing can create a movement that cannot exist without the process of editing. A good example can be found in *'burnt'* (1997) by Vera Sander and Holger Gruss: in one scene you see a man lying on his stomach on the floor. The framing of the picture shows him only from the waist up. He pushes away from the ground, lifting himself up. There is a cut and we see a woman jumping onto the shoulder of the same man standing. By this connection of the two different scenes the impression arises that the flow of energy leads from the man's movement to the woman's. It looks as if there is only one movement, even if the form of the first movement does not match the form of the second movement. By editing, movements can be created that have never been shot in this way and that could never be performed in reality. People can start a movement in one place and end it somewhere else, and much more. More of this will be exemplified in the sections **Space** and **Body**.

What is very important about editing is the rhythm of the cuts. As dance is about rhythm as well, this is a connective element of dance and film. The rhythm of the editing can influence the dynamic of the dance. When very slow movements are filmed and edited in a fast rhythm, the impression created is that of a very dynamic dance. This is true even if the dance movements are not dynamic in their first iteration. I will say more about this mode of operation in the section **Body**, which deals with the manipulation of dance and its qualities.

SPACE AND ENVIRONMENT

One possibility film offers dance is showing the dancer in an environment that cannot be built on a stage. Surroundings can be depicted which would be impossible to show without film. Additionally, thanks to editing, these surroundings can change much faster than would be possible without film.

The environment can influence the dance directly. For example, a dancer moves differently when dancing on rocks than when on flat ground. The surroundings can be used as inspiration for the movement as well, as when a dancer winds him/herself around a tree. Besides these quite obvious effects, every environment evokes certain associations and connotations. The perception of the dancer's movement depends on these associations and, thus, on the environment. For example, if a leap is performed on even ground (such as a garden), it tends to arouse a feeling of joy. If the same leap is performed in a landscape of a canyon, or bridging a gap, it is likely to be seen as more dangerous. The tension evoked in each case is completely different.

Hans Beenhakker's *Shake Off* (2007) is a good example of this, as the film consists of three (animated) sets in which the same choreography is performed.[10] The spectator watches a man dance the same choreography three times. However, since the surroundings change, each dance appears to be slightly different. Moreover, this film shows an interesting transition between these environments. First, the camera zooms in on the back of the dancer. When it zooms out again, the dancer finds himself in a different room than before. So, the change of setting 'takes place' literally, without the dancer moving.

Other examples for interesting transitions between places are *Moving Stillness: Where Aikido Meets Dance* (2007) by Wiebke Pôpel[11] and *Give me a break* (2007) by Noa Shadur.[12] In both videodances, a movement performed by one person in one location is continued by the same—or another—person elsewhere. Thus, the flow of the movement is not interrupted by the cut from one scene to another. Even though surroundings change, the movement goes on. In Pontus Lidberg's *The Rain* (2007)[13] this technique is used in a way that evokes the impression that two people would dance together, even though they mostly aren't in the same place. A man dances on a street, and a woman dances on a meadow. They perform the same choreography, each continuing the movement of the other. It looks like a duet, but actually the editing alone establishes the connection between the man and the woman. Absence and presence are interlaced. On a narrative level this might be interpreted as the man and the woman thinking of each other.

The environment can also affect the dance by giving meaning to a movement. If a dancer moves like an animal on stage, the spectator asks himself why. He tries to find the narrative or grasp the meaning of the scene. If dancers move like animals through a natural landscape as in *Afternoon of the Chimeras* (2006)[14] by filmmaker Daniel Conrad (choreography by Aszure Barton), the landscape motivates/justifies/legitimizes the style of moving. The spectator can enter into the illusion, diving into the scenario without being troubled by any cognitive processes.

In short, the spatial setting influences the perception of the dance itself. The environment can inspire or constitute movement. It can shape the movement's dynamics. A movement can transcend locations without breaking its flow. Moreover, the environment evokes associations in/with the spectator. These function as a background/frame for the dance, visually and through the spectator's act of interpretation. Thus, the environment can give the dance a certain meaning.

PERSPECTIVE

When dance is shown on film, the camera's point of view and the framing determine the view of the observer. Both can lead to perspectives one cannot have when looking at a live performance of dance. The perspective

changes the perception of space, along with the perception of dance movements. Looking at a movement from the front gives a different impression
than looking at the same movement from the side or above. Looking from
above gives a good view on how dancers are moving from A to B. We see
the spatial patterns they perform. Group formations can be easily recognized. However, top shots cannot show poses and dance movements/
figures intended for frontal viewing.

A dancer lifts and extends a leg to the front. This gesture looks completely different, depending on whether your perspective is from the front
or the side. If you see the dancer's front, the extended leg looks short.
However, the impression you get is that the dancer is coming towards
you, so you feel more involved. If you see the movement sideways, the
leg extended in the air looks longer. Instead of the feeling of being
approached/addressed, the observer feels more like an outside viewer.
Observing the movement from the side places more importance on the
way the dancer's body expands into space.

A jump seen from worm's-eye view looks higher than when seen from
the same level as the jumping person, or from above. A person rolling on
the floor, body stretched as long as possible, gives a completely different
picture if you see the entire body, than from the head or feet. The same
might be applied to framing: a close-up of one part of the body gives
a different impression than the body seen as a whole. A pirouette performed with the entire dancer seen can easily be recognized as such. What
is emphasized is the balance of a person turning on a single foot and the
grace and elegance of the posture, which is in itself stable and still. In contrast, in a close-up of the waist rotating,[15] filling the whole screen, there is
irritation about what you see. The aspect of moving is focused at the waist
and the movement looks quicker and much more intense.

With any given movement, the filmmaker can choose among many
options in presenting the movement to the viewer. Moreover, in film
it is possible to switch from one perspective to another quickly. Several
perspectives can be combined in one picture (for example, by using split
screen, explained later in this section). So, perspective is a combination
of point of view and framing. *One Flat Thing Reproduced* by Thierry De
Mey (choreography by William Forsythe) demonstrates how using different points of view and the framing of the picture influences the perception
of the movement.[16] In the beginning there is a sequence of twenty dancers
running. They each pull a table behind them. They then stop and establish
a square formation. This running is shown three times in the film. First,

a bird's-eye view gives a good overview of the number of dancers, the formation and the room/space where this happens. Then, the running is shown from the side, the level of the camera at eye height. In contrast to the bird's-eye view, this reveals the speed of the running and the power the dancers need to pull the tables across the floor. A third version shows the same running scene from the front. The camera starts from a higher level and then comes down to the height of the tables, so the dancers run directly towards the camera. This has a strong impact on the viewer. Moreover, in this last shot the focus is on the hands and arms of the dancers. They correct the position of the tables until the square formation is perfected. Now, rather than accentuating the formation (which we saw from the bird's-eye view), the work of bringing this formation into being is stressed.

Later on there is a scene in which dancers dance in the aisles between the tables and on the tables. The perspective changes between frontal view, top view, bird's-eye view, a viewpoint from the corner/side, and some close-ups. Each of these points of view stresses a different aspect of the dance. Each also gives a slightly different impression of space. For example, the frontal view leads to a certain effect/impression of flatness of the movements. In contrast, the diagonal view creates more three-dimensionality. These changes of perspective make it more interesting to look at movements that are repeated. Moreover, they add more dynamic to the dance. The viewer not only sees the movement of the dancers but also perceives the cuts as movement (as mentioned in the section on editing). Also, the fact that one can see the room from different points of view gives the viewer a feeling of traveling from spot to spot.

FRAMING

The framing of a picture is crucial to the perception of movement, as exemplified by a scene with three women sitting behind each other, each on a separate table. A man kneeling behind the last of these three tables rests his head on the table board. The three women only move their arms a little. If this were seen in full view, the man's head wouldn't attract attention. Also, the women would look quite still, as only a small part of their bodies is moving. However, the close-up focuses on the man's head and the women can only be seen from hips to shoulders. This means that their moving arms fill in a big part of the screen, so the movement doesn't look small at all. In fact, the small movements look big. A connection between the eyes of the man and the moving hands of the women becomes visible, which wouldn't be obvious in a full view. Then, the head of another woman enters the picture from the left. This is quite surprising, as you cannot see the woman approaching (because she is out of the frame). The new head appears all of a sudden and already is very close. So the process of something approaching from further away is cut out of the picture. This frustrates the viewer, since that would be the normal way for humans to perceive someone approaching. If this scene were filmed in full view, the process of approaching would be in the picture. Or, the distance from the person entering the picture would have reduced the frustration caused by her sudden appearance.

This also works in reverse. In one scene, a woman lying on a table is shown in close-up. You can only see her upper body from the ribcage up. Her arms rest above her head on the table. All of a sudden she glides out of the picture in the direction of her feet (which you don't see). Not knowing from where this move derives, the woman's abrupt exit irritates the viewer much more than seeing somebody pull the woman by her legs off the table. The close-up intensifies the moment of surprise by erasing information about what is happening outside the frame.

This elimination of information is also interesting regarding the choreography as a whole. In *One Flat Thing Reproduced*, dancers all over the room perform different movements together, forming the choreography. Every zoom or close-up focusing on one or two dancers blocks out the rest of the dancers (that is: the rest of the choreography). Parallel or synchronal movements between dancers can be cut out of the picture, which obviously alters the choreography. The choreography is fragmented and seen as if through a magnifying lens. What is seen through the lens is intensified; what is not within the lens's focus is erased.

DANCE SEEN FROM BELOW

Another option film gives to dance is that dance can be seen from below. A dancer moving on a glass plate, with a camera placed under the plate looking up to the dancer, can be seen from a perspective not common in live performance. An example for this is *Glass Perpx* (2007) by Steven Fajana.[17] The dancer on the glass plate lying down performing movements close to the plate looks similar to the view from above. However, when the dancer gets up and dances in a more or less standing position, the view from below turns out to be exceptional. Most movements performed come from a tradition that prefers a frontal view; so, the movements are conceived of as seen from the front. As the dancer on the glass plate does not adjust his movements to the viewpoint of the camera, this leads to a really new view of dance.

The use of perspectives that can't be shown on stage can also lead to a disruption of space and gravity. For example: The dancer is lying on the ground in a position as if standing. The camera positioned above him gives a clear top shot. If this picture is seen on the screen in an upright position, the viewer tends to see the dancer as if he is standing in front of a wall. The floor becomes the wall in the viewer's perception. But still, the viewer can tell that something about gravity is not 'normal.' In *'Inearthia: An Attempt to Spin the Earth'* (2006)[18] by Colateral (choreography by Simon Halbedo) this revision of gravity is played with: you see a dancer sitting on a concrete rod coming out of the wall. When the wall starts rolling along the axis of the rod, the dancer tries to keep his sitting position by shoving himself forward along the wall. Actually what is filmed here is a dancer lying on the ground next to a pillar, seen from top view. When the camera starts moving around the pillar, the dancer crouches around the pillar. He tries to stay in the focus of the camera, keeping his position as if sitting on the pillar. What happens here is that, by turning the picture ninety degrees, the ground becomes the wall and the prostrate dancer appears to be seated. The way gravity pulls on the dancer in the lying position looks odd in the sitting position. Also, this wrong pull of gravity makes the way the dancer moves look strange. In addition, the rolling/rotating of the wall confounds viewers, as walls are meant to be stable. If this film were seen as it was originally filmed, the focus would be on the energy the dancer needs to keep his sideways lying position during the whole film. In the final (rotated) version of the film this energy does not catch the viewer's attention. We have only a vague perception of something being wrong with gravity. Instead, we focus on the movement of the wall and the whole room, which seem to be the motivation for the dancer's movements. In this example the dancer's movements are designed to make the rotation of the picture look natural. He tries to keep the illusion of gravity alive, even if gravity is not pulling him in the direction he pretends.

Similarly, in *Weightless* (2007) by Erika Janunger, the floor becomes the wall of a room.[19] This film uses two living room settings. Each is completely furnished with shelves, a bed, a stool and other things that mark the room as 'normal,' when in its upright position. In each room a dancer moves around, starting in a position that still supports the illusion of a 'normal' room. Later, when the dancers move away from the ground, it becomes clear that something is wrong. The dancers seem to be free from gravity in some moments, or the quality of their movements does not respond to gravity the right way. In this film the choreography defines the perception of space. Here, in contrast to *INEARTHIA,* the dancers' movements are designed to reveal that gravity is not pulling on them as in normal life. Some moments give an illusion of freedom from gravity. Throughout the film the viewer receives the movements as strange, realizing that their quality is not guided by gravity in a normal way. Since the room looks perfectly normal, perception is tricked.

It can be said that the (different) point(s) of view, framing, and perspective in a film affect how dance is seen. For example, movements seem bigger or smaller, depending on the framing. They look flatter or more three-dimensional, depending on the point of view. Movements that almost couldn't be seen in a live performance can be focused on. And, it is possible to separate movements by turning the picture and thus loosening the standards for the perception of gravity.

Split Screen

As mentioned earlier, film can show more than one perspective at a time. This often is achieved by the use of split screen. By dividing the screen into two, three, four or more parts, each part shows a different picture. A movement can be shown, for example, in three points of view presented next to each other. In *Der Brief* by Alec Kinnear (choreography by Ingeborg Tichy-Luger and Simona Noja) split screen is used to present the dance in different views from different distances. One part of the screen always shows a room and a dancer in full view. Simultaneously, another part of the screen shows changing pictures of closer perspectives of the same dance. While the camera shooting the full view stays in one spot all the time, the other camera sometimes moves with the dancer. The images presented in the different parts of the screen thus differ in distance to the dancer and in the dynamic of the camera itself. The same dance can be perceived as close and far away at the same time. Movements can be observed in whole picture and in detail. In *Divigations dans une chamber d'hôtel (Me and my choreographer in 63)* split screen is used to show a dancer simultaneously from right, left and frontally. The movements he performs are exactly the same movements in the three parts of the picture. So, there must have been three cameras shooting the dance at once, from three points of view. This usage of the split screen is interesting, because it creates its own new choreography. If the dancer moves to the front, from one camera's viewpoint it looks like he is moving to the left. But from the other camera's viewpoint it looks as if he moves to the right. The cameras' arrangement makes it possible for the dancer to leave the frame of two cameras while staying within the frame of the third. Or, conversely, he can leave the picture shot by one camera and stay within the frame of the other two. So if the three images are juxtaposed, the dancer enters and leaves some parts of the screen, as if the choreography is about leaving and entering. In fact, a dance between the three pictures of the split screen comes into being.

DecSurveillance (2005) by Caroline Bridges and Dom Breadmore (choreography by C. Bridges) uses split screen in a narrative way. In a reference to monitoring systems, where the video technique was developed, the screen is split in four parts. Each shows a different room in the same building. Some images have titles like 'lift' or 'corridor,' giving the impression they were shot by monitoring cameras. The film presents a story of a woman and a man meeting in the building. A sexual tension arises between them, and the building's watchman follows them. The meeting, as well as the chase, is danced, so the dance has the function of telling the story. Also, the way the cameras/viewpoints, individually and combined, are used becomes part of the narrative. The viewer constantly sees more than one perspective and more than one room. Therefore, s/he knows more than the people in the story. The images help the viewer anticipate when the characters will meet. So, here, split screen functions as more than a way to show dance from different perspectives. In fact, the use of different cameras gives dance a meaning in this film.

Another narrative use of the split screen is seen in *Dos Ambientos* (2004) by Rodrigo Pardo.[20] In this film two images are placed next to each other. One shows the situations that inspired the choreographer to create certain movements of a dance. The other shows the choreography as it later comes out. So the two parts of the screen show two levels of choreography: the progress and the source of inspiration on one hand, and the final product on the other.

To recap, the choice of perspective (point of view and framing) influences the perception of space and of dance, especially regarding the dynamics of the movement. The change between different perspectives can manipulate the dynamics of the dance as well. Close-ups can show specific movements or moments of a movement in more detail. This gives a more intense impression of, but might also block out other parts of, the choreography (or the movement). Split screen offers the possibility to show more than one perspective at a time. This in turn means the viewer can choose which picture to look at when. This combination gives a richer picture of the dance than only one point of view possibly could.

TIME

Movement always unfolds in time. If the timing of a movement is changed, its quality also changes. Film can manipulate the natural course of filmed movement, whether by slowing it down, by accelerating it or by reversing it. Slowing down a movement gives the opportunity to look more closely at the moving body. When a jump is filmed and shown in slow motion, it is possible to observe the body, its posture in the air and its tension, in detail. Moreover, slow motion changes the impression one has when observing the jump. A jump is something that can't be executed slowly. As the body is always pulled back on earth by the force of gravity, the sloweddown version of a jump seems like a moment of freedom from gravitation. This can be interpreted as dreamlike, or as an enhancement of the abilities of the dancer. The acceleration of a movement can have the same effect (moving quickly is a sign of virtuosity). But the impression that arises is completely different, as it often reminds the audience of slapstick humor. A good example of this can be seen in *Car Men* (2006) by NDT/Jiří Kylián.[21] Moreover, the speeding up of a movement tends to call on connotations of passing time in a narrative way (as in *Car Men*, and *Ex Ex Ex No 1* (2005) by Michele Arena).

A special case of manipulating time is the use of reversal. As a setoff for a jump is reversed, it looks similar to a landing. But it doesn't look exactly the same as a landing, since the tension of the body is different. Maya Deren uses this technique in *A Study in Choreography for the Camera*.[22] A movement clearly dependent on gravity (for example falling to the ground), when reversed, looks wrong or false: it is impossible to go against gravity. *Ex Ex Ex No1* has a scene where a man seems to slide over a balustrade, feet up, his pelvis and body hanging on one side of the balustrade. He is not holding himself with his hands or pushing off the ground, so it looks impossible for him to go upwards over the balustrade. Nonetheless, this is how the scene looks (actually he is falling or gliding down with his pelvis first to the ground, but the reversed version shows him going up). This causes the movement to look strange. Not only does it seem impossible for the movement to be realized, the quality is affected. It looks crooked in a way, because the natural flow is gone. The same effect can be found in a scene of the videodance *Car Men*. Here, a woman dances, holding a shawl/drapery/cloth in one hand. In 'normal' timing the motion of the cloth follows her moving arms. The film shows this in reverse. It looks as if the woman's movement follows that of the cloth. The cloth in turn seems to have a life of its own. The quality of the movement is changed. With that comes a change of how the movement operates and 'feels' to the viewer. Therefore, manipulation of timing can result in a narrative reading. Or, the movement becomes unfamiliar, changing its quality (often related to gravity).

BODY

The body is the *raw material* of dance. So, if the body is changed by film, the quality of the dance is changed too. This can happen in many different ways. Computer-based postproduction offers thousands of technical tricks and effects that can be used to manipulate every picture of a film. Therefore, it is impossible to mention all possibilities. The effects I discuss represent various ways to treat the body or the perception of dance movements. The following classifications represent an overview of the variety of manipulations of the body in film. Manipulations can work directly on the body's form. They can give the body a different look. They can extend its abilities visually, or visualize the flow of a movement.

To start with, I will give examples of techniques giving the body a different look. Working with a bluescreen/blueprint is a technique frequently used to show people in an environment they have occupied.[23] The information of one film is copied into the picture of another film and the two layers blend into one. If the illusion of the person being in that environment is maintained, this effect works the same way as previously discussed in **Space**. Still, there are differences in the impression caused when for example the quality of the movement doesn't match the ground on which it seems to be performed. Rolling on the floor can be performed easily on a flat ground. Filming this movement and copying it into the picture of a rocky desert makes the ground appear uneven and rolling on the floor in this new context would be painful. The movement looks odd and unreal, even if the illusion of a person being in that environment works on a superficial level.

LAYERING

Besides this 'normal' use of the technique that keeps the illusion alive, two layers of film can be put together in a way that doesn't connect with the illusion. I will call this technique 'layering.' For example in *Pod* (Narelle Benjamin, Samuel James) landscapes and detailed pictures of natural grounds (grass, earth...) make up one layer and a second layer shows dancing people. When these two layers come together, they are not designed to fit each other in terms of size or perspective. As a result, the body looks strange, too small. Moreover, the presented space disturbs us. We can't really say where the dancers are: they dance in front or rather between giant blades of grass. The perception of space is changed, as is the way the body is seen.

If the layers are put together in a 'semi-transparent' way, the information of both films/layers can be seen in the same time. For example a person (layer A) in a wood (layer B) is seen standing in the wood. In addition, the trees can be seen on the person's body (in a theater this effect would be caused by projection). Thus, the body blends in with its surroundings. Being integrated in a landscape or another picture gives the person a less human look. This strange appearance of the body works on an associative level. Someone moving softly and fluently, 'layered' by images of flowing water, recalls a fish or aquatic plant.[24] Bodies can be overlaid with texture of rock or other elements like stone, earth, leaves, and sand. That gives rise to associations, and offers a certain quality to the movements of the dancing body.

In *Shakti Rising* by Goa Sanchez (choreography by Julie Barnsley), the sight of rails, seen out of a moving train, is overlaid with the picture of a dancing person. The rails generate a feeling of acceleration. For the spectator, this feeling is projected onto the dance that is seen at the same time. The associations of the non-dance pictures interfere with quality of the dance, thereby changing it (the timing of the dance seems to be changed).

Another example of this can be seen in *4 clips pour aufnahmen* (Nicole Seiler), a videodance-film consisting of four parts. Each part uses layering in a different way. The fourth part, titled 'plug—play,' shows a Barbie puppet overlaid with a dancing woman. Since the dancing woman stays within the body of the Barbie, the Barbie seems to come alive. At the same time, the associations evoked by the puppet influence the perception of the dance the woman performs. Her isolated stiff movements are seen as puppet-like. In these examples the body is always easily recognizable as a human body and doesn't undergo major changes regarding its form. However, film can manipulate the body itself, as I will now describe.

DUPLICATION

As one option, the layering technique can be used to show the same body several times in one picture. The duplicated person can be seen next to himself or herself. One example for this is *Divigations dans une chamber d'hôtel (Me and my choreographer in 63)*. In front of a plain black screen the dancer is seen dancing alone. Or, two images of the same dancer dance synchronously, or seem to dance with each other. Thus, a choreography, which never really occurred, with dancing (same) people is generated. It could be said that bodies are generated in a way they don't exist. The different versions of the dancer sometimes differ greatly in *size*. A huge pair of dancing feet seems to nearly step on a tiny dancer dancing the same steps as the big feet. In the process of postproduction the editor can manipulate the material and create choreographies that didn't exist as such in the process of filming.

DUPLICATING THE BODY

In *Shake Off* (Beenhakker) the dancer is duplicated and interacts with his doubles: Dancer one does a movement that nearly touches dancer two, who reacts and avoids the contact by stepping aside. Later on dancer one jumps over dancer two, dancer three ducks under dancer four and one dancer does a somersault supported by another kneeling dancer. All these dancers are the same person, duplicated. This clearly creates a different effect than the same movements would, when performed by various people. In reality it is simply impossible to interact with oneself like that. The observer knows that what looks real in the film is illusion. The knowledge about the impossibility of what is seen influences the perception of it. Associations are called upon. Is the dancer only imagining himself dancing? Or, is he really dancing, but only imagining his doppelgangers?

Duplicating the body itself also enhances the choreography, as duets, trios or group interactions can be shown with one person dancing. Of course, this changes the dance completely. Again space is affected as well, since the place of a single dancer is only defined by position in space. On the other hand, more dancers always are related to each other. 'Next to,' 'together with,' 'behind' and so on come into being, and these directions tell not only a dancer's position. They also give a meaning to the dance performed by the dancer. A kneeling position can be read as prayer, contemplation, maybe as relaxation, or even just as a part of pure dance movement. In contrast, a kneeling figure *in front of* someone standing brings forth connotations of submission. Duplications of the dancer thus manipulate the perception of the dance. On the one hand, duplication is known to be unreal and causes disturbance on first sight. However, duplication manipulates the choreography and the meaning of the dance movements by modifying a solo to become group choreography. Moreover, altering the size of the dancer's different versions provides additional alternatives for both change of perception and choreography.

Besides the layering structure, more ways of technical manipulation to convert the body exist, especially regarding its form. For example, the picture can be *mirrored* at a certain point. If the body doesn't touch this point, it looks doubled and the movements are mirrored. It gets even more interesting if the body touches this point, because what then can be seen is very strange. The two bodies melt together, building a unity, constituting an odd-looking tangle of human limbs. The part of the body that goes beyond the point of mirroring cannot be seen anymore. Some body parts are missing while others are doubled and glued together in places they normally don't belong. A person seen from the front stands so close to the point of mirroring that the torso is nearly gone, seeming to consist of only arms and legs. One leg grows out of the joint of the other leg and one arm connects to the other arm with no shoulders in between. The limbs seem to originate out of nowhere. It can be easily imagined that a dancing person moving in and out of this mirror image creates a completely new vision of the body. Sometimes the images produced by this method are quite grotesque. However, with its ever-present symmetry, the outcome reminds us of a kaleidoscope and thus it evokes the association of art. The body becomes the material that is being formed by the camera (or to be exact: by postproduction tools). An example for this again can be seen in *Divigations dans une chamber d'hôtel (Me and my choreographer in 63)*. Sometimes the dance here looks like a fight with an invisible person, as out of nowhere a hand is grabbing for the head.

Angelitos Negros by John Crawford (choreography by Donald McKayle) also uses the technique of mirroring. But, another effect is added: the body is reproduced as a drawing in motion. Sometimes the drawing-dancer serves as the shadow of the real dancer. Then again the real dancer is mirrored by the drawing-dancer or the drawing-dancer mirrors itself.

The drawing-dancer also is duplicated, with the different versions of her seen dancing the same routine but with a time-shift (like in a canon). What happens is that a new choreography of drawing-dancers develops out of a single dancer's solo. In addition to time-shifted duplications, the effect of ghosting[25] is applied to the drawing-dancer. Then, a grid/web of lines fills the whole screen. The single body is transformed to a graphic art design. Patterns appear and disappear and the original material of a human body is nearly unrecognizable. The lines become more and more wild, and change color from white/sepia to red. The image looks like a fire, no longer human. This web of lines sometimes functions as a background for the real dancer. So in *Angelitos Negros* many techniques are combined. What emerges is a piece of art that can be seen as dance, and as visual arts as well. The body is mirrored, transformed to a drawing and to a web of lines, so the form of the body is altered in many ways.

Another way of converting the body is the possibility of cross-fading between different persons, so one person dissolves to another person. This can be seen in *Impression 2–female Version* (2009) by Goar Sánchez (choreography by Julie Barnsley). A woman dancing morphs into another woman dancing, and, again, into a third woman dancing. Of course these switches impact the reception of the dance. Every body has its own way of moving and its own expression. The unexpected, transitionless switch from one body to another evokes confusion about the mixture of movement expressions (and of course about the switch between persons: as children we learn the meaning of permanence of objects and human beings). The quicker the switches are made, the more the quality of movement intensifies. A climax is produced that actually does not take place in the movement itself. This can be compared to the example of the rails layered with a dancer, discussed earlier. By morphing the dancers, the body is manipulated and the quality of the dance is affected by the disturbances evoked.

FRAGMENTATION

Another form of manipulating the body is fragmentation. A very simple way of fragmenting the body can be achieved by using bluescreen technique differently than its normal use. Operating with a bluescreen only works if the person doesn't wear blue clothes, since everything blue will be erased in the process of combining the two layers. This can be used the other way around. A person wearing blue trousers is filmed. If this sequence is then assembled with any other background, it looks as if the person doesn't have legs (for example, in *Me and my Choreographer in 63*). This oddness is very disturbing, as the appearance of someone without legs normally is connected with limited mobility. Therefore, the very mobile dancing upper body in a way forms an oxymoron, as it contradicts these connotations.

Fragmenting the body can also be done very systematically, as can be seen in *Excellent Beauty* by the Honey Brothers (choreography by Tom Sapsford). Here, the screen is split, at first in four parts, later in more. On all parts of the screen together one woman is shown dancing. So the different parts of the screen comprise one picture, but the picture seems to have been destroyed and glued together on the wrong spots. Sometimes the timing in part A of the screen is a little different than in part B. Or, a part of the body starts in part A of the screen at the bottom but continues in part B of the screen on the top or in the middle. In other words, the body and its movement are fragmented. But since the observer can put the pieces back together in his mind he will recognize the movement as in one piece. It is like a puzzle, which makes it more challenging to look at the dance than if it were all correctly connected. This way of fragmenting the body is more complex than the first example. In this case the outcome is very much planned by the filmmaker.

ROLE OF COINCIDENCE

Fragmentation of the body can also be achieved by coincidence: Part Three of *Impression 2–female Version* shows dance in layering structure with smoke. White smoke enters the completely black screen from the bottom. Clouds come into being and disperse. After a while a dancing couple appears only where the smoke is, only on the white areas of the screen (inside the clouds). This results in a dreamlike picture of dancers who dissolve with the clearing away of the smoke. The smoke can be interpreted in many ways: the dancers are unreal, in heaven, in a dream, imaginary and so on. In this use of layering, the dancers' bodies become fragmented accidentally, as chance determines the direction and the form of the smoke and clouds. The filmmaker and the choreographer designed the idea and the setting, but can't control the outcome of the filmic product. This means the original choreography cannot be seen as a whole because some movements get lost in the dissolving clouds. The dance is affected by the fragmentation of the body because movements that actually go on might be stopped. Lines the dancing bodies form in space are interrupted and characteristic movements might not be seen at all. As in most of the other examples given, the use of layering here works on two levels. First, the body is fragmented and the dance is manipulated directly. Second, associations aroused give the dancing bodies a different mood and meaning than the dance would have without the additional layer of smoke.

Within the category of manipulations of the body and the dance, I have presented examples of duplications, change of the size or form of the body (for example, by mirroring or reproduction of the body as a drawing), crossfading between different dancers and fragmentation of the body. These examples use the real body as material for the manipulations.

ANIMATED FIGURES

However, it is also possible to work with animated figures instead of real dancers. In *Aletsch piece I* by Alan Sondheim (choreography by Foofwa d'Imobilité) one scene shows two animated figures that seem to be in a constant downfall or floating. They hang in mid-air. Their limbs rotate and move to strange positions. Or, they disappear and come back in a wrong place at the body. Real people could never do that, so the use of animation gives an idea of what dance could be like if humans were not whole and restricted by the form of their body. With examples like this, the question of what is considered dance is tantamount.

CONCLUSION

I think it has become clear by now how many variations of manipulating the body itself, and its look in general, film offers to dance. Moreover, there is a form of manipulation that does not so much treat the body itself, but rather enhances the abilities of the dancing body. As I mentioned earlier, some techniques make it seem as if the dancer has much more power than humanly possible, or as if he can do magic. For example, in *Shake off* the dancer jumps extremely high while his feet move many times, quickly, alternating right leg front and left leg front.[26] This movement takes longer than possible in real life; and, the jump is higher than normal. Perhaps the dancer, whose hands and arms can't be seen during the jump, was holding onto something during the shooting of this sequence. In the film, the dancer seems to have the power to jump extremely high. This is achieved by the simple trick of not showing his complete body (also a means of fragmentation). In the same film the dancer lets himself hang sideways until his body has the shape of a bow. The curve his body builds is very strongly bent and very close to the ground. You cannot see if he is holding himself onto anything. But, there must have been something in the process of shooting: you can clearly see that his center of gravity is way beyond the point where he could hold it with his own power. In *Break* by Shona McCullagh a dancer even hovers some feet above the ground. She also lowers her body close to the ground while staying stiff like a plank. Without taking any support on her hands, this looks like magic. These examples show how filmic presentation of dance can make dancers seem capable of doing otherwise impossible things. In these cases, gravity seems to be overcome by the dancers. This dimension is an expansion and amplification of dance and can only be produced by aid of film. Depending on how it is used in a videodance film, this can function as an upgrade of the dancer's abilities, or can be interpreted in relation to the narration of the film.[27]

There is one way to manipulate the dance that does not really have to do with the body itself, but with the dance movement in space. Although perhaps part of **Space**, it seems more related to the dance and its quality, elements of **Body**: visualization. The energy of a movement or its pattern can be visualized in film. *Wire Frame* (2005) by Oana Suteu (Choreography by Ginette Laurin) gives many examples for the different possibilities to add lines[28] to the film that visualize the energy of the dance. One option is to draw a line along the pattern a part of the body produces in space. When a dancer sways his leg through the air like a fan, the foot draws a circle in space. Normally this circle can't be seen. By using postproduction techniques, a visible line can be added that follows the foot, which seems to paint the line in the air. The same of course can be done on the floor. If someone lying on the floor whips an arm in a circle or snake-like form over the ground, the line drawn can be added. The observer doesn't have to imagine it, but can really see it there. These lines can also be used to show the energy with which a movement is performed. In one scene in *Wire Frame*, the seated dancer, wearing pointe shoes, puts one foot vigorously to the ground, toes first. Since pointe shoes are quite hard in the front this creates a dull noise. In the moment the shoe touches the ground, concentric circles start to emerge around the shoe and spread around the floor. The circles resemble waves that appear on the surface of water when a stone is dropped into a pond. So what happens is that the energy the dancer gives to the ground is visualized. The visualizing of a movement pattern or of the energy of a movement emphasizes special movements.

It also helps the observer to see and recognize these patterns and energies, which can be seen as the essence of the movement. It gives a little more to the dance by enabling the observer to 'feel' more of the movement.

Film's amplifications of dance, whether they transform the body or not, make it look independent from gravity. They also use effects to visualize a movement, give the body and/or the dance a new look that could not be achieved without film. What Dodds says about television could be said about dance and film in general:

> Within television, the body does not constitute a permanent or stable entity, but is transient and unpredictable. [First,]… the televisual apparatus is able to construct dancing bodies that could not be replicated on stage. [Then,]…through the televisual apparatus, the limitations of the material body are radically challenged. Perceptions of what a dancing body can do are extended as the spectator sees bodies defy gravity, travel in slow motion and reverse certain movements, which in reality would be physically impossible. […] Video dance has the capacity to disrupt expectations. It refuses to conform to the capabilities and limitations of the live dancing body, but instead transcends them.[29]

Most of the films I analyzed work on the level of associations and connotations. Meaning is determined through filmic manipulation of the dancing body. This body become larger than life, faster or slower than its motion demands, free of gravity or moving in reverse of regular gravitational pull, and any number of other states of physicality that are thoroughly recontextualized on the film screen. This seemingly inexhaustible range of possibilities that film editing offers choreography extends the choreographer's palette in manifold ways. Film does truly enhance dance on screen, and yet we must remember that without the original movement of actual bodies in live space, these screen transformations would exist only as animated forms rather than the lived flesh and blood of humanity.

NOTES

1. The acceptance of the term 'videodance' is described in Claudia Rosiny, *Videotanz: Panorama einer intermedialen Kunstform* (Zürich: Chronos, 1999), 22. Other terms are: 'choreo-cinema' (Allegra Fuller Snyder, 'Three Kinds of Dance film: A Welcome Clarification,' *Dance Magazine* 39 (September 1965), 34–9, 'screen-choreography,' 'dance for the camera,' 'screen-dance,' and

'dance-screen,' which is also the name of a festival that includes a competition. The category for videodance in this competition is 'Kamera-choreographie.'

2. Many of the films discussed here were shown at the Dance Screen festival (2009) of the International Music and Media Centre (IMZ) in Vienna.

3. I don't mean to analyze the differences in presentation between a live performance and the presentation on a screen in general. Other factors alter spectators' perception of dance as well. These include the minimization to the size of a TV screen and the lack of the third dimension. Other writers have discussed in detail the absence of the unique perceptions a live event arouses in the spectator. Therefore, I will only address the more visual aspects. I will be referring to the content instead of the conditions and the frame.

4. Douglas W. Jessop, *Film and Dance: Interaction and Synthesis* (Boulder: University of Colorado Press, 1975), 20.

5. Sherril Dodds, *Dance on Screen: Genres and Media from Hollywood to Experimental Art* (New York: Palgrave Macmillan, 2001), 80.

6. Most scholars who have written about the topic agree on this definition (for example, Deren, Clarke, Knight, Emshwiller, Lorber, Brooks, Dodds).

7. Maya Deren, 'Film in Progress: Thematic Statement,' *Film Culture* 39 (Winter 1965): 4.

8. Dodds, 57.

9. There are many possibilities to define the different types of filmed dance (see for example, Dodds, Rabenalt, Allen, Rosiny, Snyder, or the catalogue of the International Music and Media Centre).

10. See http://www.danshans.com/shakeoff.html

11. For *Moving Stillness* see her homepage http://www.wiebke-poepel.de/

12. For *Give Me a Break*, see http://vimeo.com/12357457

13. Trailer of *The Rain* available at http://www.lidberg.se/pontus/works/

14. Clips of *Afternoon of the Chimeras* at http://www.rhodopsin.ca/films_en.html

15. See *ECORChE* by Claire Thiébault at http://vimeo.com/32836175

16. *One Flat Thing Reproduced* at http://www.youtube.com/watch?v=cufauMezz_Q

17. *Glass Perpx* at http://www.berlinale-talents.de/bt/project/ profile/26960
18. See *Inearthia* at https://vimeo.com/32709227
19. For *Weightless* see http://www.erikajanunger.com/#post39
20. For *Dos Ambientos*, see http://rodrigopardo.com/dosambientes. html
21. *Car Men* at https://www.youtube.com/watch?v=H5Ne_AJJEQA
22. Maya Deren/Talley Beatty at https://www.youtube.com/ watch?v=OnUEr_gNzwk
23. Bluescreen works like this: A person is filmed in front of a blue backdrop. A computer program erases everything blue, so the body is cut out and then pasted in front (so visually inside) any other surrounding.
24. Another example for this is *Flux* by Candida Elton.
25. In the section 'help' of the homepage of Adobe referring to the editing software Premiere this effect is explained: 'The Ghosting effect overlays transparencies of the immediately preceding frames on the current frame. This effect can be useful, for example, when you want to show the motion path of a moving object, such as a bouncing ball.' http://help.adobe.com/en_US/PremiereElements/7.0/ WSD05CB94E-7080-453e-8D32-0355B3B0ECFF. html#WSF88D1F54-4859-43a9-A698-B69833C79B39
26. This jump is known as *entrechat* or *batterie* in classical ballet terminology. The higher a dancer jumps and the quicker he is, the more he changes the stretched feet from fifth position right leg front, to fifth position left leg front. So the number of changes is an indication of his virtuosity.
27. *Break* (2004) by Shona McCullagh is an example for using manipulations of gravity in a narrative way. See http://thearts.co.nz/ artist_page.php&aid=64&type=video&video_id=113
28. The use of the lines is very much like the lines in Forsythe's DC-Rom Improvisation Technologies (DVD of the year 2000) at http://www.youtube.com/user/GrandpaSafari
29. Dodds, *Dance on Screen*, 78ff, 99.

CHAPTER 11

Maya Deren: Leaping Across Frames and Framing Leaps

Telory D. Arendell

It was like a crack letting the light of another world gleam through. I kept saying to myself, 'The walls of this room are solid except right there. That leads to something. There's a door there leading to something. I've got to get it open because through there I can go someplace instead of leaving here by the same way that I came in.' And so I did, prying at it until my fingers were bleeding...[1]

Maya Deren pried at the doors of cinematic convention until they opened enough to let the light of alternate realities stream seductively across her visionary thresholds. She was one of many artists making work in the period following the Second World War: they tried to reproduce in visual images the sense of disorientation and distortion that American society experienced in response to wartime atrocities overseas. Deren employed various surrealist film techniques and experimented with the weight and suspension principles used by choreographers such as Martha Graham, Doris Humphrey, and Katherine Dunham. Deren made films structured like dreams that defied both psychological symbolism and psychoanalytic interpretation. Her camera lens acted as a dancer, paired in a *pas de deux* with the images it captured. Her films were cinedances or choreocinematic endeavors in which the 'dance and the camera collaborate[d] on the creation of a single work of art.'[2]

T.D. Arendell (✉)
Department of Theatre and Dance, Missouri State University, Springfield, MO, USA

© The Editor(s) (if applicable) and The Author(s) 2016
T.D. Arendell, R. Barnes (eds.), *Dance's Duet with the Camera*,
DOI 10.1057/978-1-137-59610-9_11

DREAM LOGIC: SURREALISTS VERSUS IMAGISTS

Although Deren's avant-garde films use surreal cinematic principles of montage and dream sequence, Deren had an agenda that differed from that of the surrealists. Rather than using abstract dream imagery to convey symbolic meanings, Deren believed that the language of film and the language of the unconscious were separate but parallel forces. Film should not be psychologically interpreted in terms of symbolic meanings:

> I had in mind something different from montage as it was developed by Eisenstein. His use of images and the relating of them by cutting, was symbolic in purpose… When I bring two images together, it is not because of a symbolic relation between them. I do so rather, in the effort to create a new reality by creating, actually, a functioning relationship between them.[3]

Reading dreams and films from a semiotic perspective outside the context of the dream or film itself seemed to Deren a violation of these images. For her, the film and the dream each had their own semiotic systems; they made sense of images in a totally different way than either verbal language or psychoanalytic interpretation. Divorcing herself from Symbolist labels, Deren chose to identify herself instead as an Imagist:

> For the Symbolist, the image is an element only in a synthesis built up out of a succession of images; for the Imagist, the image is the synthesis itself of the thought and emotion; the direct communication of the synthesized experience. For the Symbolist, the image is a point of departure for mysterious distances, whereas the Imagist departure is limited to the vision behind the word or image.[4]

Deren has expressed a certain inability to 'talk' about her films. It is as if her films speak their own language and to properly talk about them would involve showing them and letting them speak for themselves. Abstract dance of the late 1930s, early 1940s in America worked in much the same way. This is perhaps what drew Deren to the dance medium and prompted her to try to combine the languages of dance and film. Playwrights working in this period such as Genet and Ionesco also played with the idea of letting images speak for themselves in their own language. They even treated words as if they were images, or objects in the theatrical space:

> We must remember that Ionesco sees language—words—as fully analogous to things. A stage full of empty yet 'heavy' (tangible) noise is certainly *full*,

in the literal sense of the word… In fact, words and things are both full and empty at the same time. They 'fill' space and time, and yet they signify nothingness, they represent an emptiness… a 'bulky emptiness.'[5]

The weight of Deren's filmic images resembles the weight of Ionesco's words. Both fill space but are intended to signify nothing outside of themselves. This feeling of 'bulky emptiness' is one that occurs frequently in Deren's films in slow-motion shots where 'she creates movement with "impossible" spatial and temporal negotiations [in order to distance] the viewer from such a visceral sensation, calling attention, in fact, to its lack.'[6] Perhaps in Deren's mind, this 'lack' or hollowness allowed each image to be filled in by the individual spectator's unconscious cognitive processes, the way a sleeper's mind fills the empty images of a dream.

Both her use of slow-motion sequences and the juxtaposition of frames are techniques that rely heavily on the structure of dream logic. Here, a single actor/dancer moves from one threshold through several other incongruent ones to land in a completely different context. In Deren's filmscape, we are always on a threshold, forever caught in liminal spaces as the camera arranges memories in dreamtime. Memory itself works a bit like a camera: taking mental pictures during the day of image after image, the mind's camera reorders these pictures in the unconscious at night to produce an entirely new sequence of events. This rearrangement in turn makes room for many new meanings by juxtaposing incongruent pictures.

MEANING AND ANALYSIS

I say 'meaning' rather hesitantly. Deren would no doubt stop me to explain in detail the difference between looking for meaning in art and looking for the arrangement of images which produce a piece of art. In a sense, she multiplies meaning, or makes room for multiple meanings in this distinction. A dream can be interpreted in many different ways; Freudian and Jungian analysis proved two examples of possible lenses for interpretation. However, Deren was highly invested in discarding these particular lenses to revise the unconscious on its own terms. She wanted the lens she looked through to be a mechanism of the unconscious, yet her own process of filming and editing was a highly conscious practice.

Some film theorists posit film itself as a visual dreamscape in which '"… our sense of space is somehow bracketed or held in suspense… We do not situate ourselves where we see ourselves to be." Such an "alienated space" is similar to that in dreams.'[7] In this respect, '...our experience as dreamers may have prepared us for the style and operation of film.'[8] So if film is already inherently bound to dream structure, it follows that Deren's attempts to make films borrowing form and structure from dream states created dreams within dreams. This may explain why the only identification possible on the part of the spectator of her work is an alienated identification.

FRAMING THE BODY

In Deren's 1944 silent film *At Land*,[9] alienation is achieved on a number of different levels. The film starts with an image of ocean waves hitting an expanse of beach, a fairly conventional image; however, Deren has already begun her 'deconstruction of physical reality'[10] by showing the footage in reverse—these waves are rolling backwards. The next shot we see is of Deren's body washed up on shore, unmoving and covered with sand. Her eyes appear glazed over, as if she is a corpse. This still shot, filmed in close-up and focused on Deren's sandy face, seems like a modernist forerunner to Cindy Sherman's postmodern images: women's corpses covered with garden dirt, sand, and various pieces of garbage. With Sherman's work, we don't get to see the 'next frame,' so her corpses remain lifeless, still-deaths. With Deren, however, one image never remains still for very long. The next shot of *At Land* shows her body in the same position on the beach, but cleaned up, eyes lively, curious.

CONTEXTUAL MELDING

Deren reaches out of this sandy frame into a series of shots where she climbs up a large piece of driftwood. Driftwood branches frame her face, creating a conscious frame within a frame. The next leap takes her from the driftwood to a formal dinner setting; her face peeks up from underneath one end of the long dinner table like a child banished from her parents' dinner party and too curious to remain in bed. As her arms reach to pull her torso up onto the table, the next shot shows us her feet pushing off of the beach's driftwood. Not only has Deren the actress reached from one environment to another; Deren the filmmaker has made sure that we remember the juxtaposition of these realities by letting the lower-body push from the driftwood scene propel her upper body into the dinner party scene. 'The fusion of the two images creates a new cinematic meaning not belonging to either image, but to their manipulated combination.'[11]

In this brief flipping back and forth between environments and body parts, Deren's body has spanned two vastly incongruous settings. These settings are incongruous both in terms of social definition and geographical location. This sense of reaching from one physical location to another completely unrelated setting in the space of two juxtaposed shots is a method Deren employs in a number of her films:

> The central character of these films moved in a universe which was not governed by the material, geographical laws of *here* and *there* as distant places, mutually accessible only by considerable travel. Rather, he moved in a world of imagination in which, as in our day or night-dreams, a person is first one place and then another without traveling between. It was a choreography in space, except that the individual moved naturalistically, as far as the body movements were concerned.[12]

Deren skips across geographical locations as one might span epochs in a time machine. Once up on the dinner table, she crawls down the length of it. She prowls like a panther while the guests take no notice of her and continue their conversation with each other as if she were invisible. Her dinner table prowling is intercut with images of her crawling through dense foliage. These images in tandem draw an absurdist parallel between dinner parties and jungles, forming a fairly clear metaphorical commentary on the rigors of socializing while highlighting Deren's position as an un-socialized creature. As Deren approaches a chessboard at the opposite end of the table, the guests abruptly leave, and Deren is left alone, staring at the board. The chess pieces begin to move of their own accord, Deren focuses on them intently, as if moving them telepathically; they, like the dinner party guests, are pawns in a game of her own making.

WHITE CHESS PIECE

Suddenly a white chess piece rolls off the board and slips through a perfectly round hole in a rock to be washed downstream. Once again, the edge of the table marks an imaginary boundary between an interior domestic space and the natural outdoors, Deren's body is pulled from indoors out in pursuit of the chess piece, no doors necessary for this passage. She climbs rocks to follow the ocean-bound object and ends up not by the ocean but on a country road. This she walks along alone for a while until suddenly a male companion joins her. The two of them have a conversation wherein only one of them is visible at a time. Each time the camera switches back to the man, a new man has taken his place. Deren seems unfazed by this substitution and continues to talk silently as if to the same man. It is unclear whether these men are Deren's various fantasies or are a composite of 'everyman.' The last of these characters leads her to a run-down abandoned cottage that she climbs under in order to make her way inside. The inside, however, looks nothing like the outside of this building. Inside is a well-painted, high-class room. The furniture in this room is covered with sheets, as if the room has just been painted. Under one of these sheets is a man, who is lying on a bed, watching Deren as she watches him. He is completely still, as Deren was while lying on the beach in the first few shots. What is odd about this particular connection is that every time the camera moves to Deren's face, the light on her face moves in the pattern light makes on objects when reflected off of water. This is yet another conflation of indoor/outdoor images.

Deren leaves the man to walk through the rest of the house. She opens and closes many doors, framing herself in multiple doorways reminiscent of the doorframes in *Ritual in Transfigured Time* (1946). One door finally leads her straight out onto a high enclave of rocks. There is no transition here either. One minute she is indoors, the next she appears on top of a large rock mountain. As a spectator, this first moment on the rock is exhilarating; it is a moment of intense shock and pleasure, the sort of pleasure that comes in the pure surprise of finding something breathtaking unexpectedly. Yet for Deren, this moment is disorienting. This is the only time in the film when her character seems surprised, even disgruntled by the abrupt change in environment. Taken aback, Deren falls off this rock, reaching from frame to frame in order to grab hold of the nearest surface and reorient herself. This fall combines the suspended weight and exaggerated extension of Talley Beatty's marathon leap in *A Study in Choreography for the Camera* (1945) and the slow-motion gravity distortion of Deren's fall down a flight of stairs in *Meshes of the Afternoon*. When she reaches solid ground again, she runs away, crossing dunes of sand that resemble the curves of a woman's body.

MULTIPLE SELVES

The next clip shows Deren collecting rocks on the beach. The more she collects, the more the rocks fall, but she is persistent until something outside of the camera frame catches her eye. She drops the rocks and goes to look at this scene from the very edge of the frame, as if the camera frame itself is some sort of a doorway or threshold that she can see across but we, as viewers, cannot. What she has been looking at becomes the next shot as we see two women in formal eveningwear, presumably two women from the original dinner party, sitting at a small table on the beach playing chess. At first, when Deren approaches these women, they appear not to see her; she is invisible, as she was in the dinner party scene. She stands watching them with the same intent look she had displayed while watching the chess pieces move on the dinner table board.

The film cuts to another Deren figure watching both herself and the two women on the beach from a higher perspective atop a rocky hill. When we cut back to the Deren figure on the beach, she has switched positions, as has one of the two other women. Now all three of them are on one side of the chessboard. Deren stands behind them stroking their hair as all three women tilt their heads sunward, looks of pure pleasure on their faces. Suddenly Deren breaks out of this sun fantasy moment to assume her earlier intent focus on the chessboard. The women don't notice as she reaches between them to steal back the white chess piece she had lost earlier in the film. This sense of the protagonist's sharp focus foregrounded against a dreamy social scene is reminiscent of the protagonist Rita Christiani in *Ritual in Transfigured Time*: she searches for someone through a mass of socializers, drawing the camera's focus as if she were the only real figure in the scene. As this sharper focus Deren character runs down the beach with the stolen chess piece, the two women and her former hair-stroking character watch her go, but make no attempt to follow her.

MESHES AND MULTIPLES

Deren runs the length of the beach, this flight intercut with her various other selves: the Deren atop the rocky cliff who surveys the beach scene, the Deren collecting rocks on the beach, the Deren stroking the beach women's hair, even the driftwood Deren from the beginning of the film. There is a sense here that all of these previous Derens are watching the Deren who has stolen the chess piece as she makes tracks down the beach:

> *At Land*'s multiple selves occupy contiguous spaces rather than a single space, and they provide the continuity for a series of eye-line matches that direct the narrative's activity. When each self gazes off-screen followed by

her subjective point of view of herself in another location, the woman now becomes both the originator and the object of her own gaze.[13]

This sort of split personality is a trope that Deren uses in several of her films, the most obvious example being her signature film, *Meshes of the Afternoon* (1943). In this film, Deren as the protagonist enters her home and falls asleep, dreaming of various selves. Rather than having these selves comment on each other from within separate frames, as in *At Land*, here Deren has these various selves converge at a dining room table as if to meet and make plans for the murder of the sleeping self. These Derens can all see each other within one bounded frame space. This split self in the two films allows Deren to be both observer and observed within the context of the film and outside of it; as both filmmaker and filmed character:

> In many of her early films, Deren appears as a central character, assuming the split position of filmmaker and actor. In her first film, *Meshes of the Afternoon* (1943), she is the woman who watches herself enter the house of her lover, explore it tentatively, then fall into a deep sleep, dreaming of her own suicide. *At Land* (1944) charts a similarly self-reflective journey through a variety of landscapes... Through the eye of the camera Deren is the constant observer; within the frame she is always the observed... In both *Meshes of the Afternoon* and *At Land*, Deren's cinematic self is literally split into different aspects: one watches; the other(s) act.[14]

This constant relocation of self allows Deren to escape what E. Ann Kaplan and various other feminist film theorists have termed 'the male gaze.'[15] She is both observer and observed, and doubly so as filmmaker/actor and protagonist/split-selves. This dual position as watcher/watched allows Deren to make what postmodern theorists can recognize as a subversive statement about the act of looking, the politics of the gaze. However, it is not at all clear what Deren's own politics in using this trope of multiple personality were at the time she was filming. I am assuming, in keeping with the rest of her writings about methodology and practice, that her main reason for using this trope was to highlight the feeling a dreamer has mid-dream; she is both in her body and outside of her body within the dreamscape. That is to say, a dreamer can become various selves that are 'othered' as well as watching these other selves from the body that is realistically known as 'self.' This multiplicity of selves echoes Deren's desire to posit a multiplicity of possible meanings for her films.

The final series of shots in *At Land* brings Deren back to the dinner party scene, chess piece in hand. The party people are milling around this time, and still appear not to notice Deren's presence. This time, Deren walks among them as more of a social pariah than an un-socialized other. She pauses by the chessboard, debating whether to return the missing chess piece. The next shot shows her figure disappearing down the beach, a continuation of the original flight from the beach chess table. We are left to assume that the chess piece was never returned.

A Turn Against Psychoanalysis

To illustrate the point Deren has tried to make about how not to read her films, I would like to cite the interpretation of writer Jacqueline Smetak. This author reads the chess piece as a highly symbolic object that refers to female sexuality:

> 'At Land' (1944) may be seen as an allegory about a woman, newly emerged or born from the sea, empowering herself by snatching the symbol of power, a chess piece. 'At Land' is, however, problematic because the woman (played by Deren, which would encourage a confusion between the fictive woman and the artist herself) snatches power from other women. If the chess piece is taken to have erotic significance—it is phallic—this would lead to a reading that would see the power of Eros, for women, as essentially matrilineal. Feminine sexuality... is something women get from, earn from, learn from other women who, given the configuration of the characters in this scene, guard rather than share the secret. It is not, in other words, a power to be taken lightly, nor is it easily obtained. The snatching of the chess piece may thus be taken as an initiation ritual, the second birth of the woman first born from the sea.[16]

I would venture to say that if Deren had the opportunity to read this, she would either be doubled over laughing or ranting about the narrow-minded interpretations of viewers who refuse to approach her work without some sort of psychoanalytic lexicon in tow. Her first argument might have been with Smetak's statement that Deren's role as protagonist encouraged a confusion/conflation of character and artist. Granted, Deren was very aware of casting herself as both protagonist and filmmaker, but my guess is that her intent was not to conflate these roles; rather, she wanted to use this doubling as yet another aspect of dream-self multiplicity. Deren's second argument would undoubtedly be in response to Smetak's Symbolist reading of the 'phallic' chess piece; the women in this film must secretly 'guard' it as the instrument of a ritual second birth. Again, I can hear Deren's laughter. My own reading of the beach scene with the two dinner party women recalls this interaction as a sensual female pleasure in sunbathing and caressing other women. This exists wholly outside of any notion of phallic symbols or male desire. If anything, the chess piece seems like an instrument of social rather than sexual power. It is the chess piece that brings Deren's beach selves in and out of indoor social settings. It functions not so much as a symbol but rather as a key to doors opening onto radically juxtaposed realities, a motivation for movement.

PHYSICAL MEMORY AND RELATIONAL GRAVITY

The camera itself in all of Deren's films remains forever faithful to the impetus of movement. 'We respond to the camera's actions and to the objects it finds through our own bodies.'[17] So much emphasis has been placed on space and time distortions in the movement of Deren's characters; as spectators we are both distanced by this surreal motion and drawn further into the film space by it. We are given a choice early on of either rejecting this new sense of gravity and speed, or letting our bodies absorb this illogical kinesthesia. If we choose this second option, we must be dreamers traveling along with Deren. From one unrelated juxtaposition to the next, '…we connect the parallels through our physical memory. Much of the camera's movement draws us into its path and rhythm.'[18] We follow the lens not knowing what to expect but filled with the suspense of this ignorance. We want to open doors that lead us into absurd dream-logic realities. We are another Deren self, watching from within our own frame. 'To the soul lacking an exit, the world thus turns into a succession of fleeting phenomena. And so does time waver: memories and current events fuse with each other.'[19]

Deren offsets not only the strictures of time, but also the impact of relational gravity. In effect, film techniques aided these efforts to distort space and time. One of Deren's husbands, filmmaker Alexander 'Sasha' Hammid, explains in retrospect: 'Since Maya had experience with dancing, she wanted to use film to express dance ideas in a new way by using the film technique, if anything, to free the dancer from gravity so that the dancer would seem to be floating by his own power.'[20] Her fellow artists in the 1940s and 1950s gave her much credit for these early forays into filmic portrayal of dancing forms. One of her dancers, Chao-Li Chi, confirms that 'Maya would film [movement], cut it, [and] she re-edited it, doubled it, reversed it, so that it became a continuous interplay between her and the raw movement.'[21] Part of this continuous interplay flux in Deren's pieces relies entirely on a slow-motion format interspersed with tempos that feel more live. 'What is important in a motion picture camera,' Deren tells us, 'is of course its motor. Just remember that motion picture is a time form, just as the telescope reveals the structure of matter in a way that the unaided eye can never see it, so slow motion reveals the structure of motion. Events that occur rapidly, so that they seem a continuous flux, are revealed in slow motion to be full of pulsations and agonies and indecisions and repetitions.'[22] In effect, motion in a slower speed has no room to hide. It is in its truest form, at its most basic level. It forces us to recalibrate our perception of moving pictures.

CONCLUSION

As Deren strove to pry open the cracks of various soul exits, base structures, metaphorical doors to alternate realities, so, too, do spectators strive to place themselves in Deren's virtual dream space. Deren's camerawork caresses the bodies and landscapes it touches, leaving its viewers seduced and slightly disoriented. Her films seem to posit an unconscious whose reorientation or recontextualization of images is a continuous disorientation. Her dreamers can never quite be sure of setting foot on solid ground. We arise from her work in the haze of a waking dream. We try unsuccessfully to remember the exact order of her moving pictures but are confident that our memories of these images will return them to us reordered within our own dreams. If I had been more true to Deren's cause, I would perhaps have written this chapter as a series of juxtaposed thoughts and images, letting the reader make her own kinesthetic sense of the dreamlike sequence. Yet as Deren would probably argue, each medium has its own language. Therefore to film, dreams; to the academy, prose.

NOTES

1. Maya Deren in *The Legend of Maya Deren: A Documentary Biography and Collected Works*, ed. Veve Clark, Millicent Hodson, and Caterina Neiman (New York: Anthology Film Archives/Film Culture, 1988), 99.
2. John Martin, dance critic for the *New York Times*, as quoted in *The Legend of Maya Deren*, 286.
3. Deren, 247.
4. Deren as quoted in Jan Millsapps, 'Maya Deren, Imagist,' *Literature and Film Quarterly* 14.1 (1986): 25.

5. Richard Schechner, 'The Inner and the Outer Reality,' *Tulane Drama Review* 7:3 (1963): 196–7.
6. Leslie Satin, 'Movement and the Body in Maya Deren's *Meshes of the Afternoon,' Women and Performance: A Journal of Feminist Theory* 6:2 (1993): 47.
7. Robert Eberwein, *Film & the Dream Screen: A Sleep and a Forgetting* (Princeton: Princeton University Press, 1985), 45.
8. F.E. Sparshott, 'Vision and Dream in the Cinema,' *Philosophic Exchange* 1 (1971): 120–1.
9. *At Land*, like most of Deren's film output, can be found online at various sites. See At Land (1944)—Maya Deren—YouTube. webarchive.
10. Satin, 52.
11. Millsapps, 27.
12. Deren, 265.
13. Lauren Rabinovitz, *Points of Resistance: Women, Power & Politics in the New York Avant-garde Cinema, 1943–1971* (Chicago: University of Illinois Press, 1st edn, 1991), 66. This book is now in its second edition with the University of Illinois Press (March 2003).
14. Jeanette DeBouzek, 'Maya Deren: A Portrait of the Artist as Ethnographer,' *Women and Performance: A Journal of Feminist Theory* 11 (1992): 13.
15. See E. Ann Kaplan's article, 'Is the Gaze Male?,' in her *Women and Film: Both Sides of the Camera* (London: Methuen, 1983), 35.
16. Jacqueline Smetak, 'Continuum or Break?,' *New Orleans Review* 17:4 (1990): 92–3.
17. Satin, 51.
18. Satin, 50.
19. Siegfried Kracauer, 'Filming the Subconscious,' *Theatre Arts* 32 (1948): 37–8.
20. Alexander Hammid, in Martina Kudláček's *In the Mirror of Maya Deren* (2003 original film in Austria/Switzerland/Germany, 2004 DVD: Zeitgeist Films Ltd).
21. Chao-Li Chi, actor/dancer and Tai-Chi instructor, soloist for Deren's *Meditation on Violence* (1948) as shown in Martina Kudláček's *In the Mirror of Maya Deren* (2004).
22. Documentary sound lecture recorded in Kudláček's *In the Mirror of Maya Deren* (2004).

CHAPTER 12

Valentine for Dance Historians: Astaire on Film

Carol-Lynne Moore

Until the advent of photography, cinematography, and practicable dance notation, dance was an 'artifact poor' art. Performances of famous dancers and the masterpieces of renowned choreographers were seldom recorded in coherent visual form. Dance historians, consequently, have been forced to work from fragmentary traces. It has been possible to read about great works and past performances. But it has not been possible to *see* them other than in some reconstructed or re-imagined form.

The opposite is the case with Fred Astaire. A veteran of vaudeville and the concert stage, Astaire was at the height of his powers when he moved to Hollywood. His best work was recorded and remains available for all students of dance and film to see. Moreover, Astaire exercised considerable control over how his work was recorded. In this sense he is a wonderful 'test case.' It is possible with Astaire to do what is nearly impossible with other dancers. Film makes it possible to track the development of his style during the two decades of his Hollywood career.

This essay, then, is an experiment in dance history, employing longitudinal sampling to illuminate the unique and inimitable 'Astaire style.' It begins by examining the uneasy relationship between film, movement, and dance, and then shows how Astaire handled these difficulties. Discussion proceeds to the examination of three solos: one from early in Astaire's film

C.-L. Moore (✉)
MoveScape Center Director, Denver, CO, US

© The Editor(s) (if applicable) and The Author(s) 2016
T.D. Arendell, R. Barnes (eds.), *Dance's Duet with the Camera*,
DOI 10.1057/978-1-137-59610-9_12

career, one in the middle of his career, and one from his final starring role in a movie musical. Movement analysis is juxtaposed with critical and historical views of Astaire's work, illuminating the essence of his artistic style.

FILM, MOVEMENT, AND DANCE: AN UNEASY RELATIONSHIP

The earliest attempts to capture movement on film can be traced to the 'instantaneous photographs' and 'chronophotography' experiments of the late 1800s that predate the invention of cinematography. Photographic records of human and animal movement, notably those of Eadweard Muybridge, Étienne-Jules Marey, and Thomas Eakins, opened people's eyes to action images never seen before, stimulating artistic and philosophical debate. Some artists were quick to appropriate this photographic evidence, altering their work in keeping with the newly-revealed images of motion. As Taft notes, 'Frederic Remington, one of the most celebrated depicters of the horse, soon adopted a mode of representing a horse in motion that bore a remarkable resemblance to a Muybridge photo.'[1]

Other artists, such as Auguste Rodin, objected to such visual appropriations. While admitting that the photographs were scientifically accurate, these artists also observed that the instantaneous photographs 'produced a curiously static effect' by lifting a single movement out of its temporal context.[2] What was lost was the progressive development of action, the continuity and flow that are the essence of movement.

The philosopher Henri Bergson concurred with this artistic criticism, using the portrayal of a marching regiment as an example. He proposed taking a series of snapshots of the passing parade. These instantaneous views could be projected rapidly, one after the other, to reconstitute the mobility of the marching group. Nevertheless, he notes, if we had to make do with the snapshots alone, 'however much one might look at them we should never see them animated: with immobility set beside immobility, even endlessly, we could never make movement.'[3]

Indeed, the first silent films captured movement only imperfectly, due to the limited number of frames per second that effectively cut out part of each action and broke up the continuity of the motion. The result was comedic, lending itself to later dance spoofs such as Charles Weidman's 'Flickers,' a romping send-up of silent films. Cinematography rapidly improved, of course, but Bergson's comments on the essence of movement remain salient and particularly apt when it comes to filming dance. For as he notes,

> it is not the 'states,' single snapshots we have taken once again along the course of change, that are real; on the contrary, it is flux, the continuity of transition, it is change itself that is real.[4]

Astaire seems to have intuitively grasped the need to maintain continuity when filming dance. His first film appearances in *Dancing Lady* and *Flying Down to Rio* were cameos, providing him with an opportunity to study this new medium. As he recalled:

> Knowing absolutely nothing about photographing a dance for the screen, I did a great deal of listening and studying. I was pleased with lots of things but kept thinking of what I would like to try if I ever got in a position to make my own decisions.[5]

That time would come sooner than expected. By his third film, *The Gay Divorcee* (1934), RKO Pictures recognized the star power they had in Astaire, and he was allowed to exercise more control over how his dances were filmed and edited. As Mueller explains, 'working by trial and error and largely without precedents, Astaire created a method for the filming of dance that was to dominate Hollywood for a generation.'[6]

Either the Camera Will Dance, or I Will[7]

The prevailing technique when Astaire arrived in Hollywood was to film a dance with many shots and changing camera angles. The dance was further altered in the editing process, where close-ups of the dancer's face or feet would be interjected, along with trick shots from different vantage points. 'The result,' according to Astaire, 'was that the dance had no continuity. The audience was far more conscious of the camera than of the dance.'[8] Astaire set out to alter this.

He managed to maintain the essential continuity of dance by evolving a cohesive approach to shooting and editing his work. As Mueller delineates, Astaire accomplished this by various means. He eliminated or minimized distracting elements such as cluttered camera perspectives, re-establishing shots, close-ups of feet, reaction shots, and special effects. The dancer's full body is shown, with minimal use of even medium shots.

The camera moves with the dancers, so that the viewer is aware that they are traveling by reference to the background, rather than by their motion across the camera's frame. The dance finishes fully on camera, and the overall number of cuts in the final film presentation are always small.[9] By these means, as Fonteyn notes, Astaire 'hit upon the right formula to compensate for the missing third dimension.'[10]

Astaire also exercised control over his preparation for a film and the process of actually shooting it. Known to be a perfectionist, Astaire started creating and rehearsing dances for his films months in advance. He needed privacy when preparing, and interviewers who would have liked to observe were banned from his rehearsals.[11]

While Astaire worked with a number of different choreographers, these individuals were primarily responsible for devising the larger group numbers and serving as sounding boards for his ideas. Astaire appears to have created much of his own solo and duet work. However, the close working relationship he developed with the choreographer Hermes Pan was particularly important and long lasting. As Astaire explained, 'Pan was full of ideas, and he was exceptionally good with the girls, working up a routine and teaching it to them.'[12] For his part, Pan noted that he and Astaire not only looked alike, 'we thought alike in our ideas of dance. We had the same feelings of rhythm… he expressed things that I had always felt.'[13]

Once filming began, Astaire preferred to film each dance in its entirety. This preference, combined with his legendary perfectionism, led to some grueling days on the set. For example, in *Follow the Fleet* (1936), Ginger Rogers was costumed in a heavily beaded dress with long sleeves for the 'Let's Face the Music and Dance' number. The four-minute dance had been designed to be shot in one piece with no cuts, but the beaded sleeves kept hitting Astaire or necessitating graceful ducks. As Astaire recalled, 'we couldn't get one take all through that pleased us.' So they filmed twenty takes of this 'difficult dance' in one day, until Ginger and Fred both 'were exhausted.'[14] They left the studio at 8 pm, prepared to work on the number again. The next morning when viewing the rushes, however, they found that the very first take was perfect. Although Astaire was astounded, they were able to move on to filming the next sequence—no doubt to the relief of director Mark Sandrich and Ginger Rogers both!

Astaire's sense of perfection 'shines through all his work; there is never a trace of effort,' due to his 'rehearsing and perfecting every detail.'[15] This consummate artistry is preserved for viewers today thanks to the care

Astaire exercised in using the camera. He realized that film offered certain advantages over stage performance:

> You can concentrate your attention directly on the dancer, so that the audience is able to follow the intricate steps that would be all but lost behind the footlights. Each person in the audience sees the dance from the same perspective, and I think, gets a higher reaction. He has a larger, clearer, better-focused view, and so derives a greater emotional response.[16]

Astaire claimed that he had never used dance 'as an outlet or as a means of expressing myself.'[17] Critics view his work in a different light. Croce calls Astaire 'a master dramatist. Drama clings to every move he makes.'[18] Mueller concurs, noting that Astaire's dances 'were profoundly integrated into the plot... he was crafting dramatically eventful dances whose movement vocabulary was carefully related to, and developed from, the plot situation.'[19] According to Siegel, that fact that Astaire's dancing took its impetus from the plot 'enabled him to dance so often and so effectively in so many films. We never feel we are looking at a contrivance.'[20]

While his duets are dramatic, moving the plot line forward, Astaire's solos are often more inventive. As Reynolds and McCormick observe, 'dancing alone left him freer to explore his consummate musicality and kinetic intuition.'[21] It is this inventiveness to which George Balanchine paid homage, calling Astaire 'the most elegant dancer of our times.'[22] In the following section, three solos drawn from different periods of Astaire's film career are discussed to delineate elements of this remarkable dancer's style as it evolved over time.

ROBERTA (1935)

This was Astaire's fourth film and the first in which he really began to assume control over his dances, receiving credit for their arrangement, with assistance from Hermes Pan. By now, the Astaire–Rogers partnership was well established. In this film, Astaire portrays an American band-leader whose fondness for his childhood sweetheart, Rogers, is rekindled when they meet in Paris. His solo to the Jerome Kern tune 'I Won't Dance' occurs when his band is performing in a nightclub. Astaire sings a duet with Rogers, in which he refuses to dance with her. Then he is carried from the bandstand down to the dance floor by two nightclub employees costumed as Cossacks. The solo begins with him dismissing the Cossacks with a barrage of taps.

Initially Astaire circles the dance floor, addressing the audience seated at tables and even shaking hands with two guests. The solo that ensues is 'a virtuosic, crazy-legged affair... there is a lot of limb slinging, and between furious tap flutters, he is constantly finding one leg wrapping around the other.'[23] Indeed, Astaire resembles a spinning top with a slight wobble. This is due to his placement. He tends to tilt forward from the hips while keeping his knees bent and pliant. His arms hover to each side or rapidly trace soft curves as he taps, travels, and turns. Alternately, he leans backwards and upwards, almost falling. Then he travels downstage, tapping furiously. The only time Astaire is fully erect is when he stretches upward during a turn.

Astaire's off-vertical placement contributes to his incredible mobility, for he can only barely keep from falling through rapid footwork and counter movements of the arms. Moreover, the forward tilt inclines him to keep his gaze focused downwards, slightly in front of his body. This adds intimacy to the dance, making it seem that he is oblivious to the audience and dancing only for himself. Only in the final elongated turn, when he pauses with one arm extended upwards and the other to the side, does he look at the audience, before lunging forward, with his arms reaching diagonally towards them.

Rhythmically, the dance has three sections. The first section has the most moderate tempo. During this part, Astaire travels downstage and upstage, following a diagonal path. The traveling is punctuated by occasional spins, hopping turns, and unexpected pauses, when the frenetic activity comes to a momentary stop. At some moments the orchestra stops playing, and the only sound is that of Astaire's tapping. During the second section, the tempo suddenly slows down, allowing Astaire to do a series of spectacular turns. He throws one fully extended leg behind the other in a crossed diagonal line and pivots. Then, still crossing his legs, he spirals upwards and pauses momentarily, before falling into the next movement. In the final section, the tempo becomes quite fast as Astaire travels sideways across the stage while turning, in a final, self-absorbed frenzy of inspired tapping.

While he is in evening attire, some of the elegance usually associated with Astaire's persona is lacking here. There is more of the vaudeville hoofer than the debonair gentleman in this dance, and perhaps Hermes Pan's influence can be surmised. Pan loved after-beats and broken rhythms, and taught this to Astaire. According to Pan, this was a black tradition he had learned in Tennessee and differed from the kind of tap he saw later in

New York. Orthodox tap is done on the toes, Pan explained, but 'I used to dance on my flat foot and heel, which Fred does.'[24]

Small details, such as the use of the foot, can be discerned because the camera follows Astaire and provides an unobstructed view of the dance. There are only two cuts during the dance, and a final cut to a long shot when the dance is over.

EASTER PARADE (1948)

Astaire retired from the movies in 1946, to pursue his interest in racing horses and to start a chain of dancing schools. By 1948, however, he was growing restless. When the offer came to do a film with Judy Garland, he accepted. His role was originally to be played by Gene Kelly, but a broken ankle incapacitated Kelly, who was happy for Astaire to step in.

Astaire had some qualms about doing this. Not having danced for two years, he 'wondered if the old joints would stiffen up in reaction to a strenuous workout.'[25] Astaire was somewhat sensitive about his age. After all, he was 34 when he made his first picture. By the time *Holiday Inn* was released in 1942, Astaire was in his early 40s, and the press had started making references to his age. Nevertheless, as he crept back into shape he found that 'everything was all right. I couldn't find anything different from before.'[26]

Robert Alston was the choreographer for the film, although comments in Astaire's autobiography suggest that they collaborated on Astaire's dances. Astaire was particularly pleased with his solo in 'Steppin' Out.' As he noted, 'I used the slow-motion camera… with the ensemble dancing in normal speed while I was superimposed working in front of them.'[27]

'Steppin' Out' opens with a large chorus of dancers swirling around the stage. They soon begin to sing an introduction, leading to Astaire's appearance at the top of the stairs up center. Astaire begins to descend the stairs, tapping and singing the well-known Irving Berlin tune. By now, some of the signature elements are in evidence. Astaire has a straw hat and a cane and makes maximum use of the steps, lithely skipping up and down while addressing the chorus, who line the stairs on either side.

A series of three tap duets with different partners occur once Astaire descends to the stage floor. These again follow the pattern of a moderate tempo duet, a slower and more sensuous exchange, and a final, fast tempo romp. At the end of the second duet, Astaire's partner exits, having taken his cane. Then, as the third duet ends, Astaire slowly pivots, as if looking for something, and his cane flies back onstage and into his waiting hands.

The cane now becomes his partner, as he executes a fast and showy tap solo. This is accentuated with multiple spins and jumps, as he tosses and twirls the cane. Meanwhile the chorus dancers, seated on the stairs behind him, sway in time. Astaire comes to a momentary pause and the film cuts to him dancing in slow motion while the chorus (now standing) continues to move at a normal speed.

This slow-motion section is particularly interesting because it makes it possible to study aspects of the inimitable 'Astaire style' in more detail. While dynamic qualities are distorted, aspects of bodily organization and spatial form are accentuated. His use of a soft plié and tendency to tilt forward through the torso, so notable in the *Roberta* solo, can still be seen. What emerges more strongly here is Astaire's use of the diagonal. He tends to use steps in which one leg crosses behind or in front of the other. This allows him to pivot swiftly on two feet or complete a turn with a quick two-footed jump. He seldom faces straight front, but tends to slightly twist the upper body. This twisting and tilting can be exaggerated. For example, with one leg crossed behind, he leans so far backwards and upwards that only a quick step to the side prevents him from falling.

Indeed, Astaire seems to be the personification of what movement theorist Rudolf Laban notes: 'movements following space diagonals give… a feeling of growing disequilibrium, or of losing balance. The balance is, so to speak, dissolved in the flow.'[28] This oblique orientation and use of a tilted axis contributes to the sense of Astaire as a wobbling top. And indeed, in slow motion it is possible to see that his arms trace a tilted circle as he spins around his inclined axis. This oblique trace-form contrasts the level circle inscribed during an erect pirouette.

As in the *Roberta* solo, Astaire's gaze remains focused downwards, slightly in front of his body. This facilitates his work with the cane, which he twirls, tosses, and catches in various ways. In one magical moment, he taps the cane on the floor and releases it. Then we watch it sail slowly in front of his body and hook itself over his other waiting arm. Astaire's total concentration is obvious. For the moment, nothing exists for him but the dance itself. This capacity to be completely engaged must contribute to the charm of his cinematic performances.

Interestingly, the slow-motion solo draws upon steps seen in the initial solo, but it is not the same material simply slowed down. It appears to have been choreographed independently.

In this mid-career film, Astaire sticks with many aspects of the film technique he pioneered. Cuts due to changes in camera angle are kept to a minimum. The camera follows the dancers and the majority of shots show the full body. However, he does use a medium shot showing only the dancer's upper body, although the camera rapidly pulls back to reveal the full figure. These shots make sense choreographically, for they occur at transitions in the dance, such as when he changes partners in the three duets. Astaire also employed one reaction shot of Judy Garland, primarily to link the slow-motion section with the shift back to the dancing at normal speed that ends the number.

SILK STOCKINGS (1957)

By now in his late 50s, Astaire was on the verge of retiring from dancing for the second time. But this film, directed by Rouben Mamoulian with a score by Cole Porter and dancing partner Cyd Charisse, was too good to pass up. While Eugene Loring was in charge of numbers in which Astaire did not appear, Hermes Pan was brought in to work with Astaire, who felt he needed a 'sock solo.'[29] 'The Ritz Roll and Rock,' specially composed by Porter for the film, filled the bill.

This satirical dance opens with Astaire in silhouette, with the now familiar top hat, tails, and cane. Strains of classical music are heard as the lights come up, revealing a fashionable crowd in evening attire. Then the music shifts to rock and roll. Astaire spins, freezes, and begins to pulse with one leg. He drops suddenly to one knee, then rises again. With percussive thrusts, he seems to shock elegant groups of dancers into assuming abandoned poses and starting to pulse. Then all the men drop to the floor as Astaire begins to sing.

This particular number differs from much of Astaire's other work in terms of the use of the floor. Astaire collapses on the floor, scrambles across the floor, rolls around on the floor, rises from the floor, and slides across the floor, alongside other male and female dancers. This is meant to have a comic effect, since the men are in tuxedos and the women are wearing long evening gowns.

However, Astaire's level changes are performed as simultaneous movements and lack the rhythmic and spatial complexity of much of his other work. Consequently, these motions appear awkward. One cannot help noticing that Astaire is getting older and less nimble. He twirls his cane, catches his top hat on one foot, and shimmies up a mirror. But these tricks look contrived and lack the nonchalant elegance of earlier solos. The only exception occurs when Astaire travels upstage, turns, and then jumps backward to land on a counter—a move he performs with customary aplomb.

Although Astaire's full figure remains in view for much of the dance, a number of cuts occur. As the stage scene opens, there is a cut to a reaction shot with Cyd Charisse, who has been brought to the nightclub where Astaire is performing by her Russian comrades. Medium shots are used when Astaire starts singing, and later, when he is seated on the counter. These pull back quickly into full figure shots, as usual. Other cuts occur, as when Astaire shimmies up the mirror and later when he scrambles on the floor. At the end, Astaire is filmed from above, and then the camera moves again to a frontal shot as the dance ends. This camera work, while not really distracting, contributes to the slightly jumpy quality of the number.

In contrast to the two earlier solos in *Roberta* and *Easter Parade*, the chorus is closer to Astaire and their movements are much more tightly integrated with his actions. At one point, in fact, a group of men actually cross in front of Astaire. Much of what he does seems designed to provoke a reaction from the other dancers. As a consequence, there is never that magical moment when he appears to be completely absorbed in his own kinetic experience. Instead, he seems self-conscious. The effort to dance is more obvious. Consequently, this number lacks the playful quality of earlier works. When he is sprawled on the floor at the end of the dance, Astaire smashes his top hat flat. This final gesture says it all. As Astaire reports in his autobiography, 'I decided that I had *had* musical pictures.'[30]

CONCLUSION

Even the greatest dancers are subject to changes in fashion and the effects of growing older. Astaire was no exception. He rose to movie stardom at the peak of his powers, and transformed the medium and its relationship to dance. The 'Astaire style' became legendary. It is curious that his admirers include so many luminaries of the ballet world, for Astaire's style is definitely un-balletic. Whereas the ballet dancers' legs are stiff and straight, Astaire's are bent and pliant. While they remain erect, he tends to be tilted off the vertical. When they can balance endlessly, he is always in danger of falling. Yet what seems to speak to all dancers about the Astaire style is its ludic essence.

Huizinga has characterized dance as a 'particularly perfect form of play-ing.'[31] Play, of course, is distinct from ordinary life. It is a 'stepping out of "real" life into a temporary sphere of activity with a disposition all its own.'[32] Astaire's dances have this quality. 'We're never sure what turn of events will cause Astaire to break out in a dance next,'[33] Siegel observes. 'He could dance about walking a dog, getting caught in the rain—almost anything with any action in it at all.'[34] Once he begins to dance, however, the ordinary is transformed. As Huizinga notes, play brings 'a temporary, a limited perfection' into the imperfection and confusion of life. Indeed,

> the words we use to denote the elements of play belong for the most part to aesthetics, terms with which we try to describe the effects of beauty: tension, poise, balance, contrast, variation, solution, resolution, etc. Play casts a spell over us; it is 'enchanting,' 'captivating.'[35]

Astaire had the capacity to captivate by 'playing' on screen. Perhaps dancing became less fun for him over time. Nevertheless, he has left a beautiful record of his most inspired work. His perspicacious use of the camera preserves the continuity and flow that are the hallmarks of dance. Moreover, he allows the audience to enjoy a privileged view of the dance as it unfolds. And, as in all genuine play, viewers have a 'feeling of being "apart together" in an exceptional situation, of sharing something impor-tant.'[36] Thus Astaire's films can be thought of as a kind of timeless valen-tine for all who love the dance, and for dance historians in particular.

NOTES

1. Robert Taft, Introduction to Eadweard Muybridge, *The Human Figure in Motion* (New York: Dover, 1955), viii.
2. Jean Luc Daval, *Photography* (Geneva: Skira/Rizzoli, 1982), 68.
3. Henri Bergson, *Creative Evolution* (Boston: University Press of America, 1983), 305.
4. Henri Bergson, *The Creative Mind* (New York: Philosophical Library, 1946), 16.
5. Fred Astaire, *Steps in Time* (New York: itbooks, 2008), 184.
6. John Mueller, *Astaire Dancing* (New York: Wings Books, 1991), 26.
7. Astaire, quoted in John Winge, 'How Astaire Works,' *The European Scene: Film and Theatre Today* (London: Saturn Press, 1949), 7.
8. Astaire, quoted in Mueller, 27.

9. Mueller, *Astaire Dancing.*
10. Margot Fonteyn, *The Magic of Dance* (New York: Alfred A. Knopf, 1979), 33.
11. Astaire, *Steps in Time.*
12. Bob Thomas, *Astaire: The Man, The Dancer* (New York: St Martin's Press, 1984), 98.
13. Thomas, 98.
14. Astaire, 214.
15. Fonteyn, 37.
16. Astaire, quoted in Nancy Reynolds and Malcolm McCormick, *No Fixed Points: Dance in the Twentieth Century* (New Haven, CT: Yale University Press, 2003), 721.
17. Astaire, 325.
18. Arlene Croce, *The Fred Astaire and Ginger Rogers Book* (New York: Vintage Books, 1972), 6.
19. Mueller, 23.
20. Marcia B. Siegel, *The Shapes of Change: Images of American Dance* (Berkeley, CA: University of California Press, 1985), 115.
21. Reynolds and McCormick, 722.
22. George Balanchine, quoted in Deborah Jowitt, *Time and the Dancing Image* (Berkeley, CA: University of California Press, 1988), 255.
23. Mueller, 71.
24. Thomas, 100.
25. Astaire, 292.
26. Astaire, 292.
27. Astaire, 292.
28. Rudolf Laban, *The Language of Movement* (Boston: Plays, Inc., 1974), 90.
29. Astaire, 319.
30. Astaire, 320.
31. Johan Huizinga, *Homo Ludens: A Study of the Play Element in Culture* (Boston: Beacon Press, 1950), 165.
32. Huizinga, 8.
33. Siegel, 115–6.
34. Siegel, 312.
35. Huizinga, 10.
36. Huizinga, 12.

PART V

New Technologies: Dance as 3D's Ultimate Agent

And so we return to three-dimensional space—through Philip Szporer and Marlene Millar's discussion of 3D film and their work with that medium—and our conclusion to this collection. Is 3D the new best way to present dance and the body? Is 3D an answer to questions about presentation of dance on screen, Benjamin's doubts about the performer's aura, and even how to reach a wider audience? We wrap up with a brief history of dance and site (and, sight), pondering about the future and how technology might further change our apprehension of movement—in real life, in projected moving images, and in the virtual world itself.

CHAPTER 13

Moving In(To) 3D

Philip Szporer and Marlene Millar

It was a typical hot summer morning in June 2010 when we entered the mammoth space of an old sound stage on the outskirts of Montréal. The installation crew had worked full-on overnight, and we found ourselves bathed in and dwarfed by the Kryptonite glow of a green screen studio. The place was abuzz with a multitude of technicians and associated crew—the likes of which we had never experienced in the fifteen years we've been making dance films—all at our service in this 3D adventure.

If there is a defining quality to the work we've done to date, it is an approach that provides an intimate understanding of the dance through the landscape of the body. As established dance filmmakers, we are always trying to capture the immediacy, the urgency, the subtlety of the choreography and performance. We've worked on film, video and HD, always happily surrounded by a team of collaborators—cinematographers, editors, sound designers and composers—who are keen to delve into our investigations with us. Our constant objective is to guide the viewer's eye and perception and lead them to an increased sense of the body through kinetic images that resonate in the mind.

An earlier version of this chapter appeared as an article in *The Dance Current* 14:3 (Sept–Oct 2011), 46–8. See also website Lost Action/Trace by Marlene Millar, Crystal Pite, Philip Szporer—NFB.webarchive.

P. Szporer (✉) • M. Millar
Co-founders of Mouvement Perpètuel, Montreal, Quebec, Canada

225
T.D. Arendell, R. Barnes (eds.), *Dance's Duet with the Camera*,
DOI 10.1057/978-1-137-59610-9_13

BREAKING A CYCLE OF EPHEMERALITY

Thinking about new projects and new collaborations, we always want to work with choreographers who are passionate, open, inventive and engaged. When conversations with choreographer Crystal Pite began in 2009, she was quite clear that a prime interest in creating a dance film would be to break a cycle of ephemerality, such that there could be a lasting artifact of her work seen by a great number of people.

We had initiated a series of conversations with the Montréal-based National Film Board of Canada (NFB), specifically about creating a dance film that would push our process in a new direction. With Crystal on board as a key collaborator, we proposed an adaptation of her stage work *Lost Action*, combining live action and animation.

The NFB responded by throwing in another element, the chance to explore the possibilities of working in stereoscopic 3D. Reticent at first (we weren't convinced that we would achieve the artistic vision we had in mind), we agreed to do some research. Shooting in 3D meant that we could not do what we most love: filming in close-up, working with hand-held, very intuitive cameras, and using a montage style seemingly unsuited to 3D. Any 3D films we saw during our research rendered the bodies disproportionate within the filmic space, and simply did not have an intimate sensibility. But support for stereoscopic 3D movie-making was a priority at the institution, something any of our reticent feelings wouldn't change. In the end, the lure of working at the NFB, with its reputation as a center for innovation, the hype surrounding the technology of 3D much in the air, along with the possibility of this short film leading the way towards our original 30-minute version, meant that we jumped on the project.

Much earlier, the NFB, founded in 1939, emerged as one of Canada's most important social and critical creative institutions. Federally funded, the NFB, with its French and English units, has trained and nurtured generations of filmmakers. One of its pioneers was Canadian animator Norman McLaren. He began his filmmaking career in 1934, and came to Canada in 1941 at the request of John Grierson, the NFB's Commissioner, under whom McLaren had worked at the film unit of the British Post Office.[1] In his days as a student at the Glasgow School of Fine Arts, the Scottish-born McLaren lacked the resources of film equipment—he had access to a film projector but not a camera. This inspired him to draw directly onto celluloid—scratching the emulsion to make the film stock transparent—and from there began a lifelong interest in creating new images mixed with sound.

McLaren's unfettered cues were influenced by the works of the German experimental filmmakers and the Russian avant-garde in both the graphic realm and in theater; he picked up where they left off and developed his art at a time when technologies were undergoing major changes. McLaren's is one of the most cohesive and personal bodies of work to emerge from Western animated cinema in the last century. Not surprisingly, his films appeal to the senses regardless of the subject matter.[2]

PIONEERING SPIRIT

While 3D films are making a comeback today, the NFB has been exploring the medium since the 1950s with McLaren's pioneering 35 mm stereoscopic animated films, *Around is Around* and *Now is the Time*. Later, for Expo 86 in Vancouver, the NFB produced the first 3D IMAX™ film *Transitions*.

In the shadow of McLaren's pioneering spirit, we were happy to challenge ourselves on our project, interacting with the tools, materials and technology of 3D. Ultimately we thought that the sculptural quality of the 3D body could provide some potential for research. We were also intrigued by the viewer's altered relationship to the performance via entrance into the screen space and the possibility of their having a different experience of dance and the moving body than is typical in a regular 2D film. For the first time in our careers as dance filmmakers we were in a situation where we were able to take off our producers' hats as the NFB was fully financing the project. So when offered a short, fully produced film—what the NFB calls a 'proof of concept'[3]—as our chance to test it out, we agreed to dive in. 3D production comes with a premium—it easily adds a third to the budget. The NFB recognized how the production would be pushing the boundaries both in our creative approach and the storytelling capacity inherent within the choreography and the artistic intent of the film, and the organization was also keenly aware of cost: as a public institution, its funding comes from taxpayers' dollars, and certain restrictions were set out.

Working from our 30-minute draft script adaptation of Crystal's 75-minute stage work, we had just a few weeks to distill it down to the 2-minute version the short film would be. We had to learn everything we could about conceiving the film in 3D—from which lenses and cameras to use to framing and composing with the Z access (the depth into or outside of the traditional screen plane)—and valuing the results of a slow tracking shot. Suddenly, terms not in our filmmaking vocabulary and experience to date became a big concern, such as window violation (when the subject breaks the frame in a way which can cause viewer headaches and eye strain) and interocular (or inter—axial) distance (the space between the two lenses that emulates or mimics human vision, similar to those between our two eyes, and determines how the illusion of volume is perceived).

To attain the heightened realism of 3D, there is a balancing of images, one for the left eye, and one for the right eye. The 3D image is created by the brain, which fuses the two to create an illusion of a single image that has depth on screen (or in print). Only 4 percent of people don't have the ability to see the world in stereo (3D), but even so, 'if 3D image is not done properly, it can hurt... 3D is not something that we can watch for long right now,' comments Ali Kazimi, of York University's Future Cinema Lab.[4]

The mechanism for shooting stereoscopic 3D consists of two cameras either side-by-side or with a partially silvered mirrored rig at 45° in the middle. (We used two Red ONE cameras on a Swiss Rig [Mirror Rig camera] system.) The images have to be perfectly synchronized, with identical focus, depth of field, color and contrast—not an easy task, and time-consuming. This results in a big, unwieldy mechanism with its own inherent needs, which dictate the production schedule and the shooting approach. In terms of both composition and pacing there is much that is still unknown—filmmakers, directors, and the cinematographers need to both 'see' with the Z access in mind, and develop a language that suits the production, and moves well in that world.

Added to the 3D challenge was our continued desire to work with animation, which would now need to be in stereoscopic 3D as well. This little film was quickly becoming our *Avatar*. The NFB very warmly welcomed our proposition and we understood quite quickly that this project proposed inherent challenges to the form: first and foremost, we needed to gather the right personnel, including an experienced team of operators and crew, like our stereographer, Francis Hanneman, who would ensure that the product looks good, and not be a configuration of 'brain-confusing' images, as some would suggest.[5] The fact that the choreography was performed by a group of five dancers, moving quickly, with complex execution and precise internal rhythms, was inherently problematic, too—normally this kind of movement can create strobing effects in 3D, caused by our brains being conscious of edges. As a viewer, what is so exciting, on stage or on screen, is engaging in the physical dynamics in Crystal's work; her approach to movement allows you to, for instance, watch one movement complete itself while it has already been taken over by another part of the body. Her dances have dimensionality, and people are gripped by her movement, drawn 'in' to the emotion and the dynamism of the performance, no matter what the medium. For this project, Crystal's instincts in reshaping the dance for a 2-minute film format proved inspirational.

But that length also was tricky: we needed to create a narrative within that timeframe and not simply a chapter or excerpt of her stage work, *Lost Action*. This was one of our goals, but within a 2-minute structure, originally slated to be 1 minute, how much can you say, and still elicit and honor the other element of Crystal's premise, dance's (and the body's) ephemeral nature? Leveraging these needs and wants was an ongoing discussion. The film is couched in a war narrative, with soldiers who offer the ultimate physical sacrifice; equally it is a moving homage to the art form's fleeting quality. In terms of the dance sequences that we'd chosen for the film—and clear about its duration—we recognized that there was a good arc in place, first introducing the characters (soldiers) and their camaraderie and competitiveness in wartime conflict, then the more private narrative of one solider and his memory of a distant love, and finally coming to some resolution surrounding this man's own demise.

STEREOSCOPIC IMAGE

In terms of the editing, stereoscopic images provide more information than a 2D film (given the added Z access dimension) and a slower pacing in the cutting is preferable, allowing the viewer more time to look into the image. As mentioned, Crystal's dancers moved quickly and seamlessly in some sequences, challenging the viewer's eye to 'see it all,' before cutting to the next shot. The framing from one shot to another must be carefully considered as well to avoid the shifting of our eyes' convergence patterns, as it also takes time for the eye to adjust to the spatial composition of each sequence.

Acclaimed editor Walter Murch comments on this question: '[Viewers'] eyes must converge at perhaps 10 **feet** away, then 60 **feet**, then 120 **feet**, and so on, depending on what the illusion is. So 3D films require us to focus at one distance and converge at another. And 600 million years of evolution has never presented this problem before. All living things with eyes have always focused and converged at the same point.'[6] The difficulty of having our perceptual brains work so hard, to decouple convergence distance and focal distance, is why the headaches appear, he would argue, and with the visuals different from our real 3D world.

These facts determined that we use fewer cuts than normal, with edits enhancing the sense of depth into the screen. In addition, because we were utilizing material from only one day's shooting also meant that the variety of shots to choose from was limited. More particularly, due to filming within three walls of green screen, and anticipating the challenge that would be present in post-production (tracking the movement for the animation element) we had to limit our camera movement and we could not move the camera around the dancers, as we would normally do in our 2D dance-films. So we had a perspective that generally was straight on, and it could be argued, less dynamic. However, we enhanced the possibilities for the viewer by shooting a couple of sequences at a distance and from on high, using a telescopic crane, so that it appears that the camera is perched on a slope overlooking the action.

Whatever evolution is currently occurring in 3D films, and whatever its cultural impact, the rich history of the field draws attention to a phenomenon that existed far earlier in the history of cinema, predating photography. Michael Duffy reports that the book by stereoscopic specialist Ray Zone, *Stereoscopic Cinema and the Origins of 3D Film: 1838–1952*,[7] brings up the question of narrative and its effect on the film industry. 'Did the evolution of film narrative in the early years of the twentieth century and increasingly sophisticated production techniques in some manner diminish the drive to convey depth on the motion picture screen?' he asks at the beginning of a central chapter. 'Was the inherent "flatness" of the movie canvas, in X and Y parameters only, an advantage to filmmakers somehow in telling a story?'[8]

Indeed in our case, there was a need to 'understand the interrelated juxtapositions and struggles to entertain the cause and mean to innovate.'[9] McLaren once remarked, 'Animation is not the art of drawings that move but rather the art of movements that are drawn. What happens between each frame is more important than what happens on each frame. The basic substance of the cinema is movement—at its lowest physical level, the movement of lightwaves and soundwaves... it is the motion that speaks to us.'[10]

Movement as Basic Substance of Cinema

We needed to figure out how to avoid the pitfalls of the pop-out attention-grabbing gimmicks or simply 'compelling spectacle'[11] of popular 3D movies. Navigating the world of the animator was another new challenge. Aided in no small measure by the artistic vision of Theodore Ushev, and supported in the most minute details by his crack team of assistants—Fred

Casia (compositing and rotoscoping) and David Seitz (tracking and creation of the fog elements)—we were able to assert our desire to subvert the current wave of big-budget 3D films, which thrive on the audience-grabbing bravura cinematic moments incorporating protruding bodies and objects. The vision that we strived for, and hopefully have achieved, is a subtle, poetic sense of 3D. The footage of the dancers filmed in green screen was delivered to the animation team. Then, Ushev created a neutral background in which he could start layering all sorts of qualities we'd discussed since the beginning—fog and mist, dust and particle. The viewer enters into an abstract world, not only feeling the physicality and the depth of the space, but the urgency of the choreographic proposition. For the film's environment, Ushev worked with natural ingredients creating a terrain made of soil, wood and paint. In his process, he was also sketching, getting the feeling of the movements of the dancers' bodies through lines and gestures. The music by Owen Belton, who created a score perfectly suited for the film, including voices and sampled sounds, further pushed him in his discoveries. An added feature was the inclusion of vintage First World War footage (easily obtained in the NFB vaults), which situated the film even further, and added another robust layer of narrative.

Coming out of the independent world of self-producing, it was an incredible gift to have the time and full NFB support to learn and experiment in this, which was to us, a very new medium. We worked out of the StereoLab in Montréal with some of the best minds in the field there to decipher the technicalities and provide us with invaluable feedback around our creative choices. Another first for us in the post-production phase, and for the NFB as well, was mixing the film in full 7.1 Dolby Surround Sound, placing the sound effects, voices and music strategically throughout the theatre.

CONSEQUENCES OF 3D TECHNOLOGY

Clearly none of us was interested in producing a film where viewers would be left with eyestrain and headache. But that issue does raise questions about the consequences of 3D technology, and more particularly how we see. On stage there are so many ways to get the audience to track movement, and in dance-film getting the eye to track what we want it to see is fundamental; and this was equally the foundation of much of the conversation between Crystal and us.

Sandifer comments, 'Because this system is now rooted in the anatomical eyes of the viewer, the theater is no longer arbitrary. Instead of simply framing a view of an absent object with an absent viewer, 3D depends on the actual presence of viewer and object. When an object extends off the delineated space of the screen and into the theater, the object attains a real presence and is in an actual relationship with the apex of vision, which, instead of being an arbitrary point, is now the actual viewer's eyes.'[12]

At the Toronto International Stereoscopic 3D Conference[13] in June 2011, filmmaker Wim Wenders, the director of *Pina*, delivered the keynote address about the life and work of famed German choreographer Pina Bausch, and his decision to create a stereoscopic 3D feature documentary about her. '3D as 3 times more difficult. But not to discourage filmmakers.... Today, the big question about 3D is: what sort of film can fit the new technology? How can you fill the promise of the new language? What "product" (for lack of a better word) do you have to come up with to do justice to this challenge named 3D?!' Further he asked, 'Can I do this movie in 3D to improve its commercial chances? To get more attention?'[14]

EISENSTEIN AND WENDERS

No less than Sergei Eisenstein proclaimed in the late 1940s, 'mankind has for centuries been moving towards stereoscopic (3D) cinema.'[15] For his part, Wenders, perhaps due to his own notoriety, has played an important role in the resurgence of 3D. He commented that the traditional 2D screen was 'simply not capable' of capturing and giving justice to the recently-deceased Bausch's work. Watching her dance for the first time over twenty-five years ago, he says he was moved and 'was able to understand human movement, gestures and feelings in a whole new way.' His idea of taking the viewers into the center of the action through 3D, in the middle of the dancing, was his modus operandi, and it has had definite impact, at least at the time of this writing.

That's where dance-film trumps all the Hollywood blockbuster entertainments crowding our cinemas today—seeing the intimate, moving body through a lens is affecting, the rhythms and the edits shifting our sensibilities. While it will never take away the reality of the kinesthetic sense of live performance, 3D is a startlingly optimal way of gaining access to the dynamics, emotions, sensation, and the physicality of dance.

In many ways, what Wenders refers to is what all our dance-films are about—having the viewer enter the landscape of the body, as well as saying yes to its sculptural qualities. Choosing to work in stereoscopic 3D, it was a matter of avoiding all of the pitfalls that might enter into that proposition.

Limited stereoscopic sensibilities don't reside with novice 3D filmmakers alone. Our experience in terms of the distribution of a short 3D film is proving daunting. Confronted by festivals unable to program our film, or any other 3D art film, as they do not possess digital cinematic projection technologies in their theatres, we've arrived armed with a Depth Q projector and a case full of specialized XpanD glasses. A 'making of' 2D documentary of the process in creating our short dance-film has served as another important complement to the programming of *Lost Action: Trace*, giving viewers a context for what might not be apparent at first glance. A wider industry investment in terms of equipment and resources will determine if art films attain the same widespread acceptance as the feature films coming from Hollywood, who are filming or converting into 3D with great rapidity. Though it must be stated that the new advanced digital technology is increasingly allowing for the conversion of existing theatres to 3D projection at little cost. In addition, and perhaps most importantly, you cannot pirate 3D films, meaning that there is an audience hungry for entertainment and art films that they cannot view at home, unless they switch to home entertainment units now morphing with 3D viewing technologies.

But can we confidently say that 3D is part of the future landscape, that it is here to stay, and not a mere fad? We have repeatedly discovered that there is a larger problem that has surfaced in the post-screening discussions: audiences are vocal about accessibility, including how they must focus their eyes on the plane of the screen.

Medium of Imagination

Apart from the psychophysics and neuroscience findings, which won't be discussed here, for 3D to become the 'medium of imagination,'[16] perfecting the technology to overcome some of the glitches associated with the field is a given. It's said that the success of 3D will rest with getting rid of the cumbersome glasses and lowering the cost of home-use technology so that people have greater access to the goods, providing the general public with, for instance, cheaper, smaller cameras and even smartphones.[17]

There may well be another reason for today's film studios' push for 3D: it moves the bulk spending from post-production back to the principal photography—back to the studios. This is because, once shot or rendered, 3D film can barely be 'fixed' in postproduction—only very minimally so— before heavy distortion of the image occurs. So the power is back in the hands of the DOP and camera makers.

Dance is more ubiquitous than ever, with a proliferation of on-demand alternative outlets for dance media consumption such as the New York-based digital dance network TenduTV, live streaming of dance performances into cinemas, streaming dance content for 3D download capability, and dances created specifically for cell phones, and other hand-held devices.[18] What about the future demands for 3D dance on screen?

Since we completed our film, the NFB has embraced 3D production with greater fervor, consolidating its reputation as a leader in innovation. The organization realized, however, in a delayed reaction, that what we initially feared was true: the marketing and distribution possibilities for art films in 3D are limited, at least right now. Films like ours, certainly as 'stand alones,' aren't reaping large audiences, nor the acclaim the NFB envisaged, because these films need to be marketed differently, perhaps specifically with niche markets in mind. Nonetheless, apart from the business end of things, we can confidently say that dance is an ideal form to reproduce in 3D, and the dance and art-film worlds are expanding insofar as technology is inextricably linked to dance creation and innovation.

DANCE AS ORGANIC FIT

TenduTV's founder and general manager Marc Kirschner argues, 'For dance, 3D is an organic fit.'[19] There's more to dance than a stage, he states, and 3D high-definition film productions are an interesting avenue for choreographers. Current research supports the concept that technology augments, rather than replaces, the live-art experience.[20] A must is that those 3D dances emotionally resonate with the viewer, fuel the passion for the art form, and provide a new experience interacting with dance on screen. Viewers don't want to be encumbered by the paraphernalia (the glasses), or struggle decoding the multitude of questions floating in their heads (What is the big deal about 3D? Is this more real than 2D? Why can't I just watch the way I normally do? Why am I feeling isolated behind my glasses?).

As dance filmmakers new to this genre, we're juggling what we've learned about 3D and pondering, in open-ended fashion, what we've mastered in order to contemplate other creative possibilities in the field.

For now, we've been captivated and moved to comprehend and re-learn human movement, gestures and feelings in unparalleled new ways, expanding our reach, accessing new knowledge about state-of-the-art technology, honing our skills, keeping up with national and international trends, and increasingly exploring new mechanisms for engaging dance.

NOTES

1. Philip Szporer, 'Northern Exposures,' in *Envisioning Dance on Film and Video*, eds. Judy Mitoma, Elizabeth Zimmer, and Dale Ann Stieber (New York: Routledge, 2002), 168–75.
2. McLaren's work is defined by his probings into the language of motion. In *Blinkety Blank* (1954), for instance, images were not put on each frame. He chose to explore, in this manner, the after-image, the after-image that remains on the retina although no image remains on film.

   Many critics pick *Pas de deux* (1967) to be McLaren's masterpiece—a visual poem of form and movement. The dancers (Margaret Mercier and Vincent Warren), dressed in simple white costumes, dance a slow *pas de deux* on a black shooting stage, their bodies silhouetted and contrasted by rear lighting. They move across the space (to choreography by Ludmilla Chiriaeff), a series of multiple exposures extend, leaving delayed traces of images, almost ghostly imprints on the screen, frozen in the positions, for us to contemplate. McLaren employed, in a pre-computer age, a technique called chronophotography, in which the movements of the two dancers are staggered and overlayed by the optical printer to produce this stroboscopic effect.

   In McLaren's classic, revolutionary multiple image work with the optical printer—with step-printing to de-construct the dancers' movements and to present dance on film—explored movement and space in astonishing new ways.

   Ballet Adagio (1971) has less technical wizardry, but McLaren's idea was to stimulate our appreciation of classical ballet and to allow us the observation of the techniques and mechanics of the adagio movements. He has his dancers (David and Anna Marie Holmes)—stripped ballet bare—photographed in slow motion. Slowing down the bodies allows the viewer to observe not only the beautiful and luscious movement, but also the details and the muscles, and the concentration demanded by formal dance. McLaren's genius leads you to see something that isn't obvious.

3. Michelle van Beusekom, Assistant Director General, English Programs, National Film Board of Canada, telephone interview, 21 November 2011.
4. Gurmukh Singh, 'Indian born Prof leads Canadian Research on Future of 3D,' *Dear Cinema*, 1 March 2010, http://dearcinema.com/news/india-born-prof-leads-canadian-research-on-future-of-3d/3646
5. Roger Ebert, 'Why 3D film doesn't work and never will. Case closed,' *Chicago Sun.* 23 January 2011, http://blogs.suntimes.com/ebert/2011/01/post_4.html
6. Ebert.
7. Ray Zone, *Stereoscopic Cinema and the Origins of 3D Film, 1838–1952* (Lexington: University of Kentucky Press, 2007), 7. Zone reports that Charles Wheatstone's 1830 invention of the reflecting mirror stereoscope was demonstrated to the Royal Society in 1838.
8. Michael S. Duffy, 'Stereoscopic Cinema and the Origins of 3-D Film: 1838–1952,' *The Moving Image* 9:2 (Fall 2009): 179.
9. Duffy, 180.
10. Louis Werner, 'Spontaneous Frames of Movement,' *Americas 45* (September/October, 1993).
11. Philip Sandifer, 'Out of the Screen and Into the Theater: 3D Film as Demo,' *Cinema Journal* 5:3 (Spring 2011): 78.
12. Sandifer, 67.
13. On 11–14 June 2011, at Toronto's TIFF Bell Lightbox, experts gathered to address and analyze the 'new era in 3D cinema.'
14. Wenders's talk at the Toronto International Stereoscopic Conference took place on 11 June 2011.
15. Sergei M. Eisenstein, 'About Stereoscopic Cinema,' *Penguin Film Review* 8 (1949): 37.
16. Emily Claire Afan, 'Imax Co-founder Talks 3D,' *Playback* blog, 15 June 2011, http://playbackonline.ca/2011/06/15/imax-co-founder-talks-3d/
17. Melita Kuburas, 'Spy Films launches 3D division,' *Playback Magazine*, 17 October 2011, http://playbackonline.ca/2011/10/17/spy-films-launches-3d-division/

18. Kathleen Smith, 'Micro/Macro: Dimensions of Dance on Film and Video,' *The Dance Current* 14:3 (September/October 2011): 41–51.
19. Interview with Marc Kirschner on 4 December 2011, at the Cinedans festival, Amsterdam, The Netherlands.
20. 'Digital audiences: Engagement with Arts and Culture Online,' Arts Council England, 24 November 2010; and 'Audience 2.0: How Technology Influences Arts Participation,' National Endowment for the Arts, June 2010.

CHAPTER 14

Conclusion: Where the Gaze Lands

Ruth Barnes

When looking at dance on screen, a number of questions arise: Which medium, how and why? What is the effect of the camera on the choreography, and vice versa? What place the performer? The viewer? Why this dance on screen? Why this dance on stage? Who/what affects/influences whom/what in the video-choreography exchange? How and why combine the two? How to reconcile opposing 'takes' on live and recorded dance/performance? And, where are we?

Video theorists often reply: (1) that video work affects choreography and dancers through 'mediatization'—the technological interventions of the video medium; for example, video's capacity to alter time and space of dance; and (2) that the viewer is privileged by the camera, in that s/he is seeing more of the dance and dancer. But, what of the obverse of the situation, that of how the choreography and dancers influence how the camera and editing operate? How does location affect the creators, their team and the spectator? And, what do we understand about the gaze?[1]

We can gain much by exploring dance-video relationship(s) from choreographers' and videographers' points of view. The more I read, observe and discuss, the more convinced I become that people receive/perceive events and information differently, in part because of different priori-

R. Barnes (✉)
Department of Theatre and Dance, Missouri State University, Springfield, MO, USA

© The Editor(s) (if applicable) and The Author(s) 2016
T.D. Arendell, R. Barnes (eds.), *Dance's Duet with the Camera*,
DOI 10.1057/978-1-137-59610-9_14

239

ties (for example, perhaps one creator favors the kinesthetic sense, while another favors the visual). My own perception tends more to the tactile. Therefore, when I first entertained the notion of dance video and mixed media, I imagined that by working on my visual sense I might begin to come to grips (literally: hands on—and, perceptually) with what happens in the transfer from one medium to the other, and when the two mediums are combined (and in different ways).

A Journey in Mind and Body: Video into and Out of the Glass

Understanding and synthesizing disparate conceptions of live and recorded performance became the focus for explorations I did with a camera and dance material over a period of several years. My work was both mental and physical. I exercised my mind, reading, thinking and writing. I worked with my body in the studio, creating choreographic studies and performance pieces.

The process began with a desire to make a dance, for myself. What at the time was intended as the first part of a 20-minute solo was created and performed in Fall 2002 and Winter 2003. That live solo, *Into the Glass*, was made for a proscenium setting. As part of an ongoing emerging process titled *On Reflection* (2002–2004), the solo became the seed for three further projects: a group work (also made for a proscenium setting), a homonymic dance/video, and a mixed media promenade performance in the round. In the end, everyone involved in the project—choreographer, dancers, musicians, videographer and spectators—followed a route winding through different spaces. The path bent around corners. It passed through lenses, mirrors, swimming pools and windows. It bounced back to the viewer as the movement rebounded off the floor and walls. It echoed in rearrangements of the movement, in Baroque and new music, in video projections of the dance. The mental and physical course led to *On Reflection*'s last incarnation, viewable from 360° and with video recordings of the movement as reflected by a plate glass window and a swimming pool, or as shadows. The camera angles were various, sometimes extreme: very close up; zooms in or out; point-of-view or high overhead shots videotaped using a helmet-cam. These angles and manipulations are ways of using the camera for what it does. All footage was shot with the idea of avoiding, as much as possible, additional editing or special effects. The objective was to discover and show what the lens and frame 'see,' and not rely on editing techniques to distort or 'enhance' the image.

That in-depth examination of possibility gave me a new understanding of how flexible the camera lens could or could not be, how the frame and angles work, and how real time and space impact and are impacted by the movement captured by the camera. Writing to 'parse' what I made—in the studio, on the camera—also became part of a back-and-forth process, an additional dance, between theory and praxis.

A FIVE-MINUTE MIXED MEDIA HISTORY LESSON

Creators of mixed media, site-specific work or promenade performances are manifold. Frequently cited, from the turn of the twentieth century, is Loïe Fuller, who generated her own lighting effects with her dancing. The first mixed media work I remember seeing was a performance in the mid-1960s that combined dance, film, costumes and music, all created by Alwin Nikolais. The effect was explosive, overpowering, leaving one with the impression of a gigantic impenetrable environment, with people transformed into cyphers or objects by the general apparatus. The dancers became something indeterminate, indeterminable, other than the humans they were. In a foreword written for the Nikolais Dance Theatre 1963 Souvenir Booklet, dancer, lighting designer, assistant to the choreographer and author Ruth E. Grauert says that Nikolais' work

> ...is not abstract in the sense that he 'abstracts' values from actuality to recreate aesthetic image. Rather he uses art substances themselves to generate this new reality. His theatre is based largely on the creation and resolution of tensions among structure of energies and time/space. The stage, a black cube, is carved by light into the arena for drama. It is modeled by sound until the planes of light vibrate with identification. It is tenanted with shapes which are one with the sound and light. This cube of space becomes a new place, wherein exists new adventures for man. Nikolais does this by speaking first to man's senses—sight, hearing, sympathetic touch and kinesis, his sense of balance, his knowledge of positional changes [sic].[2]

Nikolais thus transformed space and the audience's sense of time. He provided a multiplicity of relationships among all elements that contributed to the impression that one was witnessing the movement within a kaleidoscope, or observing a new world. Choreographer Mimi Garrard, in her mixed media work of the 1960s and 1970s, continued in her mentor's steps, but on a more intimate scale.

SO MUCH TO WATCH

Merce Cunningham's *Variations V* (1965) is a striking mixed media work for four men and three women with film projections by Stan VanDerBeek, video by Nam June Paik, and music by John Cage. Sensory devices (poles and discs) placed around the stage are connected to the musicians' gear. The dancers trigger the music when they enter the force fields. Microphones placed in a potted plant (which is repotted twice during the course of the performance), on a yoga mat (Cunningham executes some movements on it), in a cushion Barbara Dilley uses when doing a headstand, or in a measuring tape, also are rigged to the sound equipment. Interactivity, however, is only one element in this complex work. The movement material ranges from the simple and quotidian (walking or riding a bicycle) to patterns of complex dance steps. The liveliness of the dancers and the total environment, whether the movement is very active or very slow, is radical. A documentation video of the work leaves the spectator with the overall impression of an enormous amount of simultaneous, rather than complementary, activity. Choosing where to direct one's attention inevitably means missing some part of the whole. And, yet, with its complexity and dissociated elements, *Variations V* achieves a certain down-to-earth reality—and, does so with humor.

French choreographer Philippe Decouflé has worked with mixed media and technologically mediated performances since the late 1980s. His work is ludic, wry, with a simplicity and directness that belie the complexity of his process. In addition to dance/videos, Decouflé has produced works that combine real-time video and dance, including *Abracadabra*, in which a dancer's movement was shot into a mirror in real time and projected, while the performer simultaneously danced live. As he describes it:

> We present a ballet and a video and then film the ballet in such a way that the audience sees what we're doing and can watch the images while the film is actually being made. It gives three different ways of looking at the same thing, and then when we introduce a sequence with mirrors, there is so much going on that you don't know what's real anymore. We hide nothing so the spectator can see we're playing with reflections, yet the magic is there.[3]

This postmodernist exposing of the apparatus at once creates transparency and confusion, recalling Freud's *The Uncanny*, as well as Robin Lydenberg and Hélène Cixous's writings on that essay, cited earlier in this collection. *The Uncanny* and the writings about it hold commentaries pertinent here, especially regarding the confounding aspect of *Abracadabra*. As Decouflé states, the spectator becomes uncertain as to what is the live dancer, what is the real-time video of the dancer, and what is the dancer's reflection. Decouflé's 'magic' happens thanks to the layering of the live and the digitized, further complicated by the inversion created by the mirror.

Other choreographers in Europe have been working with mixed media and technology since the late 1980s, including the American William Forsythe when he was based in Germany. In Great Britain, as on the continent and in the United States, independent (and, in Europe, state) television stations have promoted dance and video work since the 1970s, thereby making the technology available to choreographers, and disseminating the work to a (potentially) larger audience.

MIXING MOVES

Another way of combining the two media is, of course, dance/video or video/dance, usually a collaborative project between a choreographer and a videographer. There have been many teams around the globe. The work of Victoria Marks and Margaret Williams evokes a remarkable quality of humanness, of humanity. Their choreographic and filmic intent focuses on the people in the work, as well as the performers' relationship to each other and to the camera. Whether dancer or non-dancer, old or young, able-bodied or other-abled, choreographer Marks and videographer Williams give all of the individuals who appear in *Mothers and Daughters* and *Outside in* equal attention. The result is cheerful and generous, heartfelt and touching—a visual challenge to Marshall McLuhan's declaration that television is a cool medium. Combining dance and film to address social, psychological and human issues, DV8 Physical Theatre's artistic director Lloyd Newson has created pieces about all manner of things: 'religion, freedom of speech, sexuality, power abuse, class inequality, disability, or themes like the pursuit of happiness or the role denial plays in our lives' (DV8 promo).[4] *Dead Dreams of Monochrome Men* (1990) presents an evocative and moving narrative that depicts a ghastly series of events. The piece is based on true events involving a serial killer who stalked gay men in the London bar scene to entice them back to his flat, where he abused and murdered them. Newson deliberately heightens the spectator's experience by filming in black-and-white with harsh lighting effects;

the starkness of the image creates the effect of a newsreel. The all-male cast dances fearlessly and elegantly, combining contact improvisation with very technical European dance forms; the sometimes-violent choreography and deliberately chosen camera angles and editing are the means to relate a shocking story.

SITE AND SIGHT

Trisha Brown's alternative site work, and her transformation of stage space, present other important performance encounters, sometimes mediated with apparatus, but not with video. Her *Roof Piece* (1971) uses New York City's Soho skyline as the set. This study in the use of expansive distance places lone figures dancing on a series of rooftops while spectators watch from the northernmost vantage point. All of Brown's work with harnesses in the 1970s, in which people ambulate horizontally on walls, invites the viewer to look at perspective differently. Further, in *Glacial Decoy* (1979), stage space takes on a different meaning: the dance continues into the wings, creating the impression of scanning back and forth across a field of vision that is wider than the actually proscenium space.

Meredith Monk is another innovator in site-specific performance. *Needlebrain Lloyd and the Systems Kid: A Live Movie* (1970), perhaps her most extravagant full-evening performance work, used the entire Connecticut College campus as its set. Sections of the work happened in dorm windows, on an open quadrangle, or seemed to emerge magically from a lake. The performers—including people on horseback and motorcycles—conducted the audience from one site to the next. Monk's use of perspective and depth can be equated to European painting from the Renaissance onward. Her use of time, space and narrative in *Needlebrain Lloyd...* relates directly to cinema and cinematic devices, as the piece's subtitle implies. The audience was at once on the sidelines, observing, and in the middle of the action, participating.

PROMENADE PERFORMANCE

In 1974, the Strathclyde Theatre Group presented *The Golden City*, a promenade performance directed by Hugo Gifford, at the Edinburgh Festival Fringe.[5] In contrast with work by the Wooster Group and other experimental New York theater companies, the Scottish performers had a markedly different relationship with the audience. Spectators were surprised with unexpected scene shifts in the vast space of St Mary's Cathedral. While presenting a truly horrifying event, the actors and musicians were lively, subtle, and understated. A diatribe by the fanatical leader of the sect they were representing was the sole histrionic moment. Perhaps the difference in style is cultural (British versus American): the same restraint was seen long after, in another promenade performance of another infamous tale, a 2002 London production of Stephen Sondheim's *Sweeney Todd*. As in Monk's *Needlebrain Lloyd...*, the players in these performances directed the audience where to go or what to watch. The London *Sweeney Todd* production also incorporated the audience into two crowd scenes, as 'extras.' In this way, the spectator can become part of the family, or the act. Implied is a certain intimacy. In promenade performance, boundaries between performer and public often are challenged or broken altogether.

THREE DIMENSIONS

An issue that frequently arises in discussions of recorded movement concerns the flatness of the image on video. Here, by flatness I mean lack of depth or sense of perspective. This is no doubt partly due to evolving video technology itself. But there also appears to be an aesthetic issue that might be traced to the Cubist painters (Picasso, Braque and Leger, for example). Today, I argue, video screens and, especially, online computer graphics often replicate that use of space. In his essay, 'The Moment of Cubism,' John Berger writes,

> Cubism broke the illusionist three-dimensional space which had existed in painting since the Renaissance. It did not destroy it. Nor did it muffle it... It broke its continuity... [T]he relation between any two forms does not, as it does in illusionist space, establish the rule for all the spatial relationships between all the forms portrayed in the picture... The picture surface acts in a Cubist painting as the constant which allows us to appreciate the variables... we find our gaze resettled on the picture surface, aware once more of two-dimensional shapes on a two-dimensional board or canvas.[6]

Like the canvas, the video, computer or smartphone screen is a two-dimensional surface. In the case of very close up shots, a fragmented image can fill the screen.

As stated earlier, perhaps all these various and varying understandings of what a spectator experiences in a theatre or when watching a film/video screen is merely due to the different perspectives of choreographer and video artist. Berger points out in his written dialog with Susan Sontag, in 'The Uses of Photography':

> Human visual perception is a far more complex and selective process than that by which a film records. Nonetheless, the camera lens and the eye both register images—because of their sensitivity to light—at great speeds and in the face of an immediate event. What the camera does, however, and what the eye can never do, is to fix the appearance of that event. It removes the appearance from the flow of appearances and it preserves it, not perhaps forever but for as long as the film exists. The essential character of this preservation is not dependent upon the image being static; unedited film rushes preserve in essentially the same way. A camera saves a set of appearances from the somewhat inevitable suppression of further appearances. It holds them unchanging. And before the camera's invention nothing could do this, except, in the mind's eye, the faculty of memory.'[7]

With the 'fixing' of the image by the camera, the event's relationship to real time is interrupted, and context alters. For this discussion of 2D and 3D image, the key word is 'appearance': for that is the surface of the image. And, it is the viewer who processes the image, as Cunningham so astutely recognizes. Since any image will be processed, the camera's image is processed in the same manner as for live performance. In all cases, the spectator completes the event—going beyond the appearance to create a narrative, an understanding, a deeper meaning.

We are now at a point in time and technology when 3D images are changing the relationship between spectator and screen. In Wim Wenders's elegant and moving *Pina: Dance, Dance, Otherwise we are Lost*, the liveliness of the dancing shifts dramatically. Thanks to the 3D technology, the dancers and their dancing appear lifelike: round and full. They are less like images, more like the dancing beings they truly are. At times, the dancers seem to float in the space above the spectators' heads. Beads of water appear to splash out over the seats. The boundary between audience and screen (and, therefore, audience and performers) becomes distorted, unclear. We believe we are in a room with real, three-dimensional, live people dancing and talking, despite the fact that we are watching a film. *Pina* creates a sense of presence that calls Benjamin's *Work of Art in the Age of Mechanical Reproduction* into question. With *Pina*, Wenders demonstrates that this more recent technology, when used well, is capable of creating a representation of flesh and blood that is closer to reality than previously imagined, and that we now have the possibility of truly representing live performance in recorded form—an exciting development. What better way to embody film than with dancers moving in three dimensions—and vice versa?

PEOPLE, DANCING

To return to the notion of 'humanity'... As human beings, we occupy a place at a point in time on the continuum that is history. Much of the work in video dance, not to mention multimedia works, is a direct result of spatial and movement explorations by avant-garde and postmodern choreographers of the 1960s,1970s, and 1980s. It also reflects and benefits from ground-breaking innovations in film and television throughout the twentieth century. In addition, performers and spectators, along with choreographers and video artists, are humans who are significant in the process that is video dance: a collaborative, hybrid art form that in the best of circumstances is greater than the sum of its parts. To further my argument I will examine the Victoria Marks/Margaret Williams works *Mothers and Daughters* and *Outside in*, both created in 1994.

It is indeed these two works' very concern with humanity and humanness that is their most striking element. Victoria Marks has created what she terms 'choreoportraits' for a number of years, working with professional dancers as well as individuals not trained in dance. These are performers of all ages, from toddlers to senior citizens; they have varying degrees of agility and ability, including other-abled and non-disabled dancers.[8] The appearance of non-dancers in choreographic works is not a new phenomenon. As Deborah Jowitt explains in her discussion of vanguard dance in the 1960s, 'One of the achievements of the period as a whole was the redefinition of the dancer as "doer" and the dance as whatever was done—whether that meant performing an impressive choreographic piece of offbeat dancing, sitting still, climbing a wall, reading a text, munching a sandwich, or not showing up to perform.'[9]

And, as Jill Johnston states in writing about Steve Paxton's *Satisfyin' Lover* (1967) in the *New York Times*, the performers could include: 'Any old wonderful people... in their any old clothes. The fat, the skinny, the medium, the slouched and slumped, the straight and tall, the bowlegged and knock-kneed, the awkward, the elegant, the coarse, the delicate, the pregnant, the virginal, the you name it...'[10] This incorporation of 'everyday bodies' (the title of Jowitt's chapter in *Time and the Dancing Image* that discusses the 1960s and 1970s) was a reflection of the times: the Civil Rights, Women's Liberation and anti-Vietnam War movements, as well as a general anti-elitist attitude, impacted the work of many choreographers in those highly politicized decades. The desire for democracy, for equality and justice for all, regardless of race, ethnicity, gender or sexuality is literally embodied in avant-garde performance of the period.

Mothers and Daughters includes such a diverse group of women and girls, and displays a good deal of depth and appreciation for them. Its subject, its theme, is maternity and motherliness—and, as the title suggests, the relationship(s) between mother and daughter. The opening shot, taken from above, is of four women casting shadows on the pavement. As they walk away their shadows become imprinted on the pavement and another foursome replaces the initial women, casting their own shadows next to the imprints; the second foursome then lie down on the imprints. This is the beginning of a set-up in which the women's and girls' roles are frequently confounded: at times the mothers are maternal, at times the daughters are; similarly, the playfulness associated with youth is sometimes found in the daughters, sometimes in the mothers. What is highlighted and exploited throughout the dance video is what child psychologist D.W. Winnicott termed the complex mirror relationship between parent and child, in which the two look at each other's faces; what each of them looks like is 'related to what she sees there.' Further, Winnicott posits that 'when the average girl studies her face in the mirror she is reassuring herself that the mother-image is there and that the mother can see her and that the mother is *en rapport* with her.'[11] Throughout *Mothers and Daughters*, this mirror relationship is prominent. Simultaneously, the camera work and editing contribute to the viewer's confusion about who is the mother, who is the daughter, who is taking care of whom, who is in charge. We witness a caring, gently joyful, interdependent, feminine community, abounding with love. In a sense, it doesn't matter who is the mother and who is the daughter: they all willingly, happily exchange roles.

Mixing and switching roles are generous in *Outside in*, a Marks–Williams collaboration that features members of CanDoCo, a company comprised of other-abled and non-disabled dancers. I postulate that the nature of the dancers' physical attributes demands simpler cinematic devices than does a dance video with only non-disabled performers, to enable the viewer to see and process this differently dancing body. In this instance, therefore, the choreography and especially the performers affect the way the camera and editing function.

In *Outside in*, the cuts and special effects are relatively limited. It is as if the radical aspect of the CanDoCo dancers, their various abilities and disabilities, preclude any necessity or desirability for slow motion or acceleration, for example. The impulse to create a humanistic work demands that the viewer see all the dancers as equals; and so, the image, the representation of the human body, must show each and every body equally. In this way, the very concept of the marked or unmarked is subverted and rendered irrelevant: there is no need to 'pass,' since everyone is accepted as s/he is, and all do whatever s/he is capable of doing. Included with physical limitations are gender and sexuality issues: men and women kiss each other; men kiss men; women kiss women. Both the choreography and the camera work and editing treat all performers frankly and directly. There are no 'special cases'—or, alternatively, all cases are special. Reality is reality and is dealt with playfully and openly.

Outside in uses several movement motifs and recurring images: tracks are drawn by fingers and wheels, and are used as floor patterns; kissing; air and everything associated with it (for example, breathing, sneezing, blowing); the tango; mirrors; pictures and picture frames; footprints and thumbprints; and shifts between inside and outside spaces, between a gray, disused loft and green hills.

We meet the performers as they blow kisses and pass various kinds of breathing around a circle: affection as life and life giving; the sneeze that could be an affliction; lifesaving CPR. In the next shot a wheelchair appears in the loft, starting a sequence with all six performers in which the wheelchairs draw tracks in the dust, seen in top shot. Sue Smith, a non-disabled dancer, walks on those tracks, playing with the space, making small, close steps and twisting her pelvis and torso. The scene then cuts to a floor pattern from a dance instruction manual, with black-and-white drawings indicating right and left feet, and lines detailing the pattern. David Toole looks at this pattern and performs the steps with his hands, doing a tango with his arms instead of his legs as support. The group tango section that follows is a gorgeous display, demonstrating not only the form, but also the spirit of tango: it is sexy, lively, provocative and seductive. The dynamics are open, the movement broad. The three wheelchairs become integral to the dance. The performers are paired in ways that use all possible permutations: one couple in wheelchairs, another standing, the third couple mixed—and they exchange places. Toole is the only one of the other-abled dancers who is both in and out of the wheelchair; his chair becomes occupied by his partner, Helen Baggett, who is non-disabled. In fact, Toole is so mobile, his agility is one of the most astonishing aspects of *Outside in*. There is a certain fascination with some of what he does. 'HOW does he do it?' one asks, watching Toole use his arms to travel, run and jump. In two passages in the piece, he balances on one hand while another dancer does the same movement but uses at least one foot as well as a hand to balance. Marks and Williams use Toole's virtuosity and impish appearance and personality to great advantage.

A reprise of the tango outdoors changes the ambience somewhat: a trio starts which becomes a duet with Toole and Smith, in real tango style. She drops him and goes on dancing, luxuriant and ample in her movements. There is a certain cruelty to the dropping, like a pratfall. But, because of Toole's prowess and the general mischievous atmosphere, we imagine him landing like a cat and also continuing to dance. The camera follows Smith, and then opens out to show Toole and the rest of the cast, reassuring the spectator. The joke is on us.

AN INTERDISCIPLINARY DUET

As Roland Barthes writes, '... the *interdisciplinarity* which is held up today as a prime value in research cannot be accomplished by the simple confrontation of special branches of knowledge. Interdisciplinarity is not the calm of easy security; it begins *effectively*... when the solidarity of the old discipline breaks down... in the interests of a new object and a new language neither of which has a place in the field of the sciences that were to be brought peacefully together, this unease in classification being exactly the point from which it is possible to diagnose a certain mutation.'[12] We hold Barthes's focus on interdisciplinarity and a search for this new object or language to be paramount in our own examination of dance as it meets film or video.

The statement conveyed by much dance video, screendance and mixed media work is always greater than the sum of its parts. And the parts push each other beyond dance technique and video technology to create a work that is both dance and video (or, video and dance). The collaboration between dance and the camera is like the tango that *Outside in* so successfully portrays and exploits: the two mediums, like the dancers, are mutually supportive and full of surprises, incorporating twists and reconfigurations of the material, but always maintaining a concern for how the two fit together, and a sensitivity about the actual bodies of the individuals dancing. In this way, dance and video intertwine to produce a work—and a genre—that does not and cannot exist in any other form.

NOTES

1. It often seems that the results of combining dance and video are either violent/hard-edged (looking like video games) or nostalgic/hyper-romantic. One could posit technological constraints. Or, rather, it could be that, until recently, those who had access to the technologies were from more privileged classes, and/or more conservative in their aesthetics, (meaning, that class or socioeconomics is a determining factor). Recently, equipment has become more accessible thanks to lower prices. Smartphones have become the preferred instrument of communication and recording. So, we have seen changes in the work produced in this area. Uploading videos onto online social media and file-sharing sites has become easier and more widespread. Videos range in quality. Some retain the look and feel of home movies from the 1950s. Others demonstrate a high level of sophistication and utilize editing techniques that approach the professional.

2. http://bearnstowjournal.org/1963_souvenir_booklet.htm. Accessed 15 September 2015.

3. http://www.culturekiosque.com/nouveau/intervie/decoufle.html

4. https://www.dv8.co.uk/

5. Hugo Gifford (1945–1981): Scottish actor, writer, and stage director. *The Golden City* was based on historic accounts of the mass suicide of a group of Anabaptists led by John of Leiden in the sixteenth century.

6. John Berger, *Selected Essays* (New York: Vintage Books, 2001), 84–5.

7. John Berger, 'The Uses of Photography,' *About Looking* (New York: Vintage, 1990), 50–1.

8. 'Non-disabled' is a term used by Celeste Dandecker, co-founder of London-based CoDanceCo.

9. Deborah Jowitt, *Time and the Dancing Image* (University of California Press, 1988), 310.

10. Reprinted in Jill Johnston, *Marmalade Me* (New York: E.P. Dutton, 1971), 97.

11. D.W. Winnicott, *Playing and Reality* (New York: Basic Books, 1971), 112.

12. Roland Barthes, *Music—Image—Text*, trans. Stephen Heath (New York: Hill and Wang, 1977), 155.

BIBLIOGRAPHY

Albright, A. C. (1997). *Choreographing difference: The body and identity in contemporary dance*. Middletown: Wesleyan University Press.

Arnheim, R. (1957). *Film as art*. Berkeley: University of California Press.

Astaire, F. (2008). *Steps in time* (1st ed.). New York: Harper & Row, 1959; New York: HarperCollins Itbooks.

Banes, S. (1998). *Dancing women female bodies on stage*. London: Routledge.

Bartky, S. L. (1988). Foucault, femininity, and the modernization of patriarchal power. In I. Diamond & L. Quinby (Eds.), *Feminism and Foucault: Reflections on resistance* (pp. 61–86). Boston: Northeastern University Press.

Benjamin, W. (1999). *The arcades project* (trans: Eiland, H. & McLaughlan, K.). Cambridge, MA/London: Belknap Press of Harvard University Press.

Berger, J. (1972). *Ways of seeing*. London: British Broadcasting Corporation.

Berger, J. (2001). *Selected essays*. New York: Vintage Books.

Bergson, H. (1983). *Creative evolution*. Boston: University Press of America.

Bernardi, D. (2009). *Filming difference: Actors, directors, producers, and writers on gender, race, and sexuality in film*. Austin: University of Texas Press.

Birringer, J. (1998). *Media and performance: Along the border*. Baltimore: The Johns Hopkins University Press.

Bogart, A., & Landau, T. (2005). *The viewpoints book*. New York: Theatre Communications Group.

Brakhage, S. (1963). *Metaphors on vision* (edited and with introduction: Sitney, P. A.). New York: Film Culture.

Brannigan, E. (2011). *Dancefilm: Choreography and the moving image*. New York: Oxford University Press.

Brooks, V. (2002). Timeline: A century of dance and media. In J. Mitoma et al. (Eds.), *Envisioning dance on film and video* (pp. xix–xxx). New York: Routledge.

© The Editor(s) (if applicable) and The Author(s) 2016   253
T.D. Arendell, R. Barnes (eds.), *Dance's Duet with the Camera*,
DOI 10.1057/978-1-137-59610-9

Clark, T. J. (1999). *Farewell to an idea: Episodes from a history of modernism*. New Haven/London: Yale University Press.

Clark, V., Hodson, M., & Neiman, C. (Eds.). (1988). *The legend of Maya Deren: A documentary biography and collected works*. New York: Anthology Film Archives/Film Culture.

Coontz, S. (1992). *The way we never were: American families and the Nostalgia Trap*. New York: Basic.

Croce, A. (1972). *The Fred Astaire and Ginger Rogers book*. New York: Vintage Books.

Current, R. N., & Current, M. E. (1997). *Loïe Fuller: Goddess of light*. Boston: Northeastern University Press.

Daval, J. L. (1982). *Photography*. Geneva: Skira/Rizzoli.

Deren, M. (1965). Film in progress: Thematic statement. *Film Culture, 39*, 1–59.

Deren, M. (2005). In B. R. McPherson (Ed.), *Essential Deren. Collected writings on film by Maya Deren*. Kingston: Documentext.

Dodds, S. (2004). *Dance on screen: Genres and media from Hollywood to experimental art*. New York: Palgrave Macmillan.

Eberwein, R. (1985). *Film and the dream screen: A sleep and a forgetting*. Princeton: Princeton University Press.

Fonteyn, M. (1979). *The magic of dance*. New York: Alfred A. Knopf.

Fuller, L. (1913). *Fifteen years of a dancer's life: With some account of her distinguished friends* (introduction: France, A.). Boston: Small Maynard and Company.

Garsten, C., & Wulff, H. (2003). *New technologies at work: People, screens and social virtuality*. New York: Berg.

Goren, L. J. (2009). *You've come a long way, baby: Women, politics, and popular culture*. Lexington: University of Kentucky Press.

Greenfield, A. (2002). The kinesthetics of Avant-Garde dance film: Deren and Harris. In J. Mitoma et al. (Eds.), *Envisioning dance on film and video* (pp. 21–26). New York: Routledge.

Gunning, T. (2003). Loïe Fuller and the art of motion: Body, light, electricity, and the origins of cinema. In R. Allen & M. Turvey (Eds.), *Camera Obscura, Camera Lucida: Essays in honor of Annette Michelson* (pp. 75–90). Amsterdam: Amsterdam University Press.

Hallett, H. A. (2013). *Go west, young women! The rise of early Hollywood*. Berkeley: University of California Press.

Hargraves, K. (2002). Europeans filming new narrative dance. In J. Mitoma et al. (Eds.), *Envisioning dance on film and video* (pp. 163–167). New York: Routledge.

Harper, S. (2009). *Madness, power and the media. Class, gender and race in popular representations of mental distress*. Basingstoke/New York: Palgrave Macmillan.

Harris, M. H. (1979). *Loïe Fuller: Magician of light*. Richmond: The Virginia Museum.

Hart, L. (1994). *Fatal women: Lesbian sexuality and the mark of aggression*. London: Routledge.

Haskell, M. (1987). *From reverence to rape: The treatment of women in the movies* (2nd ed.). Chicago/London: The University of Chicago Press.

Huizinga, J. (1950). *Homo Ludens: A study of the play element in culture*. Boston: Beacon Press.

Humphrey, D. (1959) and B. Pollack (Eds.) (1991). *The art of making dances*. New York: Grove Press.

Jessop, D. W. (1975). *Film and dance: Interaction and synthesis*. Boulder: University of Colorado Press.

Jowitt, D. (1988). *Time and the dancing image*. Berkeley: University of California Press.

Kaplan, E. A. (1983). Is the gaze male? In *Women and film: Both sides of the camera*. London: Methuen.

Karlyn, K. R. (2011). *Unruly girls, unrepentant mothers: Redefining feminism on screen*. Austin: University of Texas Press.

Kelly, D., & Flight, N. (2012). *Ballerina: Sex, scandal, and suffering behind the symbol of perfection*. Vancouver: Greystone.

Kloetzel, M., & Pavlik, C. (Eds.). (2009). *Site dance: Choreographers and the lure of alternative spaces*. Gainesville: University Press of Florida.

Kostelanetz, R. (Ed.). (1992). *Merce Cunningham: Dancing in space and time*. London: Dance Books.

Kracauer, S. (1948). Filming the subconscious. *Theatre Arts, 32*, 37–40.

Kristeva, J. (1984). *Revolution in poetic language* (trans: Waller, M. and introduction: Roudiez, L. S.). New York: Columbia University Press.

Kristeva, J. (1998). The subject in process. In P. French & R. F. Lack (Eds.), *The Tel Quel reader* (pp. 133–178). London/New York: Routledge.

Laban, R. (1974). *The language of movement*. Boston: Plays, Inc.

Levitin, J., Plessis, J., & Raoul, V. (2003). *Women filmmakers refocusing*. Vancouver: UBC.

Louppe, L. (1997). *Poetics of contemporary dance* (trans: Gardner, S.). Alton, Hampshire: Dance Books.

Mallarmé, S. (2001a). Another dance study: Settings and the ballet (1886a). In M. A. Caws (Ed.), *Mallarmé in prose* (trans: Lloyd, M. & Caws, M. A.). New York: New Directions.

Mallarmé, S. (2001b). Crisis in poetry (1886b). In M. A. Caws (Ed.), *Manifesto: A century of Isms*. Lincoln: University of Nebraska Press.

Marks, V. (2002). Portraits in celluloid. In J. Mitoma et al. (Eds.), *Envisioning dance on film and video* (pp. 207–210). New York: Routledge.

McLuhan, M., & Lapham, L. H. (1994). *Understanding media: The extensions of man*. Cambridge: MIT Press.

McPherson, K. (2006). *Making video dance: A step-by-step guide to creating dance for the screen*. New York: Routledge.

Miller, W. I. (1997). *The anatomy of disgust*. Cambridge, MA/London: Harvard University Press.

Mueller, J. (1991). *Astaire dancing*. New York: Wings Books.

Mulvey, L. (1999). Visual pleasure and narrative cinema [1975]. In S. Thornham (Ed.), *Feminist film theory. A reader* (pp. 58–69). Edinburgh: Edinburgh University Press.

Murch, W. (2001). *In the blink of an eye: A perspective on film editing*. Los Angeles: Silman-James.

Otake, E. (2002). A dancer behind the lens. In J. Mitoma et al. (Eds.), *Envisioning dance on film and video* (pp. 82–88). New York: Routledge.

Pasolini, P. P. (2005). The "cinema of poetry" [1965]. In *Heretical empiricism* (pp. 167–186) (trans: Lawton, B. & Barnett, L. K.). Washington, DC: New Academia.

Porter, J. (2009). Dance with camera. In J. Porter (Ed.), *Dance with camera*. Philadelphia: Institute of Contemporary Art.

Rabinovitz, L. (1991). *Points of resistance: Women, power and politics in the New York Avant-garde cinema, 1943–71* (1st ed.). Chicago: University of Illinois Press; 2nd ed., 2003.

Reynolds, N., & McCormick, M. (2003). *No fixed points: Dance in the twentieth century*. New Haven: Yale University Press.

Rose, M. (2002). Fishing for humans: Dance and the story of story. In J. Mitoma et al. (Eds.), *Envisioning dance on film and video* (pp. 228–231). New York: Routledge.

Rosenberg, D. (2000). Video space: A site for choreography. *Leonardo, 33*(4), 275–280.

Rosenberg, D. (2012). *Screendance: Inscribing the ephemeral image*. New York: Oxford University Press.

Rosiny, C. (1999). *Videotanz: Panorama einer intermedialen Kunstform*. Zürich: Chronos.

Sandifer, P. (2011). Out of the screen and into the theater: 3D film as demo. *Cinema Journal, 5*(3), 62–78.

Schroeppel, T. (2002). *The bare bones camera course for film and video*. Tampa: Tom Schroeppel.

Siebens, E. (2002). Dancing with the camera: The dance cinematographer. In J. Mitoma et al. (Eds.), *Envisioning dance on film and video* (pp. 218–223). New York: Routledge.

Siegel, M. B. (1985). *The shapes of change: Images of American dance*. Berkeley: University of California Press.

Sobchack, V. (Ed.). (2000). *Meta morphing. Visual transformation and the culture of quick-change*. Minneapolis/London: University of Minnesota Press.

Szporer, P. (2002). Northern exposures. In J. Mitoma, E. Zimmer, & D. A. Stieber (Eds.), *Envisioning dance on film and video* (pp. 168–175). New York: Routledge.

Thomas, B. (1984). *Astaire: The man, the dancer*. New York: St Martin's Press.

Vaughan, D. (1992). Locale: The collaboration of Merce Cunningham and Charles Atlas. In R. Kostelanetz (Ed.), *Merce Cunningham: Dancing in space and time* (pp. 151–155). London: Dance Books.

Wilson, A. A. (2002). Breaking the box: Dance the camera with Anna Halprin. In J. Mitoma et al. (Eds.), *Envisioning dance on film and video* (pp. 232–235). New York: Routledge.

INDEX

Printed by Printforce, the Netherlands